MEN IN THE PU

Men's domination of the public domain is obvious, yet it is often ignored in social and political analyses. How do public men, in public patriarchies, come to exert such enormous power? How and why do men dominate in the public worlds of work, politics, sexuality, and culture? Jeff Hearn explores these questions and investigates how public worlds construct public men and public masculinities in different and changing ways.

These important issues are examined by focusing on the period 1870–1920, when there was massive growth and transformation in the power of the public domains. Jeff Hearn explores the relationships between men's activity in and domination of the public domains, the domination of private domains by public domains, and the intensification of public patriarchies. An underlying theme is that the present exists in the past, and the past in the present, and Hearn demonstrates that these historical debates and dilemmas are still relevant today as men search for new, postmodern forms of masculinities.

Men in the Public Eye reveals why men's domination in and of the public domains is a vital feature of gender relations in patriarchies, both past and present. It will be essential reading for anyone interested in the social, political, and cultural dimensions of men and masculinities.

Jeff Hearn is Senior Lecturer in Applied Social Studies at the University of Bradford.

Critical studies on men and masculinities

Jeff Hearn and David H.J. Morgan (editors)
Men, Masculinities and Social Theory

David Jackson
Unmasking Masculinity
A critical autobiography

David H.J. Morgan
Discovering Men

Arthur Brittan
The Competitive Self (forthcoming)

Tim Edwards
Erotic Politics (forthcoming)

Editorial advisory board

Men in the public eye

The construction and deconstruction of public men and public patriarchies

Jeff Hearn

London and New York

First published in 1992
by Routledge
11 New Fetter Lane, London EC4P 4EE

Simultaneously published in the USA and Canada
by Routledge
a division of Routledge, Chapman and Hall Inc.
29 West 35th Street, New York, NY 10001

British Library Cataloguing in Publication Data
A catalogue record for this book is available from the British Library.

Library of Congress Cataloging in Publication Data
Hearn, Jeff.
    Men in the public eye: the construction and deconstruction of
    public men and public patriarchies/Jeff Hearn.
    p. cm. – (Critical studies on men and masculinities)
    Includes bibliographical references and indexes.
    1. Men. 2. Patriarchy. 3. Masculinity (Psychology) I. Title.
    II. Series
    HQ1090.H44   1992
    305.31 dc20   91-44397
                                                                CIP

ISBN 0–415–07619–6
ISBN 0–415–07620–X (pbk)

Typeset in 10 on 12 Bembo by LaserScript, Mitcham, Surrey
Printed and bound in Great Britain
by Biddles Ltd, Guildford and King's Lynn

Contents

List of tables and figures   vi
Series editor's preface   Jeff Hearn   vii
Preface   ix
Acknowledgements   xi

Foreword   Pluralizing perspectives: the present and
    the past   1
1 Introduction: the problem of public men   11

PART 1   FROM THE MALESTREAM TO
PUBLIC PATRIARCHIES
2 Public men in the malestream   25
3 Patriarchy, public patriarchy, and related critiques 43
4 Public patriarchy: some initial implications for men
    and masculinities   69
5 Public patriarchies, public men, public domains, and
    public masculinities   74

PART 2   PUBLIC MEN IN PUBLIC PATRIARCHIES
6 Public men as social relations   95
7 Organizations of men (1): size, structures, and
    hierarchies   140
8 Organizations of men (2): processes, sexualities, and
    images   170
9 Public men as persons: selves, psyches, and senses   208

Afterword   Beyond public men?   227

Notes   232
Bibliography   254
Name index   276
Subject index   282

Tables and figures

Tables

1.1 Examples of the ideological gendering of the private
    and the public   2
3.1 Private patriarchy, public patriarchy, and related
    concepts   54
3.2 Comparison of Walby's (1986, 1989) and Hearn's
    (1987a) approaches to patriarchy   237

Figures

3.1 Types of masculine gender-system   51
3.2 Historical timescales in conceptualizing public
    patriarchy   55
7.1 Types of organization by gender divisions   244

Series editor's preface

Gender is one of the most pervasive and taken-for-granted features of our lives. It figures strongly in the make-up of all societies. Yet it is easy to see that gender may also create problems – in terms of power, oppression, inequality, identity and self-doubt.

The growth of modern feminism and the associated development of women's studies have brought a deep questioning of women's social position. At the same time feminism and women's studies have provided continuing critical analyses of men and masculinities. In a rather different way the rise of gay liberation and gay scholarship has shown that previously accepted notions of sexuality and gender are no longer just 'natural'. This has led to a recognition that the dominant forms of men and masculinities are themselves not merely 'natural' and unchangeable. In addition, inspired particularly by important research in women's studies and the need for a positive response to feminism, some men have in recent years turned their attention to the critical study of men. These various focuses on men are clearly very different from the traditional concern with men that has characterized the social sciences, where in the worst cases men have been equated with people in general. Thus men and masculinities are seen not as unproblematic, but as social constructions which need to be explored, analysed, and indeed in certain respects, such as the use of violence, changed.

This series aims to promote critical studies, by women and men, on men and masculinities. It brings together scholarship that deals in detail with the social and political construction of particular aspects of men and masculinities. This will include studies of the changing forms of men and masculinities, as well as the broader historical and comparative studies. Furthermore, because men have been dominant in the writing of social science and production of malestream theory, one area of special interest for critical assessment is the relationship of men and masculinities to social science itself. This applies to both the content and 'results' of previous social research, and to the understanding of social theory in all its various guises – epistemology, ideology, methodology, and so forth.

Each volume in the series will approach its specific topic in the light of feminist theory and practice, and, where relevant, gay liberation and gay scholarship. The task of the series is thus the critique of men and masculinities, and not the critique of feminism by men. As such the series is pro-feminist and gay affirmative. However, this critical stance does not mean that men are simply to be seen or understood negatively. On the contrary, an important part of an accurate study of men and masculinity is an appreciation of the positive features of men's lives, and especially the variety of men's lived experiences. The series includes a range of disciplines – sociology, history, politics, psychoanalysts, cultural studies – as well as encouraging interdisciplinarity where appropriate. Overall, the attempt will be made to produce a series of studies of men and masculinities that are anti-sexist and anti-patriarchal in orientation.

Finally, while this series is primarily an academic development it will also at times necessarily draw on practical initiatives outside academia. Likewise, it will attempt to speak to changing patterns of men's practice both within and beyond academic study. Just as one of the most exciting aspects of feminism is the strong inter-relation of theory and practice, so too must the critical study of men and masculinities and change in men's practice against patri-archy develop in a close association.

Jeff Hearn

Preface

Writing exists in spaces. It is in-between: between what can be said and what can be imagined. This writing exists within a number of spaces. It spans time and place – from Bradford (1986–88) to Manchester (1988–89) and back to Bradford (1989–91). It also is in-between: between analysis and experience; structure and process; modernism and postmodernism; construction and deconstruction; men and masculinities; One and Others; and so on.

Acknowledgements

This book is the product of a lot of talking, reading, researching, writing, rewriting, and a lot of inspiration from women, men, and young people. There are very many people, groups, and organizations I'd like to thank for assistance in this process. They include colleagues and students at the University of Bradford, particularly those who have been taking courses on 'men and masculinities'; Paul Wilding and all at the Department of Social Policy and Social Work at the University of Manchester for making me so welcome during 1988–89; the Hallsworth Research Fellowship Committee for their generous award of funds to do much of this work; the Manchester Campus Workshop on the Critical Study of Men and Masculinities for providing continuity and support; the Men, Masculinities and Socialism Group and other men's groups; and librarians at Bradford University, Manchester University, and Bradford Council for their help.

Many people have helped directly or indirectly, and I would like to thank, among many others, John Barker, Jan Barrett, Harry Brod, Alan Carling, Cynthia Cockburn, David Collinson, Margaret Collinson, Helen Corr, John Davis, Harry Ferguson, Lesley Fowler, Richard Freeman, John Gillis, Kerry Hamilton, Jalna Hanmer, Jay Hearn, Øystein Gullvåg Holter, David Jackson, Lynn Jamieson, Deborah Kerfoot, Michael Kimmel, David Knights, Mary Locking, Mary McIntosh, Antonio Melechi, David Morgan, Wendy Parkin, Christine Parton, Steve Potter, John Remy, Deborah Sheppard, Liz Stanley, Gary Wickham.

I am also grateful to the participants at various conferences and other educational and political forums who have commented on papers presented on these issues. These include the universities of Cambridge, Manchester, Sussex, York; Birmingham Polytechnic; the Centre for Gender Studies, Hull; several British Sociological Association Annual Conferences; and the North East London Polytechnic/Free Association Conference on 'Psychoanalysis and the Public Sphere'.

I would also like to thank Gordon Smith, formerly of Unwin Hyman and now of Routledge, for his support, also the staff at Routledge; Sue Moody for typing the script and sorting out all the squiggles and arrows; and Amy, Jay, Molly, and Tom, whom I live with, for making fun of 'the sexuality of the masculinity of the patriarchy . . . '.

Foreword
Pluralizing perspectives: the present and the past

We are no longer private. We are not private. For better and for worse, we, men, are public, and increasingly so.

This book is about public men, or, in other words, men in public, within patriarchy – or, patriarchies. The motivation for writing this, and for publication, has been intensely personal. And although this has involved dealing with questions of society, history, and theory, the reason I have been brought to them is to understand and change myself and other men, our social locations, and politics.

Exploring these issues[1] has forced me to face, consider, and feel the enormity of men's material powers, both in public and more generally. It has also rather gradually brought me to realize, what now seems very clear, that all of this is *historical*.

In some ways writing this represents a coming together of two of my particular interests and preoccupations: men, masculinities, and patriarchy; and gender, sexuality, and organizations. Up until now I have tended to explore these two areas rather separately. Here, however, I want to look at them together; and consider their implications for each other: the gendered and sexual nature of organizations for men, masculinities, and patriarchy; and vice versa. This interconnection may (or may not) seem obvious enough, yet there are few thoroughgoing attempts to relate, say, how organizations work to how patriarchy works, or analyses of patriarchy in relation to what happens in organizations. This combination of forces again emphasizes the need for history – the interrelations of men, organizations, gender, sexuality, and patri-archies are clearly not fixed. These various interrelations also point to the need for plural, multiple perspectives. For it is very unlikely that any one perspective will be satisfactory for all the different questions and issues raised. Multiple or plural

[1]

perspectives are also important in a more general way as an attempt to appreciate the diversity and differences of lives and experiences. To put this more directly, single perspectivism and anti-feminism may go hand in hand.[2]

In looking at the enormity of men's material powers, how they have come historically to be the way they are, how they oppress women, and how they affect, and even in certain specific ways may oppress us ourselves, I have been increasingly impressed by the power of men and men's institutions in what is often called the public domain. As I shall explain later, I think now that there are in fact *a number of public domains* rather than *a* or *the* public domain – and for that reason I use the plural. So by the term 'public domains' I mean all that happens in public, and not domestically, not in private; that which happens in organizations, militaries, public workplaces, factories, offices, churches, and other corporate institutions, and in the street and other widely visible open spaces. In this sense public parks *are* different from private parks. Furthermore, the public domains are in all manner of ways associated with dominance and the dominance of men. Notions of 'public' and 'private' have become effectively gendered, and accordingly *mapped onto* a whole range of possible ideological dichotomies: 'male'/'female', 'masculine'/'feminine', even 'gendered'/'agendered', as well as many other agendered associations (see Table 1.1).

Such genderings have come to apply as much in academic analysis as in everyday perceptions. Thus dominance/public domains/public men/men are in a mutually reinforcing relation – that relation is part of the problem of public men. Furthermore, that power and dominance of the public domains and public men appears to be historically on the increase, at least in its potential.[3]

Table 1.1 Examples of the ideological gendering of the private and the public

Private	Public
Gendered (explicitly gendered)	Agendered (implicitly gendered)
Female	Male
Feminine	Masculine
Sphere of women and femininity/ies	Sphere of men and maculinity/ies

This is especially clear in the operations of the public institutions of violence, with their increasing corporate capability for destruction and genocide.

If this book has a central task, then it is to explore the relationships between men's activity in and domination of the public domains, and the persistence of patriarchy – or *patriarchies*.[4] It addresses the significance of patriarchies for understanding public men in the public domains, and the significance of public men for understanding patriarchies. So here we have two more plurals: patriarchies rather than patriarchy; and public men rather than public man. I prefer 'patriarchies' because, while there is certainly societal domination by men, this isn't reducible to one societal system or process; instead there are effectively lots of patriarchies, dominated by different types of men, operating simultaneously, overlapping, interrelating, contradicting. Similarly I prefer 'public men' to 'public man'. The notion of public man echoes the use of the generic universal Man (often implicitly able-bodied, heterosexual, and white) – of both neutral (neutered?) humanity, and as 'male'. Furthermore, whereas Richard Sennett (1977) uses the term without *explicit* references to gender, the plural term is used deliberately to speak of men *as men*.[5] 'Public men' is also simply more accurate. Thus in calling this book *Men in the Public Eye*, I am referring to men in the plural, and the way men are constructed through public visibility. This also makes clear the way in which construction of the public domains is founded on forms of (dis) able-bodiedness.[6] When I refer to 'public men', I am thinking not primarily of 'public figures' or individual 'men in the public eye', but rather of different men's presence in and relationship to the public domains. The notion of public men as 'public figures' or individual men 'in the public eye' is itself an ideological elaboration of the general construction of men in public. Their individual power accrues from the general, that is a social structural, relation of men to women, in the public domains and elsewhere. 'The eye' in 'the public eye' is not an individual eye, but a structural arrangement, the social structuring of visibility and invisibility, to which all may be subject. In another sense, the notion of public men in use here is itself ideological and could be contrasted with the notion of private man as the apparently autonomous patriarch.[7]

What I have said so far about the powers of men and of public men applies especially to the power of able-bodied, heterosexual, 'middle-aged'/older, middle/upper-class, white men. Accordingly this book is primarily about such men. This focus as 'the' primary problem suggests that not only do men dominate women, but also different types of men dominate other men – able-bodied over men with disabilities, heterosexual over gay, and so on. This applies in, first, the domination of public men over private men, and the exclusion of certain types of men, such as those with disabilities, from the public domains; and, secondly, the domination of different types of men over other men within the public domains. This book is thus partly a deconstruction of able-bodied, heterosexual, 'middle-aged'/older, middle/upper-class, white men. For although such a type of men is dominant, this description of men is itself an ideological construction; to put this rather simply, such men may rarely, if ever, exist! All the above qualifications of men – for example, 'able-bodied' or 'heterosexual' – are themselves problematic. Each qualification is a much simplified abstraction, *a transformation of relative distinctions and real, material powers into relatively fixed categories.* To say this is not, however, to limit the power of public men to such men. Other types of men, oppressed through (dis)ability, sexuality, age, economic class, ethnicity, or some other medium of oppression, may dominate in their own ways in their own public domains. This may apply both over women who are oppressed in apparently comparable ways, for example women with disabilities, lesbians, young women, working-class women, black women; and over other types of men. Thus while my discussion of public men is directed primarily towards men in dominant groups, it may also have relevance to men who are not in dominant groups in particular social contexts.[8]

Focusing on public men

As is so often the case, there are personal, political, historical, and theoretical reasons for focusing on men in public.

The personal rationale is that it is a problem area that concerns me personally. Partly this comes from my interest in the workings of organizations in the public domains. More particularly it comes from my time spent trying to work on or against sexism and patriarchy in public situations – in campaigns, demonstrations, talks, lectures, meetings, training sessions, conferences, and so on. This is itself related to changes in my 'life course' and the ages of the people I live with. Spending time in public working on questions of sexism raises practical and personal dilemmas for me – am I able to do that? have I got the necessary energy? what if I feel nervous? if it goes wrong? does it matter? how much time should I give to it? and to preparation for it? how much of myself should I share? is not enough sharing copping out? is too much sharing self-indulgent? how does all this relate to my private and domestic life? and so on. So there are plenty of solid practical reasons for trying to sort out my thinking on men in public.

Related very closely to all those questions in a way that at times makes them almost indistinguishable are the political rationales for focusing on men in public. These include the question of how do men develop a politics that is against patriarchies, and especially so in ways that do not reproduce the past associations of politics, masculinity, and oppressive power.

The problem of public men is politically important for me, and I believe other men (that is, the gender class of men), in terms of my/our relationship to feminism and patriarchy. Men are inevitably located as powerful *within patriarchies*, while men's relationship with feminism is inevitably *problematic* (Hearn 1992). What this means is that, because of men's structural location within patriarchies as members of the oppressor class, we cannot simply announce our alliance with feminism and feminists, as if that is proof of our good intentions. Words, and writing, are themselves not enough. Our relationship with feminism will always be problematic. Our positive relationship to feminism, even if problematic, will be furthered by deeds more than words alone.

Then there are social, historical, and theoretical rationales for focusing on public men. This is partly a matter of historical changes, as already noted; it is also a matter of attending to political–epistemological questions around the very construction and deconstruction of knowledge. What counts as knowledge, that is public knowledge, is so bound up with men, and men's public power, that it is necessary to deconstruct 'men', 'public men', and 'men's power'. We have to take on the 'Big Boys' of the social sciences (Canaan & Griffin 1990), their gender-blindness, and the ways in which 'men' and 'masculinity' have often been kept implicit in their accounts. Thus the investigation of public men is also an investigation into knowledge, and part of

[5]

an attempt to dismantle that taken-for-granted malestream (O'Brien 1981).[9]

In several important senses 'patriarchy' – or rather patriarchies – have changed their fundamental shape over the last century or more. The form of 'patriarchy' that is currently dominant can be described as 'public patriarchy' or 'social patriarchy' as against 'private patriarchy' or 'family patriarchy'. Though patriarchies certainly still exist, they cannot be said to do so in any simple or direct way – the power of the individual father is no longer necessary for the continuation of 'patriarchy'. In taking up these issues there is throughout a double theme: the historical changes whereby men have come to dominate women in 'modern', 'patriarchal' ways, over and above, in part replacing the ways of familial, privately based patriarchy; and impact of those changes upon men. Those two strands are of course related. The second strand itself has a kind of double thread – for those changes have both been made by men, and have in turn made men. Thus there are at least two initial sets of relations here – between women and men, and in the making of men by men. It is necessary and important to bear in mind these and other relations, because, when someone says or writes 'men', these complexities and complications are usually implicit.

Changing the private and the public

This book is also more generally about social science, men's relationship to feminism, and the explicit theorizing of men and masculinities. As Marx suggested, the way to understand the world, in this case men, is to change us/them. One way of understanding all this is in terms of my writing in gender class traitorship, of spilling the beans on my gender class – which I feel so antagonistic to, yet love so much. This book is about just a part of that gender class position – not the whole. My focus on public men is not because I see them as more important than men in private. Indeed, paradoxically again the significance of the public domains comes from their domination of the private domains. For the public domains that are dominant over the private constitute the superstructure to the base of the private domains.

My focus on public men is despite the fact that the division

[6]

between the public domains and the private domains is extremely problematic. Indeed, further to that, I see the public domains, as a material, spatial and ideological construction, founded upon (genderic) powers and contradictions of the private domains. At its simplest, the development of public domains is principally a means by which men come to wrest power from women's (potential) power in and of the private domains (O'Brien 1981; Hearn 1987a). The public domains and men's power there are in that sense rooted in the private domains. They are premised upon men's various direct and indirect dominations in and of the private domains in the constructions of private domains themselves, in the avoidance of work there, in the separation of the private and public domains, and in the control of the private domains by the institutions, laws, and procedures of the public domains. At their base, patriarchies and the patriarchal form of this society rest on the private domains and on private practice there – on practice at the various points of the reproduction of social life. Thus I am addressing one of the major, though probably not the prime, arenas and forms of domination, indeed of world domination – men's domination of the public domains, and both within and through that of the private domains. This study is therefore inevitably dealing with less than half the story: it isn't possible to do everything all the time.

I hope it will be clear from what I've already said that the public/private divisions are both important and yet very complex. It is extremely difficult to convey, especially in a concise form, the ways in which the public/private division is real, material, and powerful; and the ways in which it is problematic, 'unreal', discursive, and strangely enough equally powerful. At this stage, it is perhaps sufficient to say that the *separation* just suggested between a material and a discursive perspective on the public and the private is, in a profound sense, false, because the material is also discursive, and the discursive also material; secondly, an important aspect of the power of the public domains and of public men is the normalization, rather than problematization, of the public/private divisions. Furthermore, there is another real difficulty around the notion of 'public/private divisions', for it is certainly not a definite or complete *division*. In keeping with the arguments above, it is probably more accurate to speak of 'public/ private differences'. Thus in this text, I hope, paradoxically, to assist that problematization of public/private differences and the deconstruction of public men by focusing on the public domains and public men.

In view of all these complications, you may be wondering – well, why bother? Why not just focus on, say, men in private, and avoid some of these contradictions? My first reaction to this is – yes, that might be simpler, more directly to the point; but my second reaction is that the avoidance of contradictions is itself illusory – we live in a dialectical world, and other contradictions appear in what may initially appear non-contradictory situations and arenas. It is just that this is the area I am dealing with here. Having said that, there is a further contradiction that men's specialization in public matters is part of the context within which I came to be interested in the public domains and organization theory in particular. Having accumulated some understanding of how the public domains and organizations work, I am now turning that back against itself. Rather similarly, attention to the public domains does not imply an emphasis on 'structure' over 'agency' or over 'practice'. The form the public domains take is certainly a structural matter, but so too is the form of the private domains. The public domains are just as much based in and on practice as are the private domains. To assume specific equivalences between the public domains and structure, and the private domains and practice, is mistaken.

To explore how I am and we are the way we are as men by virtue of the increasing importance of men's power in the public domains is a task beyond any one volume. Inevitably, it is necessary to be more specific and more selective. For example, it could be argued that a crucial period of the historical development of patriarchy occurred in the early ancient Greek civilizations (O'Brien 1981). Or it could be argued that we need to attend to the beginnings of capitalism. I shall be selective and specific in two ways. First, I shall focus on particular historical processes, namely the shift to a society based on large, powerful, corporate, multi-unit institutions, the so called 'public patriarchy' – or, as I prefer, 'public patriarchies'. Second, I shall focus on the period of 1870–1920, as the prime time when this shift can be observed, even though the shift certainly began earlier and continued later, to this day. In deciding on these two focuses, there is inevitably some arbitrariness. However, my guiding principle has been where in the past I am most able to recognize the beginnings of the dominating features of the present. Third, I shall be concerned mainly with changes in Great Britain/the United Kingdom, and to a lesser extent in the United States and elsewhere.

With this particular historical focus, I like to think of this book as a kind of historical document – a description of some strange times past when things were different. Unfortunately, and even taking on the methodological and political critiques of the divisions between the public and private domains, I can't see or say that. 'Public man' and 'public men' are still very much a reality, both as ideology and as practice.

Thus, to sum up so far, in returning to the past I am talking of the present. I am interested in the past to the extent that it speaks of the present. This is so both in the general sense that speaking of the past is always speaking of the present, and in the specific sense that speaking of certain aspects or periods of the past speaks directly of the dominant powers in the present, in this case the powers of men. In my own case, I am interested in how 'modern men' feel we are moving from the modern to some other experience of 'masculinity', difficult to specify, sometimes rather grandly (*sic*) labelled 'postmodern'. Such (post)modernization of men produces all kinds of paradoxes, and especially so for 'public men', 'men in public'.

Before moving to look at the way in which this book is structured and arranged, it would be inappropriate for me to end this Foreword without turning to the question of 'difficulty'. In the course of writing, I have tried to work out why writing this book has often been so difficult. As is usually the case, I think there are several reasons. First is the chronic feeling that I am labouring under and against the *weight* of men's power in the public domains. Another is the paradoxes and contradictions already noted, especially around the focus on 'public men', and the problematic relation of the public domains and the private domains. Third is the sheer volume and complexity of material I am working on. Fourth is my attempt to work against dominant malestream paradigms. Fifth, and possibly more personally, I think arduous mental work is sometimes associated with other difficulties: emotional pain can become sublimated into the pain of mental labour. I hope that these difficulties will be eased by making them more conscious in writing.

The structure of this book

This book is organized in the following way. The Introduction
(Ch. 1) elaborates on the rise of the problem of public men. The
first main section, 'From the Malestream to Public Patriarchies',
considers in Chapters 2 and 3 the changing social and societal
frameworks for locating public men. Chapter 4 discusses some of
the implications of the concept of 'public patriarchy' for the
analysis of men and masculinities. Chapter 5 argues more fully the
case for pluralizing the major concepts to public patriarchies,
public men, public domains, and public masculinities, as already
outlined in this Foreword. The second main section provides a
detailed description and analysis of public men in public patriarchies in the period 1870-1920 – in terms of existence and
change in the major relations of public patriarchies (Ch. 6); the
size, structures, and hierarchies of organizations (Ch. 7); processes, sexualities, and images in organizations (Ch. 8); and men
as selves, psyches, and senses (Ch. 9). The Afterword brings these
historical debates and dilemmas back to the present, and to the
need to re-form the differences between the public and the
private as a way of changing men, and for men to change. It is the
order of things that makes an argument.

CHAPTER 1

Introduction: the problem of public men

In working on this book, I found a kind of passionate enthusiasm for tracking down the 'origins', historical or otherwise, of present-day masculinities, particularly the public masculinities of public men. I say this whilst being immensely dubious about the search for origins, especially those that are distant and archaic (Hearn 1987a, p. 192). This seemed different, however: it *appeared immediate*. I was drawn to discover where and how public men began to be as we are now in our public masculinities. I knew it had something to do with the enlargement and domination of the public domains, sometimes sudden, sometimes gradual, over the private with modernization and modernity, and particularly the creation of a new kind of universalization of experience. In this sense we now see ourselves not simply as individuals but as part of the mass collectivity of men, in corporation-produced images, words, deeds, and actions. This is easily seen as a huge burden, a massive negativity, that detracts from some essential and higher 'man'. This is mistaken: there is no such 'higher being'. The ever-presence of corporate, universal man is neither a good nor an evil; it is what has become. The problem of public men thus refers to both these confusions around the form of masculinities, especially public masculinities, and the intense associations of public men and power already described, and exacerbated in the technological, institutional, and organizational developments of the 'modern world'.

So how have we come to recognize the problem of 'public men'? The rise of this problem, and the rise in the recognition of the problem, necessarily involves a process of *public recognition* in the public domains (for example, in politics and academia). All men become 'public' in the process of (public) recognition, just as all discourse is public. Thus one could reasonably, if long-windedly, refer to this process as the public rise of the public problem of public men – it is only in the public domains that a 'problem', as private trouble, becomes the problem, as public issue.

Just as the way men are talked about, understood, and explained in everyday conversations is partly a question of the material impact of (particular) men and partly a question of their construction in discourse, so this is equally so in the more public debates of men, academic, political or otherwise. The changing ways in which men have been seen and are now seen involves both material changes in men and what men do (for example, the type of work men do) and changes in the placing of men in discourse. This means that to describe 'the rise of the problem of public men' is to describe both some of those material changes and the ways that they are constructed, which includes constructions in everyday conversation, politics, *and* academic study. For example, what we call 'history' is both a story of material and other changes, a discursive construction of such changes; and it is also a story about itself, in the *senses* that both the material changes and the discursive constructions include the productions of other histories. Something similar could be said of everyday conversation. Thus material and discursive changes in everyday, political, and academic speech about men are all part of themselves, and all relevant to undertaking the rise in the problem of men, especially public men.

When someone speaks about men or masculinities in everyday conversation, they are both saying something about the 'topic' and, at least if they are a man, showing something of the 'topic'. Similarly, in academic discourse on men or masculinities, the 'topic' is talked about and it is displayed, certainly within the malestream and probably also in counter-streams. For these reasons, the history of ideas about men is very much part and parcel of the central problem (of men).

In this chapter I shall look at the recognition of the problem of public men in three main and closely interrelated ways: first, in terms of cultural and historical constructions; secondly, political and other critiques; and thirdly, contradictions around public men in the context of modernization.

Cultural and historical constructions

While we live in 'patriarchy', indeed in 'world patriarchy', the manner and form of gender relations throughout the world is intensely varied. Though related, however indirectly and at least at times in some of our minds to biology, sex, and 'sexual difference(s)', gender is materially and culturally produced. This applies both to cultural variations in the signification of gender in particular societies, and more ambitiously to the category of 'gender' itself. Gender always remains a cultural, practical accomplishment (as well as a human, sensuous one as Marx might have said[1]). To see gender as cultural formation is not to subscribe to a cultural *explanation* of gender. Gender is culture, which is itself historically and materially formed. This involves transforming matter to matters of interest. Men and gender are produced in the conflicts and struggles of history and politics.

Gender and gender relations are also subject to great historical transformations, albeit with pronounced historical irregularity. At times the pace of change has been intense; often contributing to and reinforced by rapid change in a variety of social arenas and through a variety of social processes. Men's domination of the public domains has been ancient, contested, and culturally variable. In medieval society there were definite separate spheres for women and men, for example in religious, court, and military arenas. By the fifteenth century women's participation in the public domains was increasing. In Restoration England of the late seventeenth and early eighteenth centuries, political and economic changes in urbanization, industrialization, and capital accumulation, and the growth in the admittedly still small electorate were intimately connected with change in families, households, and gender relations. These in turn, it has been argued, provided the context for definitions of masculinities:

> As the structural bases of gender relations had shifted and were thrown into disarray, the meaning of masculinity itself was brought into question, debated, and in part redefined. Women's assertion of sexual agency, of an equality of desire, and of equal rights within marriage, inspired men to abandon traditional roles within the family, just as changes in the organization of work and political changes eroded their economic autonomy and the traditional system of fixed political statuses in pre-capitalist society.
>
> (Kimmel 1987, p. 134)

Amongst the affluent class, the '"new man" of Restoration England was transformed into a feminized, feminine "invert", as

[13]

vain, petty and pretty as any woman' (p. 135). While there are a number of conceptual and empirical difficulties with this kind of analysis, particularly around the assumption of the externalized (economic and political) structural bases of gender relations, it is clear that the perception of men and masculinities as a contested problem, indeed as significant at all, is historically variable and historically constructed.

As already noted, change in men and gender relations involves both social change and discursive change. Thus from the beginnings of the Enlightenment in the sixteenth century the promotion of 'rational' approaches to human affairs was also a question of gender.[2] This is most obviously seen in the association of particular forms of masculinity with the rational control of society, nature, and each other. At a rather naive level this has sometimes been seen simply as a sign of men's power to control, and hence dominate. On the other hand, it is worth noting that in the eighteenth century, both Leibniz and Bentham employed rational argument against war and militarism: men's rationality turned against another form of men's power. Bentham also emphasized the irrationality of antisodomitical violence and advocated the decriminalization of sodomy in a series of unpublished essays (Corber 1990).

The eighteenth and nineteenth centuries saw further massive transformations of gender relations. This was for many reasons – economic, political, sexual, spatial. Gender, gender ideology, and ideologies around gender became more explicit. While the words 'feminine' and 'masculine' were in use in the sixteenth century, 'femininity' and 'masculinity' did not acquire widespread recognition as significant categories for describing identifiably gendered people until the nineteenth century.[3] A central feature of this was the establishment of a series of ideologies around the notion of 'separate spheres' for women and men:[4] 'the central *belief* . . . of a male breadwinner gaining a livelihood through work and maintaining his female [and child] dependants within the home . . . . In this view, husband and wife were the archetype, but father and child, brother and sister, uncle and niece, master and servant reproduced the relationship of clientage and dependency' (Davidoff 1979, p. 64; my emphasis and insertion).

Very importantly these divisions and differences were, and indeed are, matters of ideology. As Leonore Davidoff and Catherine Hall write, with respect to the English middle class of the eighteenth and nineteenth centuries: 'Public was not really public and private was not really private despite the potent imagery of "separate spheres". Both were ideological constructs with specific meaning which must be understood as products of a particular historical time' (1986, p. 33). These shifts to the ideologies of separate spheres are usually dated around the first fifty, sixty, seventy years of industrialization from the 1780s. Connections might be made between specific cultural, literary, and ideological representations of gender and sexuality, and changing patterns of industrialization, employment, geographical mobility, and domestic organization; in short, a correspondence between the gendered and the institutional separation of the public and private spheres. There are, not surprisingly, problems with such accounts. Dating such gender shifts is in fact extremely problematic, not least because of variations by economic class. For example, early industrialization often engaged large numbers of women workers in the public domains.

A rather different perspective is provided by John Savile (1988) when he suggests that the eighteenth-century preoccupation with rampant sexuality for women and men had indeed been superseded by the 1850s by the 'Victorian' pattern of separate gendered (passive/active) sexualities. This view has in turn been challenged by A. D. Harvey (1978, 1989) through analysis of literary conventions. Even in the 1740s Samuel Richardson's novels *Pamela* and *Clarissa* were already portraying women as naturally passive and asexual, following on the previous view of women as sexual predators. By the 1810s, pornographic books dealing with flagellation of men by women were fashionable, as was gossip about predatory lesbians. Harvey suggests that these constituted the *reaction* of male chauvinist fantasy against what was then the standard model of passive female sexuality. These particular class-specific literary modes thus provide much earlier accounts of 'separate spheres'.

Either way, by the second half of the nineteenth century, ideologies of the separate spheres for women and men appeared more fully established (Pleck & Pleck 1980), and the further categorization of gendered states was proceeding apace – through medical, psychiatric, moral, sexual, and other discourses. For example, the terms 'homosexual' and 'homosexuality' were formulated in 1869 by the Hungarian doctor Karoly Maria Benkert (Weeks 1989, p. 213). Jeffrey Weeks (1989, p. 87)

[15]

describes 1885 as an *annus mirabilis* of sexual politics, in which several purity and legal campaigns came strongly to the fore, including the passing of the Criminal Law Amendment Act, which raised the age of sexual consent, and the Labouchère Amendment, which criminalized male homosexuality. According to Michael Kimmel (1986, p. 14),[5] in 1886 '[t]he words "heterosexual" and "homosexual" came into popular usage [in the United States] . . . after a review of Krafft-Ebing's *Psychopathia Sexualis* in the *New York Times* . . .'. The turn of the century saw all kinds of further gendered/sexual elaborations and institutional developments (e.g. Mangan & Walvin 1987). Frank Mort (1987) places such gender ideologies in the wider context of 'gender-specific discourse on sexuality'. In particular he notes an association between the promotion of 'manliness' within muscular Christianity and the intellectual inspirations of 'the moralized language of evolutionary science' (p. 115). He goes on to suggest that 'language of purity (for men) opened up a space for women to define their own images of female sexual identity' (p. 116).

Accordingly, the late nineteenth century has to be seen as a time of major and crucial change in the construction of masculinities (e.g. Kimmel 1987; Dubbert 1979; Pleck & Pleck 1980). Writing in the context of the United States, Kimmel notes how the twin forces of industrialization and political democracy threatened 'masculinity' – or, more accurately, *particular types of masculinities* – at that time. And, while problems remain around such notions of 'threatened masculinity' or 'crisis in masculinity' (Brittan 1989), as well as the relationship of 'gender' and the 'economic' (see pp. 96–102), the general significance of historical change at that time is difficult to doubt. In particular, and if for no other reason, present-day confusions and divergences of masculinity, so pervasive in this fracturing postmodern world, cannot be seen outside of history.

What is of profound interest here is the 'publicization' (Brown 1981) of the social world, the bringing of activities and issues into the public domains. This is important in both the growth of larger and more powerful organizational means of production, control, and indeed institutional violence, and the transformation of masculinities in their various forms. Publicization has created a set of circumstances in which there is a huge array of universalizable images and informations about what men and masculinities are or are meant to be. External information is not new to humans, nor

[16]

is it new in large quantities; what is new is its universalizable qualities – its availability to all men, its speaking to all men, *its complex combination of internalization and externalization*. We are in a profound sense alienated from whatever might be called a sense of 'self'. The potential power of both individuals and collectivities is assumed by others, so that those who work on and are responsible for the production of those mass images are not better able to see themselves.

Critiques

These cultural and historical circumstances have also brought a number of major developments that have assisted the recognition of the problem of public men, and provided political and other critiques of public men. In this way, the historical transformation of gender cannot be separated off from gender politics and the politics of sexuality.

These include most obviously the rise of feminist theory and practice. In saying this I am thinking particularly of the fact that feminist theory and practice has a long history; and not only in the late nineteenth and twentieth centuries. Feminism has long been making the invisible visible, speaking of problems that have no name, making voices, decentring the centre, recentring the other, making the private public, challenging and changing consciousness, recognizing and deconstructing patriarchy, celebrating sisterhood, and opposing the power, domination, oppression, and violence of men. Feminism has always addressed the problem of men (Hanmer 1990).[6]

A different kind of cultural and historical construction is represented by gay liberation and gay studies since the late 1960s. These have produced their own critiques of men, paradoxically through recognizing men loving and desiring men. In addition, developments as diverse as socialist organization, psychoanalysis, and critical cultural studies have contributed to the critique of public men. They can be understood as both outcomes of and responses to the universalizing tendencies of modernization, both reactions to and appreciations of the collective subject. Despite their own dominant patriarchalism, they have in some instances assisted the recognition of public men and the problem of public men. From all of these have come first 'men's studies', and then the critique of men (and the critique of 'men's studies').[7]

Feminist critiques of men, in theory and practice; gay studies and gay critiques; anti-sexist critiques; the critique of men – all contribute both to making men and masculinities explicit, and paradoxically to the deconstruction of men and masculinities. The impact of feminism on men and men's response to feminism were often at first a personal and private matter; increasingly, this has changed as men in public situations – in organizations, in business, trade unions, political parties – have had to respond to feminist initiatives. Similarly, men's positive pro-feminist responses have become more public – in groups, networks, newsletters, organizations. Critical study on men in the public domains has become increasingly recognized as a political, as well as an academic, issue.

The focus on public men in relation to these 'gender critiques' has revealed a further paradox. Feminism has shown the importance of personal experience, the political nature of the personal, the personal nature of the political, the interrelation of the private and the public; the implications of this for studying men are not simple or unambiguous. One lesson might be for men to turn to the private and the personal; another might be to consider the interrelation of the private and the public; a third might be to look again at the public face of men, but in a different light. This last possibility is the focus here. While Betty Friedan (1963) wrote of the problem that has no name when speaking of women's confinement to the private world of domesticity, men may need to address both our private subjectivity as well as the problem of public men that has no name. In saying this I am not suggesting that men in public is a problem comparable to women in private; rather, I am thinking that the problem of public men is the problem that comes from power and domination, and from its non-recognition – the problems of separation from the private domains, of the public domains being 'normal', 'neutral', and 'objective', of there being no language to make this *objectifying* sphere the object not the subject of knowledge.

So 'public men' are recognizable and are open to critique on a wide variety of grounds: direct domination over women in the public domains; the hierarchical structuring of the public domains, and the domination of some men over other men; the domination over both women and men in the private domains, albeit in different ways; the silence on the relationship of men's activity in the public domains to their/our activity in the private domains; the overarching domination of life, society, and discourses by the construction of the public domains, and hence the overriding of the private domains; and finally, in this list at least, public men's oppression of ourselves and each other.

Contradictions

Patriarchies do not exist in any simple way. This universalizing world which subsumes and separates men, which provides ample material for our misapprehension of ourselves and each other through the presence of mass images and a thousand and one other informations, is also the ground for men to appreciate the possibilities of being different and being against sexism and against patriarchies. Men's praxis against sexism is very largely a coming together of responses to feminism and gay liberation with men's particular biographies and histories. Men's praxis against patriarchies comes out of historical movements towards and within public patriarchies. Men, as individuals, groups, and collectivities, now exist with the experience of mass media, education, and corporate, organizational lives; and of struggles and resistances, personal and political, in relation to them. We try to excavate sense, and sometimes a sense of self or selves, within all these confusions and oppressions. Public patriarchies produce alienations from ourselves, as well as the social circumstances that make possible the overcoming and transcendence of those alienations, as individuals and collectivities.

The power of the individual father has been, if not superseded, then at least complicated by men's own powers in the public domains maintaining the continuation of patriarchies. The movement from private patriarchy to public patriarchies is not remorseless, or some kind of end-state to be achieved. Within this *movement* lie the seeds of the destruction of patriarchies, just as much as contradictions within the development of capitalism provide the seeds, or at least the fertile ground, for the supersession of capitalism. In the case of capitalism, the seeds include the progressive shift of use values to the realm of exchange and exchange values, and the contradiction that ensues between those relations of production and distribution and the forces of production. In the case of patriarchy, the contradictions are somewhat different; they include that between the use values of human contact and the exchange values of violence.[8] In the particular case of *public* patriarchies, contradictions develop between the experiences, signification, and appearances of the private realm and those of the public realm: all forms of (patriarchal) power, however 'trivial', can become *public*, that is, can move to signification and appearance in the public domains. What was shared 'semi-publicly' twenty years ago among friends, workmates, family members, and in consciousness-raising groups, may now be shared in the public media in the public domains. All is potentially public.

This is a new historical form of patriarchy that may catch out men (as patriarchs). The days of patriarchal power may be numbered, as all can now be known. Even those formerly secret conspiracies, cabals, cabinets, committees, clubs, chats in saunas, behind closed doors, meetings in boardrooms, 'fixes' in pubs and snugs, in locker rooms, front rooms, cafés, restaurants, offices of company directors, civil servants, politicians, monarchs, dictators, military men, police, and torturers, can now potentially be known. And the patriarchs know this, and are, if not scared, then slightly apprehensive. This is partly a technological matter of surveillance, of electronics, of bugging, of computers, of hackers; it is also a matter of politics – men can be *on the other side*. Men have long been spies, double agents, and class traitors; now men can be against patriarchies, and the patriarchs just cannot be sure who those men (potentially) are. This new historical form of patriarchy opens up a new set of possibilities for the undermining, the subversion, of patriarchies.

On the other hand, the creation of more complex societies with more powerful public domain institutions provides the conditions for yet more powerful relations for men. Any possible feelings of 'loss' for men – personal, existential, collective – may be more than 'compensated' by new orders of men's power, both individual and collective. In these ways, the movement to the modern provides innumerable *resources* for men to gain, perhaps regain, their/our power and their/our sense of being a man. Thus, while the movement to the modern, and thence the postmodern, may involve loss, it also offers opportunities for men to gain power: the possibilities of both further elaboration and immediate subversion.

[20]

Arguments and themes

Having outlined some of the problems and complications of focusing on public men, what are the main arguments and themes to follow? The main arguments, in a slightly simplified form, include:

1. (i) An understanding of men rests on an understanding of men's power.
   (ii) An understanding of men's power rests on men's relationship to the public and private domains.
2. (i) The divisions or differences between the private domains and the public domains are fundamental in a patriarchal society. To put this in a slightly different way – the creation of the public domains is a creation of men in order to wrest power from women in the private domains.
   (ii) Fundamental bases of these conflicts of powers are biological reproduction, sexuality, nurture, and violence.
   (iii) For these reasons, the private domains, and the activity therein, are effectively the bases of the public domains, and the activity therein.
3. Since the latter part of the last century or more, there has been a qualitatively significant increase in the extent and potential of dominance of the public domains over the private domains. This dominance is overwhelmingly controlled, performed, and perpetuated by men.
4. (i) All the above is culturally and discursively produced, reproduced, and enacted; culturally and discursively elaborated and elaboratable; and reflexively experienced.
   (ii) Notwithstanding the above, there are a potentially infinite number of ways of conceptualizing, explaining, experiencing, or elaborating the divisions and differences between the public domains and the private domains. In particular, links and associations may be made with all manner of other dualities characteristic of patriarchal discourses.

Accordingly, the main themes include:

- 'Totality': the 'totality' of public men in public patriarchies.
- Power, domination, and oppression.
- Difference: the pervasiveness of different kinds of difference.

- Publicization: the historical process of bringing social activities and experiences into the public domains.
- Consolidation and unities: the persistence of the consolidation and unities of men as a gender class.
- Diversifications and fragmentations: the diversifications and fragmentations of material bases and social practices of public patriarchies into numerous partially autonomous realms, and of men, masculinities, and types of men.
- Disjunctions and fracturings: disjunctions and fracturings in/of experience.
- Contradictions: the ubiquity of contradictions in social processes.
- Praxis: the interrelation of experience, work, politics, theory, as human, sensuous activity.

PART 1

From the malestream to public patriarchies

Public men, men in public, can be considered and analysed within many different frameworks – implicit or explicit, natural or social, malestream or feminist. This section reviews some of these approaches, and also constructs a deconstructionist framework for the analysis of public patriarchies. The first of these four chapters is a critical review of some of the contributions of malestream traditions (Ch. 2). This is followed by a discussion of feminist and related approaches to these issues, with a special emphasis on theories of public patriarchy (Ch. 3). The next chapter considers some of the initial implications of such theories for the analysis of men and masculinities (Ch. 4). The section is concluded by extending the analysis of public patriarchy to take account of plural perspectives and the persistent questions of deconstruction and difference. Accordingly, it is public patriarchies, public domains, public men, and public masculinities all in the plural, that are the subject of this framework (Ch. 5).

CHAPTER 2

Public men in the malestream

The 'public' and 'publicness' are everywhere. In this chapter I look critically at some of the ways in which the 'public' element in *'public men'* has been formulated. Following an initial discussion of the problem presented by the social sciences in analysing the element of the 'public' in 'public men', I consider some major contributions of the malestream to this question.

The problem of the social sciences: patriarchal public discourse

The notion of 'public men' refers to men, their existence and activity in the public domains. The concept of 'public domain' itself has different meanings, and may refer to a set of times, places or spaces (like the street or certain buildings); a type or series of institutional developments, social interchanges or activities (like organizations or sport); a more personal sensibility (like outer-directedness or self-presentation); or social discourse (see Ch. 3). Public men – that is, men in the public domains – clearly act and exist in very different ways in relation to these different meanings of the 'public domain'.

To explore these issues of publicness, the public domains, and public men necessitates some critical discussion of the social sciences themselves. This is because they not only have provided numerous specific interpretations, both implicit and explicit, of why the public domains and public men are the way they are, but they in themselves also make up one broad kind of construction of the public domains, usually constructed by public men. Indeed, the public domains and public men have been the traditional centre of concern, analysis, and prescription for the social sciences. Within them the private domains and private experiences have often been seen as unimportant, irrelevant, and of low status. The traditional social science 'disciplines' both provide explanations of the public domains, as different kinds of discourse, and constitute the public domains as discourse. This double message has to be constantly borne in mind when making critical sense of the contribution of the social sciences to discussions of the public domains, and what happens there.

Now, to argue this is not to suggest that contributions of social science are any more limited than are any other type of human knowledge. It merely introduces a degree of scepticism into the evaluation of these contributions, particularly when we consider the particular kind of personal life often lived by the men who have written and constructed the social sciences, in the safety of the public domains or their domestic study, and away from the *particular* rigours and demands of the private domains. For this reason alone, let alone more structural reasons around the societal construction of the patriarchal malestream, it is perhaps not so surprising that practitioners of the traditional social sciences have generally not seen the public domains, or the public men there, as problematic. Within this framework, social science has both echoed and supported other dominant constructions of the public domains and public men as *non-problematic*. Analyses may be developed that treat the 'public domain' as a 'closed system', within which self-referential categories are in use, in both the public domains as observed and analysis itself. Moreover, the analytical separation of the public domains and public men, and their analysis, as if they were natural objects, is often reinforced by describing both the events observed and the analysis in neutral terms. This can sometimes be done explicitly, as within some varieties of liberalism or pluralism. More usually, however, a more implicit form of neutrality is used. For example, the activity of women in the public domains may be described in terms of the categories of men's experiences. More generally, the implicitness of attention to public men in social analysis is a major way in which that supposed neutrality is maintained.

In place of an explicit and problematic treatment of these issues, the traditional social science disciplines have *reduced* public matters to something simpler and more self-contained. In the case of economics, the reduction has usually been made to the value of goods and services, exchanges of goods and services, and market forces in the public domain; in the case of political science, the reduction has usually been to the documentary indications of formal power, contract, legal–rational authority and decision-making facilities in the public domain;[1] and with philosophy, reduction has been of a rather different form – to the abstract universals of thought in the public domain. These self-references in turn portray the *possibilities* of seeing public men in terms of exchange, formal power, and thought, though this is itself rarely done in relation to public men as men, public or not. As already noted, this is not to dismiss such 'disciplines'; far from it. It is highlighting the possibility that the public domains could be explicitly and problematically theorized in terms of gendered human value, unspoken power, private thought, and much more.

Malestream accounts of public men: the contributions of the malestream

It will be clear from the introductory section above that I am very critical of the contribution of malestream social science to the understanding of gender, patriarchy, and men. However, it would be mistaken to go on from this to dismiss a few thousand years of thought and action. For one thing, even though the malestream is extremely careless in its analysis of men, there is at least a variety of misdemeanours to choose from. Within the malestream, positions have differed on the extent of the separation or overlap of the public and private domains; the diverse *bases* of social life in each of these domains; the significance given to production and/or reproduction, to productive labour and/or reproductive labour, and indeed to concepts of work and labour, as against concepts of being and existence. Furthermore, while such work usually fails explicitly to theorize men in the public domains (whilst talking all the time about them), it provides examples of patriarchal public discourse of public men – and accordingly is of interest.

In some ways to explain men's domination of the public domains is a task calling on all the insights of the analysis of gender, and of the analysis of society 'in general'. I say this with some caution, for, as noted, the bulk of agendered malestream social science has neglected this question in a desperate and profound sense. The shelves of books on economics, political science, philosophy, and sociology are mostly actually, though often implicitly, talking about men in the public domains – this especially applies to the works of their 'founding fathers', as well as to a lot of their 'sons'. There are articles, books, treatises, yearbooks, encyclopaedias, and so on, on all the institutions of the public domain – the state, party, politics, capitalist enterprises, the money markets, the military, and so on – that are actually all about men, even though they do not say so. There is this vast body of writing and research that is about men and masculinities, even though it doesn't say so explicitly.

Following this line of thinking a little further, the more specialist fields of study on, say, local government, organizations, management, and so on, present more specific theories and prescriptions on men in particular public domains, usually without naming men explicitly. Thus, focused theories of how organizations work or should work (such as bureaucratic theory or systems management theory or Taylorism) are often about men and how some men think others should be organized.

At the more societal level of analysis, similar observations can be made. Sociology, politics, and economics in particular present us with a huge array of themes and research studies on how 'society' works. Thus, structural-functionalism, conflict theory, Marxism, social contract theory, liberalism, Keynesianism, and the rest, all focus primarily on the public domains and public men, without explicitly saying so.

In mainstream sociology, the division is reproduced non-problematically, for example, in the distinction between community and association – the latter implicitly becomes the social arena in which men meet in the public domains, though this is not usually explicitly explored in these terms. Margaret Stacey (1982, p. 6) pursues this line of thought further as follows:

. . . sociological theory was created by men in the public domain in the 19C [nineteenth century] and was about the public domain. This was true of writers as disparate as Marx, Weber, Durkheim, all of whom were in their several ways concerned with problems of social order as these were manifested through the great changes that were going on in industry, state and market place, indeed in all facets of the public domain.

(Also see Stacey 1981.)

[28]

She argues from this, first, that sociology has played an active part in the creation and re-creation of ideologies which continue the oppression of women; and, second, that terms and concepts in sociological theory which adequately deal with the domestic arena are lacking. I would want to add a third and paradoxical consequence, namely, that the preoccupation in sociology, as in other social sciences, with men in the public domains has produced terms and concepts *which are inadequate for dealing with men explicitly and sociologically.*

In political science, what counts as politics at all is heavily biased towards what men do. Politics is seen as primarily formal, party, institutional politics, and as politics in the public domain, even though this is rarely made an explicit and problematic feature of analysis. This presumed association of 'politics' with men is also rarely seen as worthy of critical study within political science. A similar set of discriminations has been observed within malestream political theory, often displaying naturalistic and given assumptions about the difference of women and men. These distinctions reproduce differences recognized in political theory and political practice, at least since the times of Ancient Greece (Clark & Lange 1979; O'Brien 1981). Further parallels can be drawn between the public domains and the productive sphere and the private domains and the reproductive sphere, thus linking debates on the public/private to more conventional social and political analyses, including those within Marxism.

Economic analysis has also traditionally taken so much for granted. It has specialized in the production of laws, absolute or probabilistic, about social (i.e. economic) life. It has constructed models of how economic enterprises work or don't work, as if what happens in the private domains either just happens or isn't really important. On the other hand, recent attempts have been made to apply economic insights to private life, including family matters, marriage, and patterns of sexuality, often by extending the categories of the malestream public domains to other situations.

Part of men's task in producing critical pro-feminist studies of men and masculinities is to take on and critique these malestream traditions of the social sciences, and other dominant forms of (public) discourse. This includes giving critical attention to the traditions of social and political theory, classical and modern; particularly to how men, as intellectuals, political élites, and sometimes political non-élites, have articulated and explained their ideas about how 'society' (women and other men) should be. Usually all this has been done without much reference to women as political participants or citizens.

In making sense (or non-sense) of the malestream, let us consider the possible ways in which the relationship of the private domains and the public domains may be understood:

- as relatively unchanging;
- as the public domain progressively taking over the private;
- as the public domain progressively taking over the public men;
- as in a state of transformation, so even dissolving the boundary between them.

Of these, the first two positions are undoubtedly the most dominant; and in both cases their formulation of the relation of the public and private domains may often state, imply, or assume that public men are equivalent to the social whole. The first may be seen as broadly naturalistic: the public and private domains, and their separation, are part of a natural state, relatively unchanging and relatively unproblematic.

Naturalism: the classical legacy
The dominant tradition in the social sciences on the relation of the public and private domains is undoubtedly a flagrant naturalism. 'Men' and 'women', and the 'public' and the 'private', are as they are in a balanced complementarity. Similarly, the private and the public domains are seen as separate realms, and the division between them as given. This approach takes many forms: philosophical, political, economic, sociobiological, and so on. It is clearly represented in the works of Plato and Aristotle, as elaborate, and sometimes contradictory, rationales are provided for keeping women out of public life. In *The Politics*, Aristotle (1962) placed women alongside children and slaves. He believed that women needed a certain amount of coercion to maintain their inherent goodness and purity within the private domain. Meanwhile men provided the social norm through their domination of the public domain of 'politics'. The dichotomy continues in the liberal political tradition of Thomas Hobbes, John Locke, and David Hume. For example, Locke promotes the distinction between reason and passion, knowledge and desire, mind and body, so reproducing the public–private division, on

one side of which people supposedly act through rational calculation, while on the other they experience subjectivity and desire (O'Donovan 1985, p. 8). A more recent example is the naturalism of Parsonian structural-functionalism, in which the fundamental distinction between instrumentality and expressiveness, and many other gendered dichotomies, is reinforced within a systemic worldview.

The most obvious political form of this naturalistic division between the public and the private is in the given notion of the polis or polity – composed typically of men of a certain wealth or social status. The *public* is accordingly the domain of the adult citizen (Latin, *pubes*), until recently usually men. The public domain is accordingly the domain of law, open to the scrutiny of the polity. The public domain may be *seen* by the public: it is visible to the gaze of the citizenry. The public domain is not private and not domestic: it is outside the house and home. The private domain is, in contrast, 'one' of both exclusion of outsiders (beyond the law) and confinement of those within as insiders. This latter characteristic has clearly been of utmost importance in terms of men's control of women. Accordingly, we may very simply distinguish those confined to the private domain (often women); those in control of the private domain (often men); and those outside the private domain (often mainly men, also women).

This notion of the 'public' as 'the citizens' persists in such terms as the 'public interest', 'public opinion', and the 'public' as an electorate. The 'public sector', as the citizens' or state sector, is thus the institutional representation of the polis and polity – the public sector *on behalf of* the citizens. From this political concept of the public has subsequently developed the range of collective and semi-collective spaces and economic activities that are not private, including many that are privately owned (R. Williams 1976, pp. 203–4). Just in case this discussion sounds a little archaic and irrelevant to the present day, it is as well to realize that even women's suffrage is not universal. For example, in one Swiss canton, Appenzell Ausserrhoden, women were only *given* the vote (by the men) in April 1989; and in another, Appenzel Innerrhoden, they await it (F. Williams 1989).

More generally, the distinction of the private and the public remains enshrined in and as *law*, with the private for many centuries literally that which is unregulated and beyond the control

of law (O'Donovan 1985; Unger 1975) (see p. 126). This fundamental assumption and prescription of law is itself open to critical
questioning and social transformation (see pp. 45–7). This becomes clear when we consider the common associations of law,
language, and men's dominance (of both). In British law, the 1850
Abbreviation Act stipulated that 'all acts importing the masculine
gender shall be deemed and taken to include females' (s.4),[2] and
this was reaffirmed in the 1889 Interpretation Act. These arrangements stood until the 1978 Interpretation Act legislated that:

> In any Act, unless the contrary intention appears, –
> a] words importing the masculine gender include the fe-
> minine;
> b] words importing the feminine gender include the mas-
> culine.

Even so, public domain language, as law, usually remains
'naturally' 'male'.

The progressive power of the public domains and public men

A second major position may be understood as part of the broad
tradition of 'man'/humanity coming out of 'Nature'; similarly the
'public' comes out of and *progressively* (in both senses) overtakes
and takes over the private. This strand is therefore structured *in
change* rather than in the stability of the first approach. Change is
its rationale, so that history is often assumed to consist of the
march towards social completion – or, to put this another
(Hegelian) way, the coming unto itself of Spirit, separated from
Nature, is resolved in the end of history. Change may occur
through gradual social evolution, through modernization, or in a
series of relatively dramatic 'turning points'.

While the first approach is probably still predominant in
everyday commonsense views of the world, this optimistic and
progressive strand of the malestream remains dominant within the
social sciences, if often implicitly so. This brings together a social
naturalism with a positive and rational faith in human (that is,
generally, men-dominated) affairs. It is the particular form that
the Enlightenment and the 'bourgeois public space' so created
(Habermas 1975[3]; Felski 1989) have promoted so successfully.
'Man' and 'men' are, within this (that is, their) public sphere, the

agents of change and 'progress' – the takeover of the private by the public.

The transformative power of the post-Enlightenment public domains, and public men within them, often to the neglect of the private domains, is found in the works (both writing and deeds) of public men as diverse as Niccolo Machiavelli, Ralph Waldo Emerson and John Stuart Mill. In *On the Subjection of Women*, Mill proposed granting to women full equality in formal rights alongside those of men in the public sphere. From this public equality in the public domain, he assumed change would take place in a progressive and more loving family, itself essentially unchanged in form and content. The gender division of labour, and women's subjection in the private sphere, remained as before, though ameliorated by a 'sympathy in equality'.

Other versions of 'optimistic progressivism' have invoked notions of historical change from community to association, from Gemeinschaft to Gesellschaft, from mechanical to organic solidarity, from traditional to modern, modernization, and modernity. Such changes are indeed deeply gendered, though malestream social theorists of these transformations have often described and analysed them as if they were not. In such accounts, the progressive onset of the public domains may be related to one or several of a vast number of social changes: militarism, state formation, and the growth and centralization of nation states; the development of economy, corporate capital, and technology; the internationalization of capital and the world, imperialism, increasing travel; and a whole range of more specific social processes around urbanization, bureaucratization, professionalization; and so on – often without exploring the implications for gender relations. Modernization is also very much about the transformation of women, and of men, and of the relations between women, men, and young people. Perhaps the most significant issue for such optimistic progressive malestream social theorizing is that the onset of the public domains is rarely seen as problematic for men; indeed, the creation and expansion of public domain institutions is seen, usually implicitly, as compatible with dominant forms of masculinity, or as providing opportunities for new, equally unproblematic, forms of masculinity.

Optimistic progressivism also figures prominently in the ideas of the 'twin fathers' of sociology – Marx and Weber – though rather more ambiguously in the works of the latter. Weber, though most well known for his analysis, and indeed at times prescription, of rationalization, is also deeply ambivalent about the process, and all too aware of the limitations of rationality, especially instrumental rationality. Against this, Marx's faith in the general benefits of the overriding of the private domain by the public domain is relatively undialectical. The optimistic progressive, whether Weberian or Marxian, sees the change to the increasing domination of the public domain as operating under the rules of the public domain – rational, bureaucratic, bourgeois, revolutionary, and usually 'male'.

The location of Marxism within the swath of optimistic progressivism stems more from its Hegelian tradition than from the immediate prospects for social and political reform or revolution at any given time. While more of a total theory of history than Weberianism, the Marxist tradition has stressed a positive combination of progressive elements of the public domains. These include most obviously the socialization of both production (the bringing of the productive process into collective forms of organization, like factories, if not collective ownership and control) and reproduction (the spread of state and other collective and public domain forms of organization of the reproduction of the next generation of workers). A major and broad theme in the former is the bringing of women into the 'productive labour force' and in the latter is the commodification of household tasks – the turning of household tasks into commodities.[4]

Weber's theory of rationalization deals with both quantity and quality, both the *extent* and *form* of change. The public domain dominates not just in the spread of its domain but also in the form of the rules that operate there and increasingly beyond. And just to make the point explicit, rationalization has both in substantive histories and in its particular social form been heavily dominated by men. Moreover, although rationalization interrelates with other social and economic changes, for example capitalist development, as a process it remains paramount.[5] There are a vast number of different ways in which modernization and rationalization theses have been developed by Marxian, Weberian, and other writers. Most, however, have failed to notice the fact that they are talking implicitly or explicitly about men. In emphasizing the *progressive power* of public men and the public domains, there may be a tendency to equate, or at least conflate, the one and the other. From this it is but a small step to equate public men and the public domains with the totality of society, and so reproduce a kind of social naturalism.

The progressive reduction of public men by the public domain

Another and contrasting influential group of malestream social theorists who have stressed the importance, and even the growing importance, of the public domain have done so in terms of its impact on people's personal and private lives. While they are fully aware of the power, indeed the increasing powers, of the institutions of the public domain, these 'pessimistic progressives' have focused on the limitations or even the negative consequences of modernization for citizens – for which we can usually read 'public men'. This concern with the onset of the public domain is thus combined with a deep pessimism. Their critique is frequently developed by way of psychoanalysis, psychoanalytically informed concepts, or the psychological effects of rationalization, though in some cases a more general cultural or discursive analysis is developed. This strand recognizes the onset of the public domain, yet sees it either, like Freud, as a necessary control against uncivilizing forces, or, like Durkheim, as bringing unanticipated and unwanted consequences, or, like Sennett, as even shielding its own hidden and paradoxical collapse (hence the phrase 'the fall of public man').

Thus public men can be said to be reduced – not numerically, but qualitatively and psychologically. Modernization might thus also be taken to mean the possibility of the transformation of men's traditional gendering, and of men's status and standing in 'the community'. That historical and social 'loss' may come to be seen or experienced as a personal, even an existential, loss – and, moreover, a possible loss to men's (sense of) manhood, manliness, or masculinity. This possible historical sense of loss feeds on men's, or rather some men's, sense of being a man being based in that which is liable to be taken away. In this view, being a man is a *double negative*: it is not having lost.[6] This perspective on modernization as loss for men is of course prominent in romanticism, perhaps conjuring images of a 'Golden Age'; it also figures in some forms of Marxism, especially those that emphasize the nobility of labour (that is, men labourers), and, perhaps more interesting still, in some versions of fascism, especially those that emphasize men's (and women's) association with Nature.[7]

[35]

Interestingly, some of the themes have been prominent in recent liberal malestream social theory from the United States.[8] Among such progressive pessimism, the most influential is probably Richard Sennett's (1977) *The Fall of Public Man*. He argues that, in the movement from the eighteenth to the nineteenth century, the public domain became more firmly yet more superficially established, as in the belief in instant facts in themselves rather than in pre-existent order or systems into which apprehensions might be fitted (p. 21). Similarly, he mourns the loss of rituals of association in public life: instrumentality in the public domain destroys the public domain. Or, to put this another way, there is a yearning for community within association.[9] From this there is both a civilization of politics in the public domain and retreat into the private, narcissism, and the 'tyrannies of intimacy'. Meanwhile the personality becomes a dominant mode of public life. His text is both reductive and paradoxical. In some ways the very expansive possibilities of the public domain and its cultural processes destroy themselves – just as Marshall McLuhan speaks of the extension of the senses through the extension of the electronic media leading to a collapse of the nation, and a move against authority and towards retribalization.

Some of these themes have been explored in a rather different way by Christopher Lasch in a series of texts, often operating at the intersection of humanism (*sic*), Marxism, and psychoanalysis. In his *Haven in a Heartless World* (1977) and *The Culture of Narcissism* (1979), he extends the Marxist paradigm, especially the analysis of the socialization of production, to the self, as a complement to the work of Harry Braverman and others. In the former he puts forward a bleak tale of the decline of the patriarchal family, the patriarchal father, and the benefits he sees them bringing, with the growth of the impersonal, bureaucratic state and other public domain institutions. It is in this space that 'the culture of narcissism' grows.[10] More recently, he has moved on with a remorseless logic to consider 'the minimal self' (1984), encroached upon from all sides in the nuclear age.

A rather similar assessment is made by Russell Jacoby (1977) in *Social Amnesia*, except here the focus is much more fully on the psychoanalytic level. While Lasch mourns the loss of the patriarchal family, Jacoby regrets the loss of personalized insight. He also addresses the historical loss of attention to the insights of psychoanalysis itself (he thus presents in a sense a parallel, or rather the inverse, of Sennett's analysis). Both Lasch and Jacoby are nostalgic; some would say conservative – one for a family focus, the other for a personalized insight. Despite their differences, they share a similar *attitude* to, if not analysis of, the (patriarchal) father. Jacoby (1977, p. 107) writes:

> the bourgeois family – and monogamy – as instruments of authority are being eclipsed by more efficient means: schools, television etc. The father, as the wielder of the absolute power of condemnation or inheritance, is being phased out. The erosion of the economic content of the family unit ultimately saps its authoritarian structure in favor of complete fragmentation.

This is contentious enough (in its malestream commonsense) and as such is representative of the dangers of men suggesting that the father's power is dead or declining. However, he goes on to suggest, like Lasch, that

> the family in its 'classic' form was not merely a tool of society, but contained an antiauthoritarian movement . . . a form of humanity as well as a form of inhumanity . . . The family as an independent and (relatively) isolated unit preserved a 'space' in which the individual could develop *against* the society; as a mediator of authority, and not merely an instrument of it, it resisted as well as complied.
> (Jacoby 1977, pp. 107–8)

Jacoby's argument also works on a different level of speculative abstraction. In discussing the relation of the political left and subjectivity, he despairs at the reduction of politics and analysis to human subjectivity: '[t]he fetish of subjectivity and human relationships is progress in fetishism . . . For the cult of human subjectivity is not the negation of bourgeois society but its substance' (pp. 103–4). He continues: 'If the intensification of subjectivity is a direct response to its actual decline, it ultimately works to accelerate the decline. To the damaged subject it proposes more of the same. The objective loss of human relationships and experience is eased by their pursuit' (p. 115). This is all just one step away from a 'rampant narcissism [which] surfaces as the final form of individualism' (p. 116).

[37]

And just when it appears to be all over, we come to Jacoby's bitterness, hardly masking misogyny:

> Vague conceptions of guilt, the universal oppression of women by men, one's 'own' oppression, function as instruments of an ego that is regressing in the face of a disintegrating society. That men, too, have suffered and died in the massacre of history is affirmed or denied, but is in any case irrelevant. What counts is the immediate, and here an economism-turned-feminism is promoted as if the blind endorsement of what every worker did or thought is improved when it is blindly applied to women. . . . The jealousy with which the oppression of women, children, homosexuals, and so on, is defended as a private preserve, off-limits to others, expresses an urge to corner the market of oppression.
>
> (pp. 116–17)

The transcendence of the public domains and public men by public discourse

The transcendence of the public domains and so of 'public men' does not refer to the progressive onset or reduction of the one over or against the other; instead, it refers to the transformation, political and discursive, of the meaning of 'public' and 'private' (see Ch. 3). In this view one can no longer conceive of the public–private division as a shifting boundary; rather, if it means anything at all, it is itself, at any given time, a political or discursive reality, existing within political discourse. While these notions of political or discursive transformation may be informed by any number of traditions, in practice poststructuralist and postmodernist analyses have been especially significant within the malestream. This is because they are often concerned not just with transformation and change 'in general', but rather with problematizing the public–private divide 'itself'. This particularly applies to the work of Michel Foucault on the discursive character of what may often appear personal, idiosyncratic, and private. A good example of this is the way Foucault (1981) and others have de/constructed sexuality not just in discourse but as discourse. Seen in this way the public domain and public men are themselves concepts in/as discourse, not representations of discrete forms of special public discourse.

There are at least two major ways in which Foucault's work is of direct relevance to the questions in hand. Most important is Foucault's construction of the ubiquity of discourse as an over-whelming presence,[11] so that distinctions between private domain and public domain, and their own discourses, are themselves part of discourse – historical, particular, structured, changing. This brings a necessary discursive realism to the analysis of the relation of the domains, and in particular warns against any romanticism of the private.

A more specific argument of relevance from Foucault's work is that presented in *The History of Sexuality. Volume One* (Foucault 1981), according to which '[t]he rising bourgeois class gradually creates a new ideology for itself that shifts the emphasis from control of social process through marriage alliances to the control of sexuality as a way of maintaining class hegemony' (Ferguson 1982, p. 157). This kind of argument and interpretation is, to my mind, not necessarily at odds with the optimistic and pessimistic progressives already discussed.[12] Although Foucault explores historical discourses on sexuality in great detail, much of his writing is curiously genderless.[13] And although he again does not deal explicitly with men, his approach has major implications for the critical study of men and masculinities.

Another example of malestream theorizing that brings these discursive themes together with a modified progressivism is that of Norbert Elias. In *The Civilizing Process* (1982) he provides almost all his examples from the actions and institutions of men, yet seems unaware of this, thereby failing to theorize men and masculinities explicitly. Like Freud, Elias appears to see 'civil-izing' as predominantly a matter for men. Having said that, his work contains interesting insights, which bring together elements of optimism, pessimism, and transcendence. In describing the transition from medieval to modern sensibility, he writes,

> Medieval conceptions of hell give us an idea of how strong . . . fear between man and man was. Both joy and pain were discharged more openly and freely. But the individual was their prisoner; he was hurled back and forth by his own feelings as by forces of nature. He had less control of his passions; he was more controlled by them.
>
> Later, as the conveyor belts running through his existence grow longer and more complex, the individual learns to

control himself more steadily; he is now more a prisoner of his passions than before. But as he is now more tightly bound by his functional dependence on the activities of an even larger number of people, he is much more restricted in his conduct, in his chances of directly satisfying his drives and passions. Life becomes in a sense less dangerous, but also less emotional or pleasurable, at least as far as the direct release of pleasure is concerned. And what is lacking in everyday life a substitute is created in dreams, in books and pictures.[14]

(Elias 1982, pp. 241–2)

In this kind of transformation he suggests that the struggles and tensions move from the social to the psychological – 'the battle-field is . . . moved within' (p. 242) the individual. The central relationships of modernizing society are not between people, but between parts of people, with the '"trend" . . . always . . . towards a move or less automatic self-control' (p. 248). Elias's version of rationalization is not organizational or procedural like Weber's, but closer to Foucault's notion of 'technologies of the self':

Continuous reflection, foresight, and calculation, self-control, precise and articulate regulation of one's own effects, knowledge of the whole terrain, human and non-human, in which one acts, become more and more indispensable pre-conditions of social success.

(p. 271)

As noted, Elias is not explicitly writing of men, but his approach could be adapted to describe the modern historical situation of public men. As with Foucault's analysis, his approach transcends the public–private division: it addresses men who happen to be both 'in public' and 'in private' as public discourse. The discursive approach places 'men' and 'change' in men as formed in discourse, so that even private domain experiences are constituted in discourse; similarly, the 'division' between spheres is itself equally *in* (a) discourse. Consequently, discourse itself can be seen as transformation.

[40]

His-story so far

Most malestream accounts of the public and the private, the public domains and the private domains are inadequate on several grounds:

- they take the public–private division for granted;
- they see the division as either absolute or historically relative but not problematic;
- they are not gendered;
- they do not attend to their relations to men, men's dominance, and patriarchy;
- they speak in terms of 'division' rather than 'difference'. While there is no definite *division* between the public and the private, *differences* certainly do exist between what happens in public and in private; furthermore, people of different genders recognize and experience such differences differently. Moreover, 'division' suggests dividing into two, whereas 'difference' suggests multiple fragmentations and relations, as well as unities divided from themselves (see pp. 74–5). For these reasons I prefer to talk of 'public/private difference(s)' rather than the 'public/private division'.

On the other hand, there are useful insights to be gleaned from each of these approaches. To my mind the interest of naturalism lies principally in the way it makes clear the supposedly unproblematic association of law, language, and the public domains. Marxian and Weberian accounts provide optimistic rationales of the power of the public domains that remain fundamental within the progressive Western malestream. The pessimistic progressives provide the other side of that coin. Malestream social science has operated very much in that space, in the tension between the perceived positive and negative effects of modernization; two positions that imply each other, and are part of the same worldview or paradigm. Furthermore, both progressives and poststructuralists assist in the process of deconstruction of public men and the public domains. For a start, the public domains and public men cannot be equated. The power of the public domains and their institutions bears on men differentially, in positions of greater and lesser relative power, and they and other men, and women, experience the impacts and effects of those institutions

[41]

differently. So we can distinguish, in relation to men: institutions dominated by men; different men's different positions therein; and the experience and relation of those and other men to these institutions.

Finally, an overarching issue in the assessment of the meaning of the 'public domains' and 'public men' is the ubiquity of discourse *as public discourse*. All discourse is public, and all references take place *in* discourse. This brings a different sense of 'public' from that usually contained in the 'public domains'. These senses of reference and discourse enfold even the private domains, and private acts therein. However, to deconstruct private acts as 'merely' (in) public (discourse) in no way diminishes them, experiences of them and their effects – they remain at times happenings of pain, hurt, and material destruction (Hearn 1988a, p. 539).

CHAPTER 3

Patriarchy, public patriarchy, and related critiques

This chapter addresses the way theorists, mainly feminist theorists, have developed very different approaches and sets of concepts from those discussed in the previous chapter in order to critically analyse the significance of the public and private domains for gender relations. Such analyses have usually focused on women's relationship to the public domain, and therefore the private domain also; less often have they focused on men and men's power in relation to the public domain. An important concept which has been developed by some feminist theorists to deal with these various issues is 'public patriarchy'. However, before looking at that in some detail, I shall first consider some of the other ways feminists have analysed the public domains.

Feminist critiques of the public and the private

The contributions of malestream theorists are wide ranging, yet in most cases continue with notions of the public and the private domains that are *conceptually* relatively fixed, even if the boundaries of those domains are seen as open to change over time. Most of these malestream contributions have proceeded without an explicit analysis of men. Such procedures are effectively uprooted in feminist theory and practice, as connections between gender and the public/private question have been made clearer. This is seen in the various ways feminists have interrelated the private and the public, the personal and the political, along with moves to transcend dualism and dualities. Feminist critiques do much more than just provide the gendered counter-side to the various traditions of the malestream: they are more than just another paradigm shift.

There are several reasons for feminist concern with the issues of the relationship of the private domains and the public domains. One is summed up in the phrase, 'the personal is political'. Indeed, there are all sorts of ways in which what is personal or private is potentially political or public. Then there is the related argument that the movement of women's experiences, problems, and struggles from the private to the public domains is a vital part of the process and progress of women's liberation. This can be seen most obviously in the way that problems that were seen as private, outside the law, or 'had no name', such as men's domestic violence to women and young people, may become public(ized) at particular historical times. It is partly for this reason that the boundaries between the public and the private domains are especially important practically, politically, and theoretically for all interested in gender construction. Likewise, historical change around these boundaries is important as both evidence of change and inspiration of further change. Some of the more specific historical changes around the interface of the public and private domains have been summarized by Margaret Stacey (1982, p. 13) as follows:

- women doing tasks and filling roles which were formerly men's, and vice versa;
- tasks which were at one time undertaken in the private domain moving into the public domain;
- increasingly invasive attempts by the public domain to control the private domain; and
- the development of professional skills to replace domestic skills (see Stacey & Price 1981).

Historically, many of women's tasks, such as health care, education, agriculture, the production of goods, and midwifery, have been transferred, at least in part, from the home to organizations, with their frequent re-closure, usually by men.

Then there are a series of ideological critiques of the private and the public. One example is the view that what counts as 'private', and what counts as 'public', is largely ideological. Warfare and the military may be seen as 'public', yet they entail the takeover, and sometimes the destruction, of people's homes, the barracking of soldiers, the private worlds of army camps, and all manner of private experiences, some distressing and damaging beyond belief. 'Family life' or 'home life' may be considered private, yet may entail interrelations and negotiations with all manner of other institutions and organizations. Then there is the question of the fundamental gendering of the public and private domains, and their relations. Public/private 'divisions' or differences are made problematic simply by seeing them as *gendered*. For example, Joan Kelly (1979) has argued that the public/private 'division' is false in the sense that women's experience, personal and social, is shaped by the simultaneous operation of the relations of work and sex. The division represents 'a false division between personal experience and knowledge, between the subjective and the objective' (Humm 1989, p. 179).

In *The Anti-social Family*, Michele Barrett and Mary McIntosh (1982, p. 90) argue that 'the distinction between public and private domains has been constructed historically and ideologically' and that 'this distinction should be an object of analysis and not a conceptual tool'. The different ways in which the public and private domains, and men's public or private appropriation of women, have developed historically have become a broad area of increasing concern for feminist writers and theorists. Relevant questions include: In what ways are the public and the private gendered? Is that gendering changing? How does the public/private issue relate to patriarchy (or the 'male dominated gender order', Stacey 1986, or the 'masculine gender-system', M. Waters 1989)?

The division of society, ideologically and materially, into public and private domains is itself a particular form of power. The separation of private and public domains is part of patriarchal society and malestream discourse, and as such subject to anti-dualist, feminist, and postmodernist critiques. As a consequence, one broad direction for analysis, deconstruction, and change involves attention to cultural and discursive meanings and lived experiences – not as some collection of free-floating subjectivities but as material gendered existences.

Reproduction, law, and culture

Feminist accounts of the public and the private domains, and their interrelations, have made questions of gender central. Even so, definite differences are recognizable between feminist accounts in terms of variable emphases on the political, the economic, the cultural, and so on, as well as on different historical periods. In some ways these differences parallel differences within the male-stream (see Ch. 2), but more fundamentally they often rest on the analysis of patriarchy and related concepts.

Some theorists argue that the public/private division is fundamentally gendered, in terms of the structuring of reproduction, patriarchy, or a patriarchal society. Mary O'Brien (1981) sees the division as a pre-capitalist construction, arising from men's appropriation of the child 'in law' following the social discovery of paternity, and the creation of the (public) institution of (private) fatherhood. Katherine O'Donovan (1985) focuses on the institution of *law*, especially in the transition from feudal to market society, arguing 'that the root of inequality of the sexes lies in the dichotomy between private and public, and the clash of values involved' (p. xi). While O'Brien emphasizes a dialectical materialist analysis, based in biological reproduction, O'Donovan constructs a more diffuse, gendered analysis, privileging the public–private division through the perspective of values. Rather similarly, Diane Polan (1982) suggests that law in general is fundamental to patriarchy, as opposed to Marxist interpretations of laws emphasizing their instrumental, albeit class-based, purposes.

O'Donovan argues that '[t]he division between women and men has its counterpart in the dichotomy between private and public'. In her analysis she links this gendering specifically to law, such as 'the stipulated meaning of private is non-regulation, an absence of law' (1985, p. 81). In this kind of account, attention is primarily directed to the *distinction between the public and the private domains in the first place*, even though that distinction is complicated by historical change. She notes: 'The boundary between spheres regulated by law and the unregulated shifts over time and in accordance with cultural, economic and legal factors . . . particularly . . . in areas of the personal, such as sexual and reproductive conduct' (1985, p. 59). The way in which the private domains may have been in the past beyond the law needs considerable clarification. This is not just because of cultural diversity, but more particularly because the immunity of the private domain to law has still had to be recognized and maintained in the law of the public domain. This applies whether or not the private domain was defined in relation to 'legal' marriage or some other element of the private domains. Furthermore, in recent years, and particularly over the last century, this distinction has broken down as more and more laws operate on the private domain, either in a specific way or without regard to the public–private 'division'.

These questions have also been taken up by feminist anthropologists. Michelle Rosaldo (1974) argued that in all societies women are assigned to the private, domestic sphere, and men are assigned to the public sphere. This is partly through confusion between 'women', women's reproductive capacity, and women's caring and parental abilities. This is important in highlighting the notion of 'cultural value', the locus of which, according to Rosaldo, lies with men. Women's association with the 'domestic' rather than the 'public' is also often linked to an association with 'nature' rather than 'culture' (Ortner 1974). Culturally based arguments can be constructed, not just for the construction of gender, but for the complex material and ideological interplays of gender divisions, the public and the private, 'culture' and 'nature', and so on. Accordingly, Henrietta Moore (1987, p. 21) suggests:

> The 'domestic' versus 'public' model has been, and remains, a very powerful one in social anthropology because it provides a way of linking the cultural valuations given to the category 'woman' to the organization of women's activities in society.

She goes on to examine 'the arbitrary and culturally specific nature of the "domestic"/"public" division' through a critical discussion of the false assumptions about mothering and the family upon which it is based; in short, the public/private division is cultural.[1]

Patriarchy and patriarchies

To consider the relationship of public men and the public domains to patriarchy is to begin a new approach to the questions in hand, and to risk entanglement with complex, and perhaps irresoluble, conceptual difficulties. On the first count, the public domains (and public men) may be seen, in both form and content, as symptomatic of patriarchy; on the second, what is actually meant by patriarchy, and indeed whether the concept is valid or useful at all, is highly contested.[2] In making sense of the main debates about patriarchy – such as dualism, particularism, generalism, determinism, separability – it is useful to bear in mind that 'patriarchy' is merely a word; so what is possibly important is what lies behind the word, rather than being for or against the case of the concept in itself.

Patriarchy refers literally to the rule of the father or fathers. However, beyond that the complexities start, for not only is there much disagreement about possible explanations of patriarchy, but there is wide variation in the meaning of the term, beyond its literal meaning. In particular, patriarchy is sometimes used to refer to the rule or power of men (that is, adult men) over others. This is sometimes spoken of as viriarchy (M. Waters 1989), androcracy (Remy 1988, 1990), andrarchy (Summers 1989) or phallocracy (Miles 1988). While some or all of these alternatives might be considered more accurate concepts than 'patriarchy', I have continued to use the term and its derivatives for several reasons. This is mainly because there has yet to be a full evaluation of the claims of these various alternative terms. Additionally, 'patriarchy' has the advantage of referring to both hierarchy, even outside its literal sense, and a social construction, that is, fatherhood and its derivatives. In contrast, terms like 'androcracy' and 'andrarchy' are ambiguous in referring to both 'men' and 'males'.

Further distinctions may be made between patriarchal, patrilineal, patrilocal, and patrifocal societies and social structures. Furthermore, surnames might be passed on patrilineally, while inheritance of property might or might not be patrilinear. In these senses, it could be said to be mistaken to call this society a patriarchy, even though it might be appropriate to call certain social relations, specifically those in families, patriarchal. Jean Bethke Elshtain (1981, pp. 214–15) provides a clear statement of the ways in which the father is no longer all powerful, for example in the control of the education and arrangement of marriage of progeny, through the growth of state and compulsory education and changing kinship patterns, respectively. Arguments for and against the usefulness of the concept of patriarchy are often largely arguments about politics and methodology – and the usefulness of conceptualizing social existence in terms of *societal* social structures. My own past conclusion on this was that:

[48]

despite . . . various difficulties . . . there remains a case for
retaining the concept of patriarchy that is fundamentally
social structural. . . . it can be of analytical, and possibly
political, use in focussing on the social structuring of gender
relations and oppression between men and women. It can
prompt the understanding of possible social structures
underlying both institutional inequalities and everyday
action. The concept above all highlights the possibility of
different social bases of control and thereby oppression *by
men* (and indeed between men in some respects) from those
that arise from industrial, capitalist organisation, and the
socialisation of productive labour.

(Hearn 1987a, p. 43)

There are a variety of such social bases of patriarchy, including
sexuality and various aspects of reproduction.[3] These in turn often
emphasize the fundamental importance of forms of labour other
than those defined narrowly in relation to production.[4] Within
the large literature on patriarchy, critiques of the concept and the
complexity of the arguments about its use have also partly been a
reflection of the relationship of feminism, poststructuralism, and
postmodernism. Critiques of the concept of patriarchy can be
placed alongside critiques of political economy and of the notion
of class, whether it be economic class or gender class.[5]

At about the same time (in the late 1970s) that some feminists
were dismissing the *concept* of patriarchy, others were working on
these difficulties by making clearer distinctions between *types of
patriarchy*. If patriarchy refers to a monolithic structure, then it is
as limited as any monolithic concept, say, a monolithic concept of
capitalism. Similarly, some theorists have been at pains to attend
to the complexities of patriarchy in terms of different sites of
patriarchal relations (Walby 1986), types of specifically patriarchal
relations (Hearn 1987a), and the contradictions of patriarchal and
other relations (Ramazanoglu 1988). Some of these distinctions
between types of patriarchy have been drawn in relation to
capitalism – hence the term 'capitalist patriarchy'; others have
been focused on the private and the public domains – hence the
terms 'private patriarchy' and 'public patriarchy'. These are
powerful concepts for examining the problem of public men and
public masculinities explicitly in terms of gender. They also give
a rationale for the need to talk of patriarchies rather than just

[49]

patriarchy; rather than seeing patriarchy as a social monolith, there are many different patriarchies – of different shapes and sizes.[6]

Capitalist patriarchy and extended viriarchy

The term 'capitalist patriarchy' has largely been developed by Marxist feminists and socialist feminists to refer to the kind of society that is both capitalist and patriarchal. The exact way in which those two elements relate is itself open to dispute.[7] One can alternatively argue that the, often Western, society in question is best seen as:

• a patriarchal type of capitalism;
• a capitalist type of patriarchy; or
• some more integrated or interrelated form of capitalism/ patriarchy.

What has this got to do with public men? Well, unfortunately many theorists of 'capitalist patriarchy' do not really attend to this problem. They usually provide convincing accounts of the inter-relations of women's oppression and capitalist oppression (of women and men); much less usually do they spell out the implications of their analysis for men, either in terms of men as oppressors, the oppressor class, of women, or in terms of the oppression of men *as gendered people* under capitalism. Similarly, public men and public masculinities are not usually explicitly addressed in theorizing capitalist patriarchy.

Having said that, theories of capitalist patriarchy do provide important implicit accounts of public men and public masculinities. So what do some of the significant elements of these implicit accounts look like? Men are assumed to be the main controllers of the capitalist production process, both as owners and as managers; to constitute the more valued parts of the paid labour force; and to dominate the content and process of trade union organization. Men workers may well seek contradictory strategies, as men and as workers: as men they may exclude women workers; as workers they may seek to defend workers' interests, including actual or potential women workers. Some feminist commentators (e.g. Cockburn 1983) have investigated the way in which men's solidarity in the capitalist workplace may serve their interests both as workers and as men. In the sphere of social reproduction, men are seen as dominant in the control of families and households, the performance of less domestic work, and the management of public institutions of education, health, and welfare. Though the public/private division is implicit in most analyses of capitalist patriarchy, it is rarely explicitly spelt out. It is also difficult to find any sense of men *as a class* in such accounts; instead we find different types of men in different *economic class-related* locations, sometimes acting under contradictory imperatives.

A rather different way of approaching capitalist patriarchy has been put forward by Malcolm Waters (1989) as part of his analysis of the rather strangely termed 'masculine gender-systems'. He has distinguished two distinct dimensions in looking at the public/domestic division: the degree of differentiation between the domains, as relatively high or low; and the primacy of the public or the domestic domain over the other. Combining these possibilities gives four main types of system: *direct patriarchy* (domestic primacy, low differentiation); *extended patriarchy* (public primacy, low differentiation); *direct viriarchy* (domestic primacy, high differentiation); and *extended viriarchy* (public primacy, high differentiation) (see Figure 3.1).

Waters' notion of viriarchy refers to the rule or dominance of adult males, in contrast to the literal rule or dominance of fathers under patriarchy. The most interesting case for our purposes is that of extended viriarchy. This includes the type of masculine gender-system associated with advanced or late capitalism – the form frequently described as 'capitalist patriarchy'. The notion of public patriarchy is not explicitly referred to, but Waters clearly

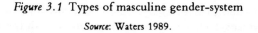

Differentiation (public/domestic)

		Low	High
	Domestic	Direct patriarchy	Direct viriarchy
Primacy (public/domestic)	Public	Extended patriarchy	Extended viriarchy

Figure 3.1 Types of masculine gender-system

Source: Waters 1989.

[51]

has in mind the form of dominance by adult males that entails men's monopolization of the public sphere, through their control of cultural representation, their covert discrimination against women, and other means. Extended viriarchy is characterized by the replacement of location in a kinship system by an idealized notion of individual achievement, performance, or credentials as a basis for the distribution of labour and power: 'Under such conditions a direct gender basis for these allocations is a contradiction.' He continues by suggesting that such a 'contradiction can only be sustained where there is a developed system of cultural and social reproduction articulated between the domestic and public spheres' (p. 207). What is under discussion here is one of the central contradictions of public patriarchy – the public ideological 'neutering' of men, and yet the perpetuation of public material dominance of men, partly through that ideological neutering. This is a continuing theme in subsequent chapters.

Varieties of public patriarchy

The concept of public patriarchy, or, as I prefer, public patriarchies, is clearly a development of the generic concept of patriarchy – the former presupposes the latter. Whereas the concept 'capitalist patriarchy' attempts to relate capitalism and patriarchy, or more precisely capitalist and patriarchal social relations, the concept of public patriarchy focuses on the way in which patriarchy is formed with respect to the public domain, and the public–private division. Although different writers, as we shall see, provide different descriptions and explanations of public patriarchy, all in some way refer to historical change in the power of men in the public domain vis-à-vis the power of the father and men in the private domain. Public patriarchy is thus usually contrasted with private patriarchy. As already noted, the clarification of the concept of public patriarchy is part of the broader attempt to specify different types of patriarchy and patriarchal society. In some cases, public patriarchy is used as an approximate equivalent to capitalist patriarchy; in others, a distinct type of patriarchy is conceptualized. In this section the concept of public patriarchy is examined, stressing both its uses and its limitations.

The concept of public patriarchy represents, on the one hand, a gendered, usually feminist, reworking of the long-established malestream tradition of the development and extension of the public domains over the private domains, the shift from traditional to modern society, from mechanical to organic solidarity; on another, it represents a reworking of the concept of patriarchy to take account of both differentiations between different types of patriarchy, and the power and dominance of the public domains. Thus the concept of public patriarchy is both a development of a particular malestream tradition, and an expression of the restructuring rather than the end of patriarchy. It also brings together feminist debates on patriarchy and feminist debates on the public and private domains.

Just as the word 'patriarchy' means different things within different frameworks and politics, so the words 'public patriarchy' have a variety of meanings. There isn't just one theory of public patriarchy. They are, however, brought together in giving some kind of prominence to the power and dominance of the public domains in patriarchy. Usually this is contrasted with the prominence of the private domains under private patriarchy; and usually too there is an assumption of an historical shift from private patriarchy to public patriarchy.

Theorizing public patriarchy has involved a number of debates and disagreements. First, there are substantive differences on the basis or bases of public patriarchy. Alternative formulations include those that emphasize particular elements in gender relations (e.g. sexuality), institutional developments (e.g. state law), or the growth of the public domain itself more generally. Men's private and public appropriation of women includes not only women's labour, but also other aspects of women from sexuality to psychological and emotional care. Andrea Dworkin (1983) has argued that there are two major forms of patriarchy, a private and a public type, in which women's sexuality is controlled by men within the private domain and the public domain respectively. The weakening of private patriarchy is in turn accompanied by the massive growth in pornography and other public forms of men's control of women's sexuality, in both material practice and imaging. Secondly, there are variations around the historical movement from private patriarchy towards public patriarchy, and whether it is the introduction of waged labour, monopoly capitalism, the post-war state, or the modern welfare state that is seen as the crucial social, and generic, shift. Thus, if private patriarchy has indeed changed towards public patriarchy, we need to specify the form of that change. Different descriptive accounts of this change are in effect different explanations – in terms of

[53]

capitalism, the state, men, certain categories of men, and so on. Thirdly, and linked to the previous point, there are differences in cultural and national context. Fourthly, the nature of the relationship of private patriarchy and public patriarchy is contested. Fifthly, there are differences in the interpretation of these changes, as welcome or unwelcome, as actually or potentially liberating or oppressive.

The earliest use of the term that I know of is by Carol Brown in 'Mothers, fathers, and children: from private to public patriarchy', published in 1981 in the *Women and Revolution* collection edited by Lydia Sargent on the theme of Heidi Hartmann's (1979) classic famous article 'The unhappy marriage of Marxism and Feminism . . . '. In the same year, Zillah Eisenstein elaborated the rather similar notions of family patriarchy (or the patriarchal family), and social patriarchy. Several other feminist commentators have developed similar notions contrasting public and private forms of patriarchy, through slightly different conceptual frameworks (Table 3.1), along a variety of historical timescales (Figure 3.2).

Table 3.1 Private patriarchy, public patriarchy, and related concepts

Private patriarchy	Public patriarchy	Brown 1981
		Dworkin 1983
		Walby 1990a, 1990b
Family patriarchy	Social patriarchy	Eisenstein 1981
Familial patriarchy		Ursel 1986
Private domain	Public domain	Laurin-Frenette 1982
		Guillaumin 1980
Private appropriation	Collective appropriation	Stacey and Davies 1983
Personal forms of dominance;	'Structural' dominance	Holter 1984
'Patriarchy'	Reorganized patriarchy	
Direct, personally exercised and legitimated dominance	Impersonal dominance	
Private dependence	Public dependence	Hernes 1984, 1987a, 1987b, 1988a, 1988b
		Borchorst & Siim 1987
		Siim 1987, 1988

1750	1800	1900	1940	1960	1980
Wage labour (Ursel)		Monopoly capitalism (Brown)	Post-war state (Hernes)	1960s' welfare state (Borchorst & Siim)	

Figure 3.2 Historical timescales in conceptualizing public patriarchy

Carol Brown (1981, p. 240) begins by suggesting that:

The labor force and the family are specific elements in what we can call public patriarchy and private patriarchy . . . patriarchy is not just a *family system*. It is a *social system* which includes and defines the family relation. It is in the family system that we find the public aspects of patriarchy: the control of society – of the economy, polity, religion, etc. – by men collectively, who use that control to uphold the rights and privileges of the collective male sex as well as individual men. The husband's family-centered control over his wife's daily labor is upheld by the publicly-centered marginalization of job, property, knowledge, etc. by men.

She continues:

as monopoly capitalism developed there was a shift from private patriarchy centered on the family to public patriarchy *centered on industry and government*. Children are no longer valued as they were in earlier times for their unskilled labor but rather they are valued today for their future skilled labor . . . children themselves and the labor required to rear them have changed from a valuable family burden that men wished to control to a costly family asset that men wish to avoid. Simultaneously, public patriarchy takes over more directly the labor of women in child bearing and child rearing through state policies, public support and professional caretaking. Male-headed families are no longer needed to maintain patriarchy.

(p. 242; my emphasis)

[55]

Conventionally, she identifies the rise of monopoly capital in the period 1880–1920, and its consolidation in the 1960s. Most of the remainder of her analysis details legal and social changes in children and family law, divorce laws, child custody, and child support, particularly in the period 1880–1920.

It seems that Brown is identifying two aspects to public patriarchy: (1) the public aspects of patriarchy in general; (2) the historically specific forms of those public aspects at certain historical times, the latter representing shifts in the form of the former. Indeed, she is quite explicit in stating:

> I am not arguing that the private family is dead or dying . . . the public patriarchy continues to uphold and encourage male domination within the family. I do argue, however, for the increased importance of public patriarchy and for the decreasing importance of private patriarchy in structuring the reproductive labor of society. . . . The relationship of husband's income and wife's labor is *increasingly mediated by the formal institutions of public patriarchy*.
>
> (p. 246)

Brown's account is a very important contribution. In particular she identifies the historical dimension to public patriarchy as most significantly, though not exclusively, the development of monopoly capitalism from the 1880s. In this respect, her specific reference to monopoly capitalism can be compared with the more general analysis of capitalist patriarchy. Indeed, one way of connecting these terms is that capitalist patriarchy is one specific form of both capitalism and patriarchy; it may also be one form of both public patriarchy and monopoly capitalism. These three overlapping types are historically interrelated but not identical. However, she limits herself to two sites of labour – paid work and domestic work, and this stands as a limitation; her account is also based primarily on United States experience.

It may be useful at this point to note that a number of feminists have provided positive critiques of the concept of public patriarchy. Particularly useful is Nancy Fraser's commentary on Carol Brown's use of the term public patriarchy, which she considers is too simple on two counts:

First, . . . I prefer not to use 'patriarchy' as a generic term for male dominance but rather as a designation of a specific historical social formation. Second, Brown's public/private contrast oversimplifies the structure of both laissez-faire and welfare state capitalism, since it posits two major societal zones where there are actually four (family, official economy, state, and sphere of public political discourse) and conflates two distinct public/private divisions.

(Fraser 1989, p. 158)

Accordingly, Fraser locates the concept historically as a set of dynamic social processes, rather than something to be accepted or rejected as either a total explanation or totally inadequate.

Zillah Eisenstein (1981) in *The Radical Future of Liberal Feminism* introduces the concepts of family patriarchy, in which the locus of the oppression of women is in the family and the private sphere, and social patriarchy, where the locus of male domination is in the public sphere. More precisely, she distinguishes between 'the hierarchical sexual organization for reproduction of sex-gender' in the *patriarchal family* and 'the organization of sex-gender as it exists throughout society as a totality', that is, *social patriarchy*. The development of patriarchal relations is seen by Eisenstein to be partially autonomous, and partially in relation to both capitalist relations and the ideology of liberalism. Thus the state acts as a mediator of conflicts and contradictions, and is not just a site of patriarchal relations. In summary, social patriarchy is (1) located in the public domain, (2) the organization of sex-gender throughout society, and (3) historical.

A number of similar accounts are given by other feminist authors. Some, like Jane Ursel (1986), writing in the Canadian context, take a long-term historical view. She argues that:

The essential condition for the subordination of women within any patriarchal system is *control of women's access to the means of their livelihood*. By making women's access to subsistence contingent on entry into particular reproduction relations or by restricting their ability to be self-sufficient, women's labour, both productive and reproductive, becomes subject to comprehensive control. This control is the essence of patriarchy, its universal function and effect.

(p. 153, emphasis in original)

[57]

She goes on to specify different types of patriarchy in relation to the concept of the mode of reproduction. These are:

> (a) *Communal patriarchy*, which corresponds with pre-class, kin-based social systems; (b) *family patriarchy*, which corresponds with class-structured social systems characterized by decentralized processes of production; and (c) *social patriarchy*, which corresponds to advanced wage labour systems.
>
> (p. 154, emphases in original)

Like both Brown and Eisenstein, Ursel appears to see the distinction between private/family patriarchy and public/social patriarchy as both an historical discrimination between two types, even periods, of patriarchy, and substantive discrimination between different elements in society. Thus on the second count, Ursel writes:

> familial patriarchy is the hierarchical sexual organization for the reproduction of sex-gender identities and relations as it exists in the family; in contrast, social patriarchy is the social organization of sex-gender relations through rules and laws concerning marriage, property, inheritance, and child custody.
>
> (p. 154)

She appears to use 'family patriarchy' and 'familial patriarchy' interchangeably. She continues:

> What distinguishes social from familial patriarchy is the increasing centralization of control, with access to resources dominated by the employer on the one hand and the state on the other. The individual patriarch is no longer the central force in the maintenance of control over reproduction. The employer's interest in the maintenance of patriarchy is a distant second to interest in the extraction of surplus; when the two conflict it is a foregone conclusion that the interests of surplus extraction predominate. Thus the state stands alone as the entity which has an interest in preserving patriarchy and the material resources to do so.
>
> (p. 157)

These shifts towards social patriarchy are located in the development of capitalism. More specifically, she suggests that:

> Familial patriarchy remained a viable system of control throughout the transition from the feudal mode of production up until the early commercial stages of capitalism . . . . Industrial capitalism centralized the process of production and its successful expansion was dependent upon the predominance of the wage labour system. . . . Gradually, the household lost all productive resources other than the labour power embodied in each member. This transformation seriously undercut the material basis of the patriarchal family for control of productive resources was the basis of the patriarch's own authority . . . under the centralization of production, industrial capitalism upsets the delicate balance between centralized and decentralized authority which had permitted a complementary co-existence between class and patriarchy in earlier types of society. . . . The state, charged with preserving the system as a whole, is faced with a major challenge in attempting to mediate the now fundamentally contradictory spheres of production and reproduction. It is under these conditions that social patriarchy emerges as a new regulatory role for the state.
>
> (pp. 156–7)

This apparent distinction is, however, partly clarified by Ursel in the following paragraph:

> Both familial and social patriarchal structures operate in class societies. While social and familial forms of patriarchy are complementary, under differing material conditions one aspect will emerge as the critical locus of power and authority over women with the other form playing a secondary or facilitative role. In a familial patriarchal mode, power and authority over women is decentralized, operates at the household level and is based upon the patriarch's exclusive control of women's access to necessary (survival) resources. Within this system social patriarchal rules are facilitative, empowering the patriarch with such control through marriage, property and inheritance laws. In the social patriarchal mode, the power and authority to control women's

[59]

access to resources is *increasingly* vested in the state through the promulgation of labour, welfare and family law. Within this mode, *familial patriarchy is essential* in providing the structural unit of reproduction in the nuclear family, but is secondary as the source of power over women.

(pp. 154–5; my emphases)

Thus social patriarchy *does not supersede* familial patriarchy: the relationship of one to the other changes historically – under the 'social patriarchal mode', social patriarchal rules and structures in the state become increasingly important, even though familial patriarchy *remains essential*. Thus, such transformations are not some kind of simple takeover of 'the family' by the state, the market, or other organizations.

According to Ursel,

[a] problem, variously described in the Victorian rhetoric of the early reformers as 'the woman problem', 'race suicide' or 'child saving', was that of the disorganization of reproductive relations occasioned by the lack of fit between the old patriarchal order and the new economic system.

(p. 158)

Not only is there a strong functionalism in this account, but also social patriarchy is defined partly in terms of the development of the state – as against a description of either an historical period or a set of structural elements (in the public domains). The state is both the locus of social patriarchy, *and* the *mediation* between production and reproduction – or, as Ursel puts it, 'the state is the guarantor of the rules of class and the rules of patriarchy and must insure that one system does not disrupt the other'. The state is both the technical and social relations of reproduction, meaning by 'social', the mediation of those and other relations.[8]

Finally,

as some of the patriarchal relations of the family were undermined through social and economic developments, the state, through the system of social patriarchy, attempted to *reinforce familial patriarchy*. Hence the peculiar paradox of our time: the liberalization of family law, the emergence of women's and children's rights, while appearing as the end of patriarchy, are, in fact, a manifestation of the growth of social patriarchy

(p. 158; my emphasis)

- 'a *restructuring* of patriarchy' (p. 188; emphasis in original).

In the excellent article 'The women's movement, anarchism and the state', the Canadian feminist Nicole Laurin-Frenette (1982) addresses the double oppression of women in the domestic (private) and non-domestic (public) spheres, and the way '[i]nstitutions other than the family have gradually assumed the organization of a considerable part of production and regulation of activity previously performed within the framework of the family' (p. 27). Her subsequent analysis stresses the control on women exerted by modern institutional forms in the public domain, especially in the state. The late nineteenth century and the early twentieth century saw the upsurge in feminism, especially around women's suffrage, the reorganization of the family, the entry of women into the liberal professions, and the steadily downward trend in the birth rate. 'As the sphere of domestic production shrinks . . . its functions are increasingly subject to extra-domestic control' (p. 32).

> Places [allotted on the basis of sex] and relations, . . . especially the exploitation and domination of women by men – tend to appear to the agents and particularly the female agents as arbitrary. The force of the dominant party has been partly undermined; the consent of the dominated has been partially withdrawn. Women are 'discovering' the gratuitous nature of domestic work. Children 'no longer recognize parental authority'. Men are 'losing' their sense of responsibility.
>
> (p. 33)

Alongside this, 'new forms of "domesticity", and "conjugality" are . . . imposed by the central institutions of control' (p. 34). 'The new "domesticity" brings about a certain weakening of traditionally work-related masculine solidarity' (p. 35). Meanwhile, new models of femininity are constructed both in the labour market and in claims to the state. Even 'the women's movement has formulated its main claims in the language of the State'.

[61]

Although not using the term public patriarchy, Margaret Stacey and Celia Davies (1983, pp. 11–12) have summarized similar changes across and between the public and private domains as follows:

> imagining a patriarchal society before the emergence of the state and with a sexual division of labour, the society was male dominated but there was a territory where women had the expertise within the domestic domain: there they had power and authority notwithstanding the overall patriarchy and from there they could influence the male world. . . . When the state was developed and a public domain created by men who set up public institutions away from home it was inevitably male. . . . Further changes took place when production was removed from the home, women were then taken in considerable numbers into the public domain but in subservient roles. . . . As the power of the state increased and the welfare state began to emerge the relative scale of the domestic and public domains changed . . . , there is an invasion of the private domain by the state, the so-called 'democratic egalitarian family' developed and the area of women's control was lost, but women have not achieved equality in the public domain with men and the domestic domain remains in many ways patriarchal. . . .

Both Laurin-Frenette's and Stacey and Davies's accounts place the growth of the modern state and the professions as central in the recent historical forms of gender domination. Similar themes have been developed in a number of recent Scandinavian feminist studies, focusing especially though not exclusively on the recent and current development of the welfare state. Harriet Holter edited and contributed to the Norwegian collection *Patriarchy in a Welfare Society* in 1984, and set out a distinction between 'direct, personally exercised and legitimated dominance' and 'indirect, "structural" dominance. . . . Structural dominance is further seen as either impersonal or personified, that is, mediated through a person [meaning a particular person]' (p. 18). She argues that:

> One of the historical changes brought about by capitalist industrialism is a shift from direct, personal forms of dominance to indirect or 'structural' ruling of the weaker groups

and classes. This is true of male oppression of women too
and forms part of the *reorganized patriarchy*.

(p. 19; emphasis in original)

In this kind of patriarchy it could be argued that the im-
personality of men's dominance not only directly uses the law, but
also less directly needs law and refers to law itself to overcome its
potential illegitimacy.

Other Scandinavian feminist writers on this theme include
Helga Maria Hernes, Birte Siim, and Anette Borchorst.[9] Hernes
focuses on the shift from private dependence in families to public
dependence on the state that has occurred particularly in the
post-Second World War period in Norway. She argues that the
'welfare state' has developed through two phases of incorporation
– the first wave of reforms affecting mainly market activities, and
thus mainly men, leading to organizational developments such as
trade unions, socialist parties, and employers' associations; and the
second incorporating reproductive areas, and affecting mainly
women (1984, p. 40; 1987a, 1987b). In this scheme, the state is
analysed as an institution to which women (and men) relate in
three major ways: as citizens, clients, and employees. Subsequently, Hernes (1988b) has explored in more detail the complexity of public domain and private domain dependencies,
characterized nowadays by a 'public/private mix' rather than a
'public/private split'. She identifies four major institutional settings: the state, the market, the public sphere of opinion formation, and the family, with the state being the dominant institution
designed to administer this mix since the turn of the century.[10] In
this more recent work (1988a, 1988b) she has also emphasized the
primary importance of the 'citizen' role for women, with the
'client' and 'employee' roles for women being determined by
women's and men's relations to the state as citizens. Thus for
Hernes the welfare form of the state does have some potential for
women but it is a potential that is structurally constrained, particularly through women's dependencies on, lack of control over,
and definition as objects by public domain institutions controlled
by men.

Borchorst & Siim (1987) pursue a related, and partly optimistic, theme in discussing Danish experience of the welfare state
since the 1960s. They see state change as an important element in
the changing position of women, but view such change as

[63]

contradictory, between a further extension of 'social patriarchy' and 'a new form of social citizenship' (Siim 1987, 1988). They seem to suggest a developmental theory of the welfare state, in terms of women as, first, mothers/clients (as in Britain and the United States), then employees (as in Denmark and other Scandinavian states), and then citizens, as potential determiners of their own social needs and political interests. Thus, despite contradictions, they suggest that 'a strong public service sector seems to be one precondition for [women] avoiding becoming solely dependent on the state as clients' (Borchorst & Siim 1987, p. 146). Having said that, they are cautious about overstating the emancipatory power of the state for women. For example, Siim (1987) has usefully distinguished between women's dependence on the state and women's involvement in state decision-making. Thus, in rather different ways, Hernes and Borchorst and Siim prioritize the need to transform state structures and processes, thus increasing women's participatory control and decreasing women's definition as objects.

All these various changes entail movements in the delimitation and social construction of what is 'public' and what is 'private'; they entail movements in the relationship and association of different areas of human activity and the public domains. While varied, these accounts see the shift from private to public patriarchy as part of the *restructuring of patriarchy, not the end of patriarchy.* This shift is generally seen as *integrally related to or even reproducing private patriarchy.* Most of these accounts do not offer 'either–or' analyses: types of patriarchy can be conceptualized as changing along continua or dimensions, not simply as falling into one of a small number of defining boxes.

Aggregation, synthesis, and difference

Having surveyed some of the major approaches to public patriarchy, what sense are we to make of the range of definitions, explanations, and historical treatments? What significance might these differences have? Different uses of the term 'public patriarchy' could be taken as commentaries on fundamentally different phenomena. Alternatively, they might indicate either different interpretations of the same phenomenon or different commentaries on different societies or societal situations. For example, some interpretations might emphasize 'economic' explanations (capital accumulation, form of surplus value, and so on), while others might emphasize 'political' explanations (state formation, publicization of political rights, duties, and obligations).

Different kinds of explanations tend to emphasize different major historical events in particular societies, particularly events that entail relatively rapid social change. Thus, for example, while North American uses of public patriarchy (e.g. Brown, Ursel) have emphasized change in capital and capitalism, Scandinavian uses (e.g. Hernes, Holter) have emphasized change in the state. These differences speak to important questions on what have been the crucial, determining changes in particularly public patriarchy, and the gendering of the public and private domains over the last hundred years or more. Thus these questions of semantics are also questions of conceptualization, ideology, and socio-historical context.

In the majority of these accounts of the shift to public patriarchy there is a combination of references to, first, the increasing power of the state and state laws over the family and the father, and the changing relation of women to the state as clients, dependants, sometimes employees and citizens; and, second, the increasing importance of monopoly capitalism over factory and other simpler forms of capitalism. The focus is usually on one of these two major institutional blocks of the public domains – the state or the capitalist/market sector – and rather less so on the public domain institutions of opinion formation – including *culture and media*. Indeed *cultural accounts* and explanations of public patriarchy or accounts of *cultural change* in public patriarchy are rare.

There are several possible ways forward in the face of this variety. One is to develop a composite approach to public patriarchy. Most notably, Sylvia Walby (1986, 1989) has argued that patriarchy cannot be reduced to the economic. Instead she has identified six structures of patriarchy: the patriarchal (household) mode of production, patriarchal relations in paid work, the patriarchal state, male violence, patriarchal relations in sexuality,[11] and patriarchal culture. She has further developed this account to argue that the change from private patriarchy to public patriarchy 'involves a change both in the relation between the structures and within the structures' (Walby 1990a, p. 24). Thus, she criticizes accounts that are limited to one or two structures, and suggests that '[w]hen all six patriarchal structures are included the account is more satisfactory' (1989, p. 228).[12] She has also argued that first-wave feminism, from around 1850 to 1930, is 'a significantly under-rated political movement' (1990b, p. 150), and that in Britain 'a move towards public patriarchy . . . was a result of the successes of first-wave feminism in the context of an expanding capitalist economy' (1990b, p. 157).

An alternative approach might be to synthesize differences rather than aggregate them. Thus, not only is it possible to compare 'economic' and 'political' accounts, it is possible to interpret 'political' accounts as another form of the 'economic', and vice versa. For example, in early industrializing societies, we can understand the movement from pre-capitalist patriarchy to patriarchy where capitalist relations also operate as the beginnings of a kind of public patriarchy. In this situation, there may be *an extension of pre-capitalist relations of dominance in the private domains into the public domains.* Capitalist enterprises developed and expanded by the extraction of absolute surplus value, by the extension of the working day, and by the employment of cheap labour. In the case of cotton textiles in Britain, and particularly in Lancashire, women and children were the cheapest labour, and constituted the majority of the workforce – 82.3 per cent in 1818 (Hutchins 1915, p. 72). Relative if not absolute gender segregation of the workforce operated. However, early in the nineteenth century the potential power of women in the employed workforce was realized by men. In 1829 a national conference of men spinners excluded women from their trade unions. Subsequently a combination of forces, including trade union action, state legislation, and employers' hiring policies and practices, excluded women from such employment, re-establishing or maintaining patriarchal relations of dominance that preceded capitalism. Towards the end of the last century we see the culmination of these forces in the institution of the 'family wage' for the man head of the household/ wage earner. State responses here can be understood as following the earlier gendered abstraction of absolute surplus value.

In contrast to this kind of account, let us consider a later industrializing society, such as Norway.[13] There capitalist industrialization occurred much later in the nineteenth century than in Britain, primarily through the extraction of relative surplus value. Technological improvements, for example, in the power and engineering industries, were used to maintain men's domination of traditional industries. Gender segregation was maintained by the late nineteenth century but by a different historical route, and without the early introduction of women's industrial employment. Thus later industrialization can be understood as an extension of pre-capitalist patriarchal relations of dominance *directly* into and through the public domains. As previously, the family wage and welfare state formation could still be introduced upon this economic base. Through these kinds of arguments, explanations of gender-segregated wage labour (enforced outside or inside the law), the family wage, and welfare state formation may be developed in relation to patriarchy and public patriarchy.

An alternative kind of synthesis that moves from the 'economic' to the 'political' is represented in the contrast sometimes drawn between patriarchy (the rule of the fathers) and fratriarchy (the rule of the brotherhoods). A recent example of this approach has been outlined by John Remy (1990) with patriarchy and fratriarchy seen as two arms or modes of a unitary system of dominance of rule by men. The relationship of the two modes may be antagonistic but more often is overlapping and asymmetrical. It is the historical evolution of the patriarchal–fratriarchal dynamic within androcracy that is most significant. While patriarchy is generally a conservative social force with a vested interest in maintaining order, fratriarchy is a dynamic and volatile system of domination. Fratriarchy involves the allegiance of fratrists to the organizational expression (or social forms) of fratriarchy, the fratriarchal men's hut – the frat. While much of this analysis focuses on the relatively small-scale frats, such as bands of, often young, men bent on terror, he also looks more broadly at the development of fratriarchal and fratristic social movements, such as Nazism, Japanese fratri-imperialism, and the American super-frat and macro-fratriarchy (Remy 1988).

Public patriarchy might be understood as combining elements of both (private) patriarchy and fratriarchy. The general corporate form of public patriarchy may be fratriarchal (rule by brotherhoods), while specific organizational processes may be patriarchal, in terms of the hierarchical domination. Alternatively, public patriarchy could be understood as characterized by public domain processes that are simultaneously patriarchal (hierarchical domination by men) and fratriarchal (collective domination by men).

[67]

Another possible kind of synthesis is around sexuality. If, as Catharine MacKinnon (1982) suggests, sexuality is at the heart of patriarchy, men's domination, and gender relations themselves, then how does the development of public patriarchy reinforce, alter, elaborate, or challenge that centrality? And what is the significance of such change for the more specific impact of organizations in the construction of men's power, masculinities, and sexualities?

A third alternative to the diversity of commentaries on public patriarchy differs from the aggregated and synthetic approaches, and attends instead to the question of difference. Rather than trying to produce *the* single account, all incorporating or all reducing, it is perhaps more helpful to recognize the possibility of difference in analysis, in the operation of public patriarchies, and in public men and public masculinities. Feminist theories of public patriarchy are to my mind the most important set of recent contributions to debates on public men. They can be usefully supplemented by attention to the implications of diversity and difference (Ch. 5). However, before discussing that perspective I shall attempt to spell out some of the initial implications of public patriarchies for the analysis, understanding, and change of public men and public masculinities (see Ch. 4).

CHAPTER 4

Public patriarchy: some initial implications for men and masculinities

Having looked at both malestream accounts of public men and feminist accounts of public patriarchy, I want now to ask – how can we go on to construct a pro-feminist/anti-patriarchal account of public men and public masculinities? To do so I think it is necessary to engage in a contradictory way with the concept of public patriarchy. This involves, on the one hand (in Ch. 5), a sympathetic critique of the concept, on the other (in this chapter) an extension of the concept to include explanations of and initial implications for public men and public masculinities. For, although there is a clear diversity of views on what might be understood by public patriarchy, it is possible to spell out some of the implications of this broad approach for the analysis of men. Thus, I am attempting to develop a constructive critique of public patriarchy in order to understand, change, and deconstruct public men and public masculinities.

In dealing with public patriarchy, it is clear that we are concerned with the development of new historical forms of public domains, patriarchies, and 'public men'. This necessarily concerns the interrelation of different elements of analysis – in particular, the societal form of public patriarchies, the modern character of the public domains, and the nature of public men and public masculinities. A number of particular types of relationships between these societal, domain, and generic levels of analysis are of special importance. These include:

- the apparent relative separation of the public domains and the private domains;
- the changing definition of the public domains and the private domains and the inclusion of more activities and interests from the private domains within the public domains;

[69]

- the relative power of the public domains over the private domains;
- the construction of the public domains through public institutions, such as the state;
- the increased public powers of public men through the development of new and larger public institutions;
- the impact of these changing formations upon public men and public masculinities.

All of these features are 'produced' and enacted by and through men, and all 'produce' men; this dialectical relation of the public domains and men is implicit in the notion of 'public men'. Indeed, in a very real and material sense the power of the institutions of the public domain both is produced by men and produces men. 'Public men' thus refers to that dialectical relation of men and public-ness, that facet of men located in the public domains. The term 'public men' is a shorthand for 'men acting in the public domain' – themselves enacting public power and patriarchal institutions, and produced by these powers and institutions.

The construction of 'public men' entails matters of both form and content. Indeed matters of form – the fact that there are socially constructed public–private differences, the fact that certain activities have moved more fully into public concern – sometimes seem to be of more lasting importance than the matters of detailed and substantive content. This is especially important in the changing historical nature of 'public men' and the changing historical construction of public masculinities.

While public patriarchy is often characterized by changes in the form of the oppression of women, such oppression persists in structured relations, themselves obviously gendered. Such oppression is not enacted by neutered non-agents; it is enacted by men as oppressors, both collectively and as agents (though not necessarily in all individual cases). Changes in the form of public patriarchies and in the oppression of women therein *necessarily* mean changes in oppression by men. And changes in oppression by men necessarily mean changes in men, or at least in some men. A focus on public patriarchies thus also produces a case for the examination of masculinities. Such masculinities in public patriarchies may themselves be public or private, hegemonic or non-hegemonic.

The argument that the development of public patriarchies has more impact on and relevance for women than for men seems to be closely related to the argument within some varieties of Marxist feminism that an understanding of capitalist patriarchy needs to address the gendered nature of women's work, but less so the gendered nature of men's work, or the gendered nature of men's power, domination, and oppression over women. This last area remains neglected within most varieties of Marxism, so that men's domination both of capital and of the state is seldom explored. Movements towards public patriarchies are likely to involve changes in the position and indeed the experience of significant numbers of men.

Let us consider why this is likely to be so. First, if men's power over women shifts to men in the public domains, then at least some men in public domain institutions will be involved in those relative increases of power, and perhaps of authority. This is perhaps most obviously seen in the association of men, men's power, and 'masculine dominance' with the development of the state (Burstyn 1983). It is also apparent in the development of 'instrumental rationality' and 'technocratic consciousness' as 'the quintessentially modern masculine style' under 'late capitalism' (Winter & Robert 1980, p. 271). Public domain channels of influence offer possibilities for patriarchal alliances between men across economic classes, for the integration of men into political processes, and for the differentiation of women and men.

Secondly, there are the variety of impacts of first-wave feminism and of women more generally upon men, and specifically upon public men. Although women did not achieve universal national suffrage at 21 until 1928, women's increasing political participation in the public domains from the late nineteenth century had numerous implications for individual men, men collectively, and the scope and structuring of the public domains.

Thirdly, the accruing of power to *some* men in the public domains has numerous sometimes contradictory implications for *other* men in the public domains who are in positions of less relative power there. Differentiations of power are not just between women and men but also between men.

Fourthly, there are implications for men in the private domains – both directly, in terms of the power of, say, state laws over men in the private domains, and indirectly, in terms of the impacts upon law and other public domain powers over women as objects of men's policies, which in some cases at least affect men with whom they are or have been associated.

[71]

Fifthly, and bringing together the two previous points, there is the possibility of the distinction, perhaps the increasing distinction, being made between private masculinities and public masculinities, with the development of new models of public men.

Sixthly, there is the relevance of public domain processes for men and masculinities in terms of both the increasing impact and power of the public domains and the psychological development and psychodynamics of men.[1] The growth of increased and powerful public domain arenas for men also develops through the reverse process of importing family and other private domain dynamics and authority structures. Necessarily these private dynamics within public forums develop differentially over time, with feudal forms dominant in early capitalism (Winter & Robert 1980, p. 251), to be later transformed in the movement to managerial class relations (see pp. 160–9).

Thus, although I have already provided a limited critique of the pessimistic progressives and poststructuralists (Ch. 2), particularly on the grounds of either their absence of a treatment of gender or their patriarchalism, they are important, in the context of public patriarchies, in raising a certain kind and level of analysis. This lies in addressing, albeit in very different ways, the more personal consequences of change in the public domains, and indeed public patriarchies, for public men. In general terms, the pessimistic progressive accounts of Lasch, Jacoby, and others seek a supposed 'humanist', if often patriarchal, perspective on the personal, whereas the poststructuralists attempt to deconstruct the personal to show that the personal is (located in) discourse.

Change in public men and public masculinities occurs in association with and in relation to (the construction of) what men do 'in private'. Managers, civil servants, and other public men have their own private worlds, and this means that there are all manner of complex possible associations between these public and private constructions. For example, the expansion of the civil service and the great business corporations occurred at a similar historical period to both the growth of mass film-going and Freud's and others' statement of seduction theory. In this perspective men (including managers, civil servants, and other public men) were accused as fathers, of sexual abuse, in reality or potentiality as well as in fantasy.

Seventhly, there is the argument that the state under public patriarchies may create not only client dependence and employee status for women, but also the potential for women, as citizens, to determine their own needs through a transformed state.[2] This is clearly a more closely defined political strategy towards the state (and stands in opposition to the anarcho-feminism of Laurin-Frenette 1982, for example). However, such analysis also has considerable implications for the position and experience of men. If the state can be and is to be transformed, as Hernes suggests, this will entail a transformation of the structure and staffing of the state, with consequent change for men working in the state, perhaps their replacement by women, and further less direct effects for men beyond the state, both as citizens and in the private domains in households.

Public patriarchies are also patriarchies, and as such analyses of them must take care not to reproduce their own patriarchalism. Public patriarchies are not just one-dimensional structures of inequality; they are complex, structural, and processual. They entail the rule of the father, the rule of men, and also the rule of public men; women may be oppressed twice over, in private and in public. Public patriarchies are also social, historical terrains, not of our own making, upon which social relations are reproduced and social actions enacted. Deconstructions of public men and public masculinities need to reflect these complexities.

CHAPTER 5

Public patriarchies, public men, public domains, and public masculinities

In the last two chapters I have mentioned, somewhat in passing, a number of problems around the idea of 'public patriarchy'. I now want to focus explicitly on some of these concerns. These stem largely from my attempt to hold together in tension two insights: that organizations and men (within them) are increasingly powerful in the public domains; and that the distinction between the public and private domains is itself problematic. Both represent an academic commentary on social change and a personal comment on my own experience of the relationship of the public and the private.

In particular I want to reconstruct/deconstruct the concept of public patriarchies by focusing on issues around diversity and difference – to develop a sympathetic critique of 'public patriarchy' that acknowledges both (the) gender class (of men) in patriarchy and cultural differences. In speaking of difference here, a number of issues are highlighted.[1] First, difference is one way of referring to difference between the experiences of women and the experiences of men, as in sexual difference (Barrett 1987). Second, there are differences between men, and between masculinities. Third, there is the more fundamental notion of *différence* (Derrida 1973, 1978) as the prime active force of sociality. In this sense, *différence* refers to *a unity simultaneously divided* from itself: a feature intrinsic to all social forms, and constitutive of human discourses. In this view, *différence* is a form of self-reference, in which social terms contain their own opposites and so refuse any singular meaning. In this sense, references to differences between men, as between other terms, invoke an endless process of *deferral*, and are always at best *partial* truths, at worst misleading falsehoods. Fourth, there is the associated anti-foundationalist approach to difference in which reference is made not just to many subjects

[74]

but rather to the undermining of defining any bases for knowledge and epistemology (Halbert 1989, p. 7). These latter two approaches might also be seen as raising difficulties for attempts to treat 'men' and 'masculinities' in terms of types, partly on account of the inherent fluidity and change of social life. Needless to say, these explorations of the implications of difference are conducted in tension with the need to recognize, first, social structures and structural relations, and, second, tendencies towards dedifferentiation.[2] They are an attempt to elaborate the different ways men maintain power in patriarchies, not a dilution of the importance of (gender class) power.

Approaching this deconstructive task necessarily involves a critical, yet sympathetic, engagement with the concepts 'patriarchy' and 'public'; making gender, men, and men's power explicit; deneutralizing the neutralizing hand of concepts and ideology (Griffin 1982); and attending to diversity in debates around 'public patriarchies' and their historical change.

It is in keeping with this approach that I have already spoken of 'public patriarchies'. Indeed, this may be a convenient time to review the major reasons for pluralizing 'patriarchy' to 'patriarchies', and 'public patriarchy' to 'public patriarchies'. First, there are a number of different material bases to patriarchies. Secondly, there are specific localized varieties of patriarchies, as, for example, when individual organizations or communities operate as relatively small semi-autonomous patriarchies. Thirdly, there is the broader engagement of patriarchy and postmodernism: there is in effect no centre to patriarchy. Fourthly, women, men, young people, may experience patriarchies differently: we may all know, have, be in, reproduce our own patriarchies. And fifthly, to use 'patriarchy' in the singular is to risk reifying 'society' and dominant patriarchal definitions of the nation, spatially and socially. There is a strong case for retaining the concept of 'public patriarchy', if by pluralizing it to 'public patriarchies' its complexities and fractures can be recognized, and the deconstruction of public men and public masculinities can be aided.

Closely linked to this pluralizing of concepts is the need to problematize dualities – not to create further false unities, but to deconstruct what appear as complementary pairings ('halves' that make up falsely unified 'wholes') in order to recognize them as relations. The most obvious relevant example of this is with

[75]

respect to the notions of public domains and private domains themselves. Such problematizing of dualities and emphasizing instead of the relational are themselves major themes within both feminist and postmodernist theorizing.[3]

In simultaneously critiquing public patriarchies and developing a framework for analysis, I shall focus on four major interrelated questions. In each case I shall consider how the notion of difference problematizes one of the major concepts in use, respectively public patriarchies, public men, public domains, and public masculinities:

- *Public patriarchies*: what is their conceptual status in time and space?
- *Public men*: how are we to deal with the interrelationships of the public domains and private domains, so that public men are understood in relation to both?
- *Public domains*: how are we to reflect the diverse material bases and multiple meanings of public domain?
- *Public masculinities*: how might all this relate to the complexities of lived experiences, both men's experiences and others' experiences of men?[4]

These issues of power and difference are now considered in turn.

Problematizing public patriarchies: concepts in time and space

While public patriarchies refer to a number of major historical shifts in gender relations, there are a number of ways in which the concept can be subject to critique. Certain critiques follow from general critiques of the concept of patriarchy, for example, in the extent to which gendered systems of dominance can be separated from other systems of dominance, such as capitalism, imperialism, socialism. Similarly, there are arguments against seeing gender and gender relations in terms of (sex/gender) classes, around the (in)applicability of models based on social and economic inequality (Gilligan 1982); additionally, arguments against the concept of economic class[5] may be re-applied to gender *as class*. It could also be held that the concept of public patriarchies is a contradiction in terms, if patriarchy is used literally. 'Public patriarchy' in its literal sense would refer to the *rule* of the father(s) in the public rather than the private domains.

For these reasons it is important not to make public patriarchies into yet another 'grand narrative'. To do so is to fall into one of the pitfalls of single logic malestream thinking. To put this another way, in using and developing the concept of public patriarchies, it is necessary to avoid conceptualization preceding oppression. History does not take place through a grand narrative of orderly stages: it takes place. Partly for this reason it may be more accurate to speak of *movements towards* public patriarchies rather than the *establishment of* public patriarchies. Similarly, Leonore Davidoff (1990, p. 229) has noted how since the early 1970s there has been a move by social historians 'against unilinear, "Big Bang" or "before and after" models, whether modernization or Marxist', and towards 'a more holistic approach' for which 'the methodological metaphor often used is the single web of meaning among innumerable variables'.

Nor does history consist of 'Golden Ages' transformed at specific 'turning points' to the 'modern condition'. Thus we need to be wary of histories of patriarchy that run simply from a pre-modern account of men's oppression of women to a modern account, whether based solely on private property, wage labour, capitalism, instrumental rationality, modern science, monopoly capitalism, the state, the modern state, or the welfare state. 'Turning points' may of course occur in the sense that at and during certain historical times there are relatively rapid changes in social relations, in this case in men's public domain domination of women. But turning points may not be once and for all; they do not 'accomplish' *polar* changes in society. Any such shifts have occurred in the context of previous shifts; they accumulate; they are placed in their own specific historical, social, and spatial locations.

Whatever the significance of these particular historical changes, the movement from the first situation to the second is not part of some smooth evolution. The concept of public patriarchies is itself simply a reference to some elements, albeit important ones, of societies characterized by gendering and gender domination – and thus is like all social life founded in social practice. Patriarchy can be reproduced in the careless use of concepts.

These issues of difference apply as much in space as in time. A very broad (that is, global) framework for understanding them may be developed through a focus on differential *movement* and differential *access* – to *places, spaces, times, resources, other people, even 'the self'*. People's *differential* movement and access to other things and other people does not vary simply, smoothly, or incrementally. Rather, some groups or classes of people, generally those with relative power, have *considerably more* powers of movement and access than people in less powerful groups or classes. Marked disjunctions[6] between social groupings may reproduce divisions between the public and the private domains: the private being domains of relatively less movement and access; the public being domains of relatively more.

Differentiations between the public domains and the private domains are consolidations, coagulations, and congealments of these various *disjunctions* in powers of movement and access. Most obviously, this includes men's control of women and women's movement and access. It also includes, however, other forms of control over movement and access, by age, ethnicity, economic class, sexuality, and (dis)abilities. For example, the able-bodied may *deliberately* construct the public domains so as to make them inaccessible to those with disabilities, such as the blind and the immobile.[7] Men, public men, are both a gender class with power over such movements, and are ourselves spatially differentiated through various social divisions and differences.

To get here we have had to travel through time and space; public patriarchies have developed not through a smoothly centred journey but through an amalgam of individual and collective journeys, historical and spatial. The present state(s) of public patriarchies is the outcome of the mass(es) of historical changes and changes in movement across the world (and beyond), including imperialism, world travel, even space travel. World patriarchies are a geographical and spatial fact (Foord & Gregson 1986; Mies 1986).

We have also, in our own biographies, often travelled from the private to the public domains. We are usually conceived in private domains, and indeed, even where conception occurs in public domains, the activity or the event may be redefined as 'private'. However, private conception, and indeed private sex more generally, increasingly take place in the context of *publicly defined* modes of sexuality and biological reproduction, for example, in terms of contraception, 'sexual orientations', marriage, and family law. Such movements to the public have been reinforced by the publicization of birth, as in hospital births, and in recent decades by the spread of publicly organized means of conception, reproductive and genetic engineering, and (artificial) insemination by donor (AID or ID). Furthermore, each life reproduces humanity, historically and spatially.

From the private activities of sex, conception, procreation, and nurture (O'Brien 1981), there has been a long-term movement to the power of the public domains over time (history) and across space (geography). Urbanization and changing, often quicker, means of transport and travel have transformed 'space–time continuums' – the particular social constructions of space, time, and their interrelations that appear in particular societies or particular social sites or situations.

Problematizing public men: back to the private

In this section I consider the category 'public men', and the deconstruction of our power in the public domains – a process that will return us to the private domains. In discussing the public domains and public men, a central difficulty is that the prefix 'public' appears to be useful conceptually and practically, and indeed refers to a social reality; and yet that reality, that public reality, material and discursive, is extremely problematic. This is so in at least two main ways: first, as already noted, the separation of the public and the private is not as definite as might be inferred; and secondly, what is called as a shorthand 'public' consists of a very complex mixture of activities and processes. This is partly a substantive matter of disputing the accuracy of this description of historical change from other forms of patriarchy, most obviously private patriarchy, or the accuracy of this description of society now. The concept of public patriarchies may thus be further criticized as suggesting too sharp a divide from private patriarchies; as reifying the public domains, wherein power is supposedly located; as not sufficiently recognizing the interrelations of the private and the public domains; as wrongly suggesting a dominant takeover of the family by organizations and organizational powers; as not attending sufficiently to the impact of the powers of private domains on the public domains.

[79]

So how are we to locate public men in relation to the public and private domains within public patriarchies? In some formulations of public patriarchy the private domain is effectively *overridden* by the power and dominance of the public domain; for example, by the state or monopoly capitalism. More usually, public patriarchy is conceptualized so that the private domain and the private power of men are still seen as important, but not the predominant or most widespread form of men's power.

I want to go one step further down this path in conceptualizing public patriarchies. For although I see the concept of public patriarchies as useful in emphasizing the importance of historical change around the power and dominance of the public domains, *I see public patriarchies as materially founded on men's power and dominance in and over the private domains*, particularly around *biological reproduction, domestic work, sexuality, nurture, and violence* (Hearn 1987a). In this approach, and *par excellence* that of Mary O'Brien (1981, also see 1990), the private domain, the 'public/ private division', and men's appropriation of the private in and through the public domain are inherent structures of patriarchy. In O'Brien's view, patriarchy predates both feudalism and capitalism; it is the form of patriarchy that changes; it both derives from and (re)produces the 'private/public division'. The form of patriarchy is clearly subject to immense change both within and between the public and private domains. According to O'Brien, the public domain (and its separateness from the private domain) is itself an essential instance of patriarchy; thus transformations in the public domains are presumably determined by the relative constancy of patriarchy. In developing this approach, I am not advocating any fundamental supremacy for the public domains over the private domains. Indeed, the private domains are bases to the public domains in the following ways:

- the public domains are a domination of the private domains, the private domains being so (potentially) powerful as to require domination by men;
- those in the public domains also live and act in the private domains;
- the oppressions of the private domains have persisted, and perhaps increased, with the growth in the size and power of public domain institutions.

Public patriarchies are particular forms of patriarchies in which the power and dominance of the public domains are prominent though *premised* on men's power and dominance in the private domains. Reference to the public domains, within public patriarchies, should not imply their reification; on the contrary, seeing public patriarchies *as patriarchies* suggests reference back to the pre-eminence of the private domains and the problematizing of the public domains. This kind of approach necessarily further questions the very idea of the/a *division* between the public domains and the private domains; as already noted, we can more usefully think of 'differences' between domains.

I have previously argued that patriarchy is founded on men's appropriation of reproductive labour powers (the potential to labour) of others, particularly women and children, but also other men (Hearn 1987a). In referring to reproductive labour powers, I was concerned predominantly with four types, often not referred to as labour at all – namely, sexual, procreative, nurturing, and violent. In addition, I also referred to the reproduction of labour power and ideological reproduction. These appropriations are themselves organized in relation to 'public/private divisions' or 'differences'. In other words, the public domains are social constructions by men to secure power from women, whose labour power resides primarily in the private domains. Patriarchies are fundamentally men's domination of reproduction, in its various forms. Thus, private/public differences are fundamental features of patriarchies, though the historical forms these differences take vary greatly.

In reconceptualizing political economy in terms of reproduction rather than production, men are not seen just as employed workers or as 'economic men' in different 'class positions'; instead men can be analysed in relation to various phases and processes of reproduction, and the associated labour that is done, not done, avoided, organized, and managed. These processes include birth, childcare, adult nurture, sexuality, violence, and death. Furthermore, what is usually called 'production' can itself be *re-seen* as 'reproduction'. Working on the factory floor or in an office, or managing a 'productive enterprise', are also forms of *various* reproductive labours and *avoidance* of others, most obviously childcare.

These processes are enacted through dominant institutions, each patriarchal and each with their own dynamics. Hierarchic heterosexuality and fatherhood appear located primarily in the

[81]

private domains, yet also function in the public domains; both are certainly ancient. The professions and the state appear located primarily in the public domains, yet also function in the private domains; and both have developed relatively more recently. In addition, the institutions of productive work and ideology are typically patriarchal, though not inherently so. Even though my current focus is on the public domain aspects of patriarchies, that is, on public patriarchies, much of this analysis remains relevant. Hierarchic heterosexuality certainly operates *throughout* the public domains; fatherhood is in many ways an institution *between men* in the public domains. Both institutions, clearly visible in the public domains, have become intensely intermingled with the operation of the professions and the state, as well as public domain productive work and ideology.

Thus a rather complicated and problematic relationship exists between public men, public domains, and private domains. Public men dominate public domain institutions, even though those institutions and indeed the public domains themselves are founded in the private domains. Meanwhile public men clearly have their own private lives; moreover, the whole of this process is historically constructed, including probable increases in the power of public men and public domain institutions.

Public men can also be analysed and located in diverse ways: as a gender class, as collectivities, as specific types, as individuals. This involves attention to men's different forms of labour in reproduction – direct, indirect, management. These locations are, however, not just matters of reproduction and reproductive labour; they also exist in culture and discourse, just as public/private differences are both material and discursive. Public patriarchies do not supplant private patriarchies. Public patriarchies are best thought of as referring to the public domain aspects, however problematic, of patriarchies, in which the private is paramount. With the existence and change of public patriarchies, private patriarchies persist.

The category 'public men', like the category 'men', also needs to be deconstructed in a different way. Men's domination and oppression of women has been and is reproduced through the differentiation of different types of men who are in an hierarchical and oppressive relationship to each other. Men continue to oppress women, by way of older men oppressing young men, white men oppressing black men, able-bodied men oppressing men with disabilities, heterosexual men oppressing gay men, and middle- and upper-class men oppressing working-class men. These differences between men operate in the bringing up of men (as in the oppression of 'boys' to become certain kinds of 'men'), in the workings of hierarchies of particular organizations (as in the oppression of workers by management), in the performing of particular oppressions (as in military men killing each other), and in the very separation of public men from private men, or men in public from men in private. In such ways we (men) oppress each other, and in turn ourselves.

This kind of differentiation of 'men' may be helpful in acknowledging some of the interrelations of oppressions. It may also be an argument for casting some limited doubt on the unity of the category 'men'. However, even these differences are not enough. Indeed, the arguments of the previous paragraph can be equally applied to other forms of oppression – by age, bodily facility, economic class, 'race' and ethnicity, sexuality. In this view, what we call 'men' and 'women' are differences for reproducing other oppressions. And although I have emotional difficulties with such an argument, I can see that it does provide the death knell for 'grand narratives'.

Problematizing public domains: material bases and multiple meanings

The concept of public patriarchies may be further refined by the pluralizing of the private domains and the public domains, acknowledging their diversity of meanings, and seeing them as/within discourse. This section explores some differences as a basis for an assessment of the relationships of the public domains and public patriarchies, and public men.

The word 'public' is used in all manner of different ways: the public sector, public lavatories, the public interest, public life, the public. Going to 'work', the street, crowds, secret meetings, government, writing, voting, may all in different contexts be perceived as 'public'. Likewise, the private is used in a great variety of ways, and may be applied to a wide range of situations, arenas, people, and places. Indeed, there is something of a paradox in the apparent disaggregation of the private domains, in 'separate' families, households, dwellings, and private spaces, and yet their greater unity and ease of definition; and the apparent aggregation of the public domains, in collectivities and public spaces, and yet their greater diversity and difficulty of definition.

The diversity of private domains and public domains comes from two main directions: first, as noted above, the various material *bases* to the private–public differences, for example, in terms of biological reproduction, sexuality, nurture, and violence; secondly, the different meanings that the private and the public have in different *modes* of analysis – spatial–temporal, organizational–collective, interpersonal, psychological.[8] I would like to look in a little more detail at these four major ways of seeing the private and public domains:

Spatial–temporal extent

Private domains are particular and limited in extent; public domains are general/universal and broad in extent. This may apply over time – in history – or over space – in geography, in places, in buildings. Thus public time and public space are relatively extensive; private time and private space are relatively limited. These differentiations may apply to time and space on micro or macro levels. Sleeping and night-time are usually (outside the polar regions at least) seen as private (domain) activities, while working and daytime are usually seen as public (domain) activities. Particular moments in time and particular localities in space are likely to be constructed as private, but the broad sweep of time or space is likely to be constructed as public.

Organizational development and collective resource accumulation

Public domains are the domains of organizational development and collective resource accumulation; private domains are the domains of the non-organizational and non-collective resource accumulations. Even individual or non-collective resource accumulation may tend to move activity towards the public domains. Private or family fortunes, unless they are just stored 'under the mattress', need public management and may indeed lead to or be based on the ownership of public domain organizational resources. Similarly, as reproduction is socialized or collectivized it is moved into the public domains.

Interaction, intersubjectivity, and visibility

The public domains are formed in interaction, intersubjectivity (often called objectivity), and visibility. The private domains are formed in isolation, subjectivity, and invisibility. The private domains may refer to the relatively more frequent contact of relatively fewer people; the public domains to the relatively less frequent contact of relatively more people. This distinction broadly parallels that between primary and secondary social relationships and their associated social activities, such as 'community'/'association', 'status'/'contract'. Furthermore, the interactional and the intersubjective are usually more visible to others; while the isolational and the (intra-)subjective are usually less visible, even invisible, to others.

Boundaries of selves

The public domains are where public selves, that is, the selves presented for others, are; the private domains are where the private selves, that is, the selves presented for themselves, are. Alternatively, certain situations or experiences may be labelled or perceived as private, and others may be labelled or perceived as public. Public selves might thus be seen or experienced as less central to the person, and the private as more central to the person.

The earlier account of public patriarchies can now be supplemented by the variable characteristics and definitions of the public and private domains – including their spatial and temporal aspects; collective organization; interpersonal processes; and individual psychologies. In addition there seem to be many current movements towards pluralization – not just in the multiplicity of forms of public domains, but also in the multiplicity of social, political, national, generic, ethnic, and other social forces. Accordingly, there are numerous possible types of public men and numerous public masculinities. These differences should not, however, obscure the ways in which men, public men, remain unified as a gender class in terms of our power relations with women and young people.[9]

[85]

Problematizing public masculinities: overlaps, resonances, paradoxes, and other experiences

Public patriarchies are experienced in complicated and contradictory ways. The public and the private are historically, ideologically, and culturally problematic; they are also problematic in experience. This is important in understanding both men's experiences and others' experiences of men. Again, the notion of difference is useful in illuminating this question.

Overlaps

Men's experiences of the public and the private are complicated by the fact that the distinctions discussed in the previous sections are rarely experienced *separately*. For example, experiences may be simultaneously spatial, temporal, social, and psychological, or simultaneously and ambiguously both public and private.[10] They may be simultaneously experiences, in public and in private, of public masculinities and private masculinities. Accordingly, public men and public masculinities are not coherent unified phenomena; they cannot just be read off as predetermined or given from our location within public patriarchies. We are *differenced*, contradictory, inconsistent, fragmenting, fractured. The experience of masculinities, whether public or private or both, is an experience *in relation to* being a man; it is not a fixed thing.

Another kind of overlap is described by Margaret Stacey and Celia Davies (1983) in terms of 'the intermediate zone'. These are (zones of) social experiences where the public and private domains overlap and features of both occur. Examples may be found in, say, children's homes and hospitals, especially long-stay ones. As there are a multiplicity of public domains and private domains, it follows that 'the intermediate zone' isn't a single zone; rather it is a series of zones. For example, on the one hand, a zone can be intermediate in a *spatial sense*, as in the case of, say, a children's home. The very term 'home' for such institutions illustrates the intermediacy of that space (Parkin 1989). On the other hand, a zone may be intermediate in terms of *social experience* or *personal meaning*. In such ways public masculinities may be experienced as confused and confusing, characterized more by blurrings than by clear definitions.

[86]

Joshua Meyrowitz (1986, pp. 46–9) attends to something similar, not in terms of whole institutions but as cultural constructions within them. He extends Goffman's model of 'back' and 'front' regions and region behaviours to talk of the 'middle region'. This develops at the cultural, perceptual, and presumably discursive levels 'when audience members gain a "sidestage" view. That is, they see parts of the traditional backstage area along with parts of the traditional onstage area; they see the performer move from backstage to onstage to backstage' (p. 47). This dramaturgical approach is applicable to many situations, for example, 'children' at an 'adult' party. In gender terms, 'intermediate zones', 'middle regions', or 'public privacies' (Hearn 1987a, p. 145) may thus develop not just in particular institutions, but equally interestingly *within* institutions – whether at particular times, like the office party, or in particular structures, like the introduction of equal opportunities policies into patriarchal organizations. Such complications may produce further contradictory experiences of and for public men and public masculinities.

Resonances

Cultural definitions are further elaborated by resonances with other social distinctions. Experiences of the public and the private interrelate with a whole range of other societal differentiations – most obviously between production and reproduction, but also economic, ethnic, age, (dis)able-bodied, as well as gender and sexual differences. More generally, public/private differences may resonate with all manner of other dualities, with their own *One/Other* relations, their own hierarchies and systems of deference. Meanings of the public and the private are thus mapped onto the meanings of other *hierarchies* of male/female, masculine/feminine, masculinity/femininity, heterosexuality/homosexuality, and many more that are indirectly gendered (see pp. 17–22). Thus experiences of public masculinities may resonate with the experiences of adults, or some other social category, especially those invested with power.

Paradoxes

Experiences of the private and public domains also often entail deep paradoxes. For example, public domains are often more open to social interchange and social influence; they are less enclosed. Yet because of this men may be or may feel less open in themselves and in their relations with others. Also the fact that public domains are more open to social influence is often premised on the relative closure of particular institutions and organizations, and may lead to the further institutional closure of others to protect and extend power, for example in the growth of state power. In contrast, private domains may appear more enclosed, yet may often be more open to newcomers, especially those who are socially similar, than much of the public domains. Various facets of publicness and privateness are often in conflict or tension in particular situations, for example when 'private' grief at a disaster becomes front page news the next day. Men's experiences in public domains are often private experiences; public masculinities are not necessarily characterized by non-intimacy.

Public masculinities may often involve contradictions between intimacy and rigidity, between women's confinement and men's property, between women's exclusion from the public domains and men's exclusion *of others* from the private domains, between flexibility and traditionalism in the gender divisions of labour. Clearly private domains should not be assumed necessarily to be places of intimacy, as shown most dreadfully in men's violence to women and children in the home.

For all these and other reasons, to treat the public men and public masculinities as fixed entities is to indulge in imaginary fictions. Instead the task here is to attempt to deconstruct them, particularly in terms of the processes of gender domination. Public masculinities are continually subject to blurrings and re-definitions. The elements from which the public and private domains are constructed are rarely in unison, and may instead be in deep conflict, in a kind of living deconstruction of their own. These fracturings have to be understood in relation to the many deep associations of men and masculinities with the public domains (and indeed the many other further associations of the public domains, such as the world of production). One such association is that within discourse; with all discourse being public in some senses, the public is 'reproduced' as supposed generality, and the private as supposed particularity. Universals, abstracts, generalizations are routinely constituted and elaborated in and of the public domains. The public domains are sites of the world of men: power, language, the phallus, men ourselves. Meanwhile, the private domains are routinely constituted as the sites of silence, the individual, the idiosyncratic, absence. Personal relationships, intimacy, desire, the person, the personality are *supposedly* resident in the private – that *special* and *important* sense of the masculinity of the (supposed) individual man.

The private and the public also exist as contradictory experiences of men's public masculinities, not just in terms of thoughts, beliefs, and feelings, but in the very sense of our bodies. The body may be in public but may be experienced internally and sensuously as private. Inversely, what is felt as private is a record of the past and the public. As David Jackson (1990, p. 48) has written, 'Even though my body seems the most private and hidden part of me, I carry my life history in my body, almost like the way age rings of a sawn tree trunk reveal a process through time.' Men's public presence is reproduced in the very material fabric of our bodies, in how we tense ourselves, have muscles, maintain posture, use our bodies on ourselves and on others, lovingly, routinely or violently, how we stride, walk, stoop, and die.[11]

Towards cultural reproductive materialism

In struggling with this chapter, I have been aware of the difficulties of writing constructively and deconstructively at the same time – of how to build on the notion of public patriarchies and how to provide a critique of it; of how to recognize the gender class of men, and differences in men and masculinities; of how to speak of the 'public' whilst acknowledging the 'private'; and so on. This has involved engaging with two major 'narratives' as convincing ways of theorizing public patriarchies. A first, more modernist and more categorical in its references to 'men', including 'men' as a class, theorizes patriarchy in terms of reproduction, in its variety of usages. Thus Shulamith Firestone (1970) focuses on biological reproduction by developing a materialist analysis of 'sex classes'; Mary O'Brien (1981) also bases her analysis in reproduction though within a Marxist–Hegelian dialectical materialist framework; Catharine MacKinnon (1982) draws parallels between sexuality, gender, and feminism and work, class, and Marxism respectively; I have developed these approaches in arguing for a dialectical materialist analysis not just of biological reproduction and sexuality, but also of generative labour (including nurture and carework) and violences (Hearn 1987a). Ferguson & Folbre (1981) coined the term 'sex-affective production' to speak of biological reproduction, mothering, nurturance, and sexuality. All these approaches (with the possible exception of MacKinnon's) focus on reproduction as labour: they are concerned with labour and activity that effects the furtherance and/or the destruction of human life. These labours are not necessarily purposeful; for example, nurture may be nurture without being intended as such. Their focus is reproductive materialism.

A second approach, more postmodernist and less categorical in tone, is a means to deconstructing 'men' and 'masculinities', to different references to different types and statements of 'men' and 'masculinities'. In this view, there are no essences, no grand narratives, no fixed categories – only significations, references, locations, and sites within discourses. Its focus may be culture, discourse, sometimes cultural materialism.

Now, are these two approaches reconcilable or irreconcilable? How do they relate to each other? Are they in fact describing the same thing in different terms? Let us consider briefly some ways of seeing them in relation to each other.

First, there is the position that the modernist materialist narrative of reproduction is fundamentally at odds with the postmodernist 'idealist' (end of) narrative of culture. At first sight, this is an attractive proposition, and one that would, in some ways, save us a lot of time and trouble. There would simply be two different accounts, needing two different theories, histories, descriptions, and explanations of experience – two different books. However, the problem with this is that, although these two approaches may come from different traditions, and with different philosophical and other assumptions, they are both here now. And they are both (im)mediately relevant to the understanding of men's domination and power. They both address how we, men, are. So the problem of their relation to each other isn't in the object of their attention; it is, if anywhere, in the limitations of their conceptualizations. Indeed, if both perspectives are relevant and valuable, we can develop both to understand and change men.

A second way of relating these two approaches is in terms of reciprocal relevance; i.e. they are both relevant, but they are relevant in different ways – they have to be added on to each other to gain a 'full(er) picture'. The cultural, in this argument, describes slightly different things from the reproductive. Although this seems a somewhat naive and dualist position, in some ways it has the advantage of conceptual clarity.

This leaves four closer forms of relation of the two approaches:

- the cultural operates within the context of the reproductive;
- the reproductive operates within the context of the cultural, as within discourse;
- the cultural is reproductive; or
- the reproductive is cultural.

Strange as it may seem, I think all of these possibilities represent accurate and useful reconstructions of the relationship of the two approaches, and useful ways of proceeding towards a cultural reproductive materialism and an embodied discourse analysis. For example, the social arrangements of reproductive labours are definitely structured. They are clearly *not* performed randomly, nor are they performed by all people in the same way. Among the most important social structures that determine the arrangement of this reproductive work in this society are the divisions/differences (presumed to exist) between the public and the private domains. As already noted, these are not by any means absolute; rather they are complex, relative, and shifting, both material, in representing shifts in the material organization and arrangement of people and their labour, *and* cultural and discursive, existing in and recognized in discourse. The private and the public are perhaps best seen both as ideological simplifications and distortions and as systematic and structured variations and inequalities in access to places, spaces, time, resources, people, and selves.

The development of a cultural reproductive materialism necessitates drawing on, though not necessarily together, a range of theoretical and practical stances, including dialectical materialism, feminist materialism, cultural materialism, discourse analysis, semiotics, psychoanalysis, and politics of the body. Among other things, these stances stress labour, corporeality, intersubjectivity, recursiveness and reflexivity, process, and sexuality. And it is these and other related themes that will inform the historical analysis that follows, and that make multiple methods and perspectives necessary in the analysis of public men.[12]

PART 2

Public men in public patriarchies

This section looks at the implications of the reformulated concept of public patriarchies for the analysis and change of public men and public masculinities. Not only does it draw on the previous critiques, it also relates these questions to historical change, particularly in the period 1870–1920. It is thus the product of the interrelation of theory and 'history' – as if they are ever separate.

Public patriarchies aren't just one thing – they are phenomenal totalities of all that follows; sets of social structures; series of social processes, qualitative changes, discourses, signs, and symbolizations; patterns of agency, psyche, and praxis. They are *not*, however, to be understood as a number of *levels* of analysis or operation. Instead they are interleaving forms; they do *not* rest in hierarchical levels one above the other. Furthermore, particular *arenas and institutions* of public patriarchies may be most easily considered in relation to and may be linked with these different *forms of analysis* of public patriarchies. All arenas and institutions are relevant to all forms of analysis, and vice versa, but in order to avoid repetition and to stress what seem to be convenient affinities of topic and method, content and form, certain arenas and certain institutions will be discussed in certain chapters. For example, the development of the mass media, though clearly important in terms of social relations, organizational growth, and individual agency, is considered here mainly in terms of its relation to the qualitative change in organizations and experience (Ch. 8). Similarly, the institutional development of psychoanalysis will be examined in relation to the focus on agency and psyche, even though again it remains relevant to other forms of analysis. The four chapters comprising this section thus explore different dimensions of public patriarchies in terms of men and masculinities. Chapter 6 analyses new and changing elements of public patriarchies as structural contexts and constraints of public men and public masculinities. It attends to the creation of new and changing forms of interrelations between the public and the private domains, and to the creation of new organizations. Chapter 7 focuses on new and changing forms and structures, particularly hierarchical structures, of organizations, and the relevance of these changes for the construction of public men and public masculinities. This includes discussion of organizations which were men only and those dominated by men but staffed also by women. This is followed (Ch. 8) by an examination of changes in selected aspects of organizational processes, especially sexual processes, and the related changes in public men and public masculinities. This necessitates analysis of the creation of new and changing cultural discourses and organizational dynamics. The final chapter of this section (Ch. 9) discusses some changes in the construction of public men as persons.

CHAPTER 6

Public men as social relations

This chapter is the first of four that look at the detailed implications of the reformulation of public patriarchies (in the last chapter) for the analysis of public men, and public masculinities. Here I focus on public patriarchies, public men, and public masculinities in terms of social relations.[1] By social relations I mean those structures and patterns of relations in and of social forms, social elements, and social institutions (like the state, heterosexuality, the economy, and so on) that exist over and above individual, interpersonal, and inter-group relationships. Furthermore, social forms, social elements, and social institutions do not exist in isolation, but exist in relations with each other. Seen in this way, public men and public masculinities also exist in social relations, and are understandable *as* social relations. Public men and public masculinities exist as social relations in relation to the relations of social forms, social elements, and social institutions. No one element is *the* material base.

Thus in this chapter I want to unearth, deconstruct, and criticize the pervasive attempt to frame 'grand narratives' (so often central in the Man/Male/Masculine One) of historical and spatial existence and change. To consider, to reconsider, the conceptualization of public men and public masculinities in this way is necessarily to engage with social theory and social theorizing. The account in this chapter and the accounts that follow (Chs 7–9) are not mutually exclusive: they are in their own sets of relations – it is difficult, if not impossible, to speak of all social relations at once. Thus the analysis presented here seeks a qualified totality, through complexities and interrelationships not through closure. While such an analysis places public men and public masculinities in historical and spatial contexts, it does not do so through a 'quick run-through' of history or through reconstructing an objectivist or rationalistic account, as if such an account is possible.

In looking at public men in these terms we need to critically address the nature of change in a number of arenas. We need to specify what are the major elements in the existence of public patriarchies and public masculinities. Moreover, there is a need to recognize the extent of the complex, mutually reinforcing nature of men's power, as a class, and the diversity of men and men's power. The brief survey of some of the alternative approaches to the beginnings and developments of modern public masculinities that follows is an exercise in the history of the present. While seeking a qualified totality, it is and is not intended to be 'comprehensive'; indeed such an ambition is empty. I focus, though not exclusively, on the period 1870–1920, as this *has appeared* as the historical means by which men and masculinities came from the heroic 'heights' of industrial capitalism in the mid-nineteenth century to become 'modern men' of this century. We need to ask and explore how the different elements of public patriarchies worked. Thus the relationships of public patriarchies and change in public men can be analysed through a number of *relationships* through a focus on procreation, sexuality, and violence; on the family and family–state relationships; the changing relations of the public domains and private domains; the growth of law and the state; cultural change; as well as changes in the form of public domain economic relations; and much more. All are no doubt important and relevant. These various social arenas and social relations all have implications for the (de)construction of public men.

The economic and the movement from the economic

Let us begin on apparently 'safe' ground and consider the coherence of what is doubtless the dominant approach to these questions, namely the 'economic': the transformation of the capitalist economy, particularly in terms of the movement to monopoly capitalism, and the relevance of that transformation for public men and public masculinities. There are many ways of developing a primarily economic explanation for the movement to public patriarchies. Most of these are variations on the theme of the movements from factory capitalism to monopoly capitalism. The features that might be emphasized in such explanations include:

[96]

- the growth of the scale of production, and of the Gross National Product;
- the development of technology and the means of production to more complex forms;
- the increased commodification of more spheres and activities;
- the increasing separation of ownership and control, and of control and labour;
- the increasing division of labour and diversification of skills and functions;
- the falling rate of profit;
- the internationalization of capital and capitalist development, including the growth of imperialism as the general rather than the pioneering mode of exploitation;
- the movement from manufacturing capital and towards tertiary, and especially finance, capital;
- growth of the organization of labour, especially trade unions;
- the extension of limited liability and corporate financial arrangements;
- the extension of vertical and horizontal integration in the economy;
- the increased interlocking of the organization of capital and labour.

These features are of course not materially exclusive or strictly separable: any of them can be related to any of the others. For example, the falling rate of profit may facilitate a greater commodification of activities formerly within the private domains, and so bring them into employed labour of the public domains, under the control and ownership of men, as either managers or owners. Furthermore, the development of monopoly capitalism, while founded on integration and growth, is also necessarily characterized by unevenness in the growth of economic sectors. Unevenness of development also occurs between capitalist and state sectors, and within state sectors. Emphases on the economic in explaining public patriarchies usually combine elements of relative decline and of relative expansion. For example, the movement towards public patriarchies (as monopoly capitalism) can also be seen in terms of the differential and uneven development of capitalist sectors of employment. This can be seen in the relative decline in the 'small-scale trading' of, say, the agricultural sector and domestic service sector. (Between 1871 and 1901 'male employment' in agriculture, forestry, and fishing in Great Britain declined from just over 20 per cent to just over 10 per cent of the respective totals.) In the first case there was a marked absolute loss in the employment of men, and in the second a marked absolute loss in the employment of women. Meanwhile other sectors of employment saw relative and absolute increases in their employment around the turn of the century. Most typically the major industries in which the development of monopolies and oligopolies was most intense were those employing large numbers of men in large bureaucratic organizations. Such organizations accounted for an increased proportion of production of goods and services, both capitalist and state. They were also subject to corporate concentration; they provided new hierarchies for men to occupy and new sites for the formation of public masculinities (see Ch. 7).

From about the end of the 1870s there was the beginnings of Britain's transition from a manufacturing to a service economy. The 1878 Factories and Workshops Act consolidated the various Factory Acts and related acts of the previous sixty years; the invention of the Gilchrist–Thomas process of steel-making is sometimes seen as the start of the decline in heavy industry in Britain; and in 1880 the Employers Liability Act was passed. On the political front, working-class organization was undergoing shifts towards a more social democratic socialism, away from varieties of Marxism and anarcho-socialism (as in the conversion of H. M. Hyndman to socialism and the subsequent rise of the Social Democratic Federation).

Changes in economic classes were accompanied by the beginnings of the transformation of *class itself*. Not only was there increasing occupational specialization, but arguably the movement of class from an economic/social relation to an occupational relation, with its own characteristic gendering for women and men. This concerns not just the division of people into strata of economic categories, but the very nature of *work itself*, as work became more rooted in *social interactions* and *social relationships*. Men, as the relatively privileged members of most economic organizations, were the first to experience these changes on a large scale. The transformation of work, particularly from local manual to less local service work, set up demands, both individually and collectively, for men to reassert particular forms of power and masculinities, through men's solidarity in workgroups and workplaces, sexual harassment, trade unionism, craft practices, and rituals.

In many conventional malestream histories, class, including 'the working class' and 'the middle class', has been constructed as 'male' (Alexander 1976). Much recent labour history 'has focussed primarily on working class men and the antinomies that have been posited about them: the "labour aristocracy" as against a heterogeneous non-aristocracy; artisans and labourers, the "independent", "intelligent", and "respectable" as against those without those qualities' (McClelland 1989, p. 165). Such categories may represent limitations as accounts of public men.

Qualitative shifts in the form and extent of capitalist ownership and capital accumulation didn't just create new forms of masculinities, they constituted 'men' and particular types of men differently and in different social locations. Men may be seen and may see themselves in terms of their 'economic' situation, their economic class, their employment, their occupation, their paid work, or their unemployment. Their manhood may be defined or appear to be defined through such economic class locations. For men in the owning economic class, their manhood may be defined, at least partly, in relation to their property, actual or potential; their inheritance, in the past, present, or future; and their associated legal and familial statuses, for example in trusts.

At times of rapid economic expansion, men may assume that their economic, especially monetary, gains are the result of 'their own efforts', rather than of the state of the (public domain) economy or simply of their own (generational) ageing. The last quarter of the last century with, in Britain at least, rural and agricultural depressions, as well as general capitalist 'booms' and 'slumps', brought shifts in the geographical distribution of people in occupational structures and in the social fabric from which optimism, pessimism, senses of self and of masculinities developed. Towards the end of the last century, trade union organization, capitalist interests, and men's gender interests all promoted the increasing demands for the 'family wage' for men – with accompanying definitions of men as the 'rightful' *earners* of such wages.

Economic change also operated internationally, particularly through imperialism. While in the United States the loss of the frontier was being experienced at the same time as the move to mass production, in Britain we see a slightly different complex mixture of forces. On the one hand, the extension of imperial powers through industrialization, the growth of state and military power, and the improvements in transport technologies increased Britain's power in the world; on the other, Britain's power declined, particularly relative to Germany and the United States.[2] Expansion and decline went hand in hand. In Britain, these complexities were found (rather than expressed) in public debate around the 'population problem' – a set of uncertainties and remonstrations on the centrality of 'race' to nations and its possible 'dilution' (Mort 1987), and a specific British national response to the coming decline of British imperialism. While the Empire was still extensive, there were the first signs of doubts at its immortality – hence also the preoccupation with manliness and sporting prowess at the end of the nineteenth century. These were not just a question of which nation's imperial powers were in the ascendant; paradoxically they also represented the beginnings of the *transcendence* of the nation and national economy by international organization and economy, nation-less in character.

As noted, rather different factors were at work in the United States at this time. A number of American scholars have recently focused upon economic determinants of the changing form of masculinities, in the move from factory capitalism to monopoly capitalism, at the turn of the century. In evaluating these accounts it is important to emphasize that such 'economic changes' are not necessarily the most important; they are simply one element or a set of elements in the development of public patriarchies that have received particular attention. These accounts are mainly from the United States, and focus primarily on white men and typically, though to a lesser extent, on middle-class white men. They also, significantly, usually focus on the economic development of the nation, with little regard to imperialism or its racial–sexual subtext. For example, in *The American Man*, Joseph Pleck and Elizabeth Pleck (1980) distinguish between 'the commercial period' of 1820–60, in which industrial capitalism expanded and the beginnings of *separate spheres* for women and men were recognized, albeit within a system of patriarchal domination, and '*the strenuous life period*' of 1861–1919, in which there was a reassertion of the values of muscular Christianity, in sport, boy scout, and other similar movements, which were 'pioneering' in theory rather than practice; and, indeed, in contrast the labelling of some men as effeminate. This has some parallels with Joe Dubbert's

(1979) analysis in *A Man's Place*, with the later period discussed in terms of the 'Bull Moose Mentality' in the 1890s and the 'Rise of Sport in 1880–1920'. The loss of the frontier and the recreation of an imaginary frontier in sport, outdoor pursuits, and so on, had a strong cultural significance in the very idea of the American Dream, in the western novel, and subsequently in the western film genre. Michael Kimmel (1987) has developed a different kind of account, focusing on the impact of women and women's demands in producing a *crisis* of masculinity at specific historical periods of rapid economic and political change, including turn of the century United States, 1880–1914. Men's responses to women included anti-feminist backlash, the pro-male backlash, and the identification of pro-feminist men. His analysis thus brings together economic, political, and interactional perspectives.

Another example of an American commentary on these economically led changes has been provided by Harry Brod, in terms of the shift from pre-capitalist to capitalist patriarchy. He writes:

A transfer of power from the hands of the individual patriarchs to the institutions of capitalist patriarchy is an essential component of this shift. This transfer is part of the widening depersonalization and bureaucratization of human relationships in the development of capitalism, which individuals experience in and on various forms of alienation. Capitalism increasingly creates a *gap* between institutional and personal power.[3]

(Brod 1987, p. 13)

Brod (1983–4) earlier presented a similar analysis in writing on the economic class basis of the (ideology of the) current United States 'men's movement'. He suggests that this recent 'new' form of masculinity is actually a subculture that fits into a certain class niche in American society. Changes of men and masculinity arise from *within* not outside the system. First, there is 'the pattern of twentieth century industrialization in which more and more of everyone's personal life is directly dominated by economic and political forces beyond their personal control'; secondly, the transformation of the economic system from manufacturing to services, in the form of information processing, public and private sector services, and so on; thirdly, the transition from the work ethic to the consumer ethic, from production to consumption. All these changes are particularly important for the middle classes, and middle-class men. Brod continues: 'The values espoused by the "new male" – co-operation, self-expression, sensitivity, etc. – fit smoothly [sic] into this new economic reality.' The office or service worker sells their (or, in this context, his) self, as in the public relations component of the job: the shift to the consumer ethic has involved more energy being put into self-gratification through leisure, loosening the rigidities of traditional masculinities, including moves to so-called 'sexual liberation'; and self-definition and identity more through consumer purchase rather than work alone. According to Brod, these economic and social changes produce new forms of masculinity. They can also be seen as the basis of new sexualities for men. For example, the selling of the self may involve the selling of congeniality, emotions, sexuality, and their interrelations. Furthermore, the selling of the self means that even aspects of the self that are not sold in specific forms of work, perhaps including sexuality, may be mediated by that selling. Such contemporary developments of masculinities have, if not their origin, then at least their clearest early expression in the 1870–1920 period.

These 'economic' accounts share a concern with the effects of economic change upon public masculinities. They also show marked differences. For example, Brod is relatively deterministic in causally connecting economic class change and the production of the 'self' of men. Kimmel is more eclectic in linking economic and *other* societal changes with demands from women for change, and then *reactions* from men to such demands. In this way he develops an interactionist account, in which the agency of (groups of) men figures.

There are several problems with such 'economic' explanations of masculinities. These include methodological problems of relative economic determinism – at root the overarching causal emphasis on capitalism as the motor of change in masculinity; and the related question of the place of men's agency. There is also a more general danger of attributing (simple) causes to (simple) effects. Economic explanations may also tend to neglect more autonomous change in social relations other than capitalist social relations, including pressure from women, feminism, and women's political organizing. There are many other elements that make up the existence of public patriarchies and public men. Movements from private patriarchies to public patriarchies may be understandable both *in terms of* transformation in the capitalist economy and *alongside* those transformations. More significantly, 'economic' (i.e. capitalist) transformations may also be seen as the reflection or appearance of other fundamental changes in (public) patriarchies. 'Economic' explanations clearly have some validity but are not *the overriding cause* of public men and public masculinities. To present them as such is to move a partial explanation towards a 'total' one.

Economy, (hetero)sexuality, and procreation

Men, masculinities, and manhoods exist in definite sets of social relations, including the social relations of sexuality, procreation, nurture, and violence. A full account of public patriarchies and public men would consider all permutations in the interrelations of these elements. While hierarchic heterosexuality, fatherhood, the professions, and the state predate the movement to public patriarchies, their importance persists in the creation of men, masculinities, and men's sense of manhood at the turn of the century. Indeed, the expansions in the professions and the state were two of the constitutive elements of the movement to public patriarchies. Feminist analyses of that period have tended to emphasize social changes around gender relations, reproduction, sexuality, and the restructuring of patriarchy. Relevant changes in the move to public patriarchies include the breakdown of the Judaeo-Christian arranged marriage; the beginnings of mass-produced contraception; feminist, purity, and other political organizing around sexuality, motherhood, morality, and related issues; the establishment of modern scientific professions; increasing state intervention in childcare, public health, medical regulation, sexuality, contagious diseases, prostitution, homosexuality, and immigration; and the legal supersession of paternal authority by state authorities.

'Patriarchy' isn't just another 'economic' system; 'it', including public patriarchies, develops through *differential* relations, historically and interpersonally, of creation and destruction. The 'economic' mode(s) of production is itself also a *variant* of the *modes* of reproduction, of creation and destruction. The Industrial Revolution entailed massive transformation in not only the mode

[103]

of production, but also the modes of reproduction. This applied in two main ways: first, the mode of production is also, *indeed is*, a mode of reproduction (Hearn 1987a, p. 101); secondly, the modes of reproduction – of sexuality, procreation, nurture, and violence – have degrees of autonomy of their own.

Accordingly, change in masculinities in the Industrial Revolution, as at other times, cannot be reconstructed from change in the patterns of paid work and economic class relations alone. Historical change in the modes of production, in sexuality, procreation, nurture, and violence, involves attention to change in the technologies of reproduction and their social relations, including the nature of the (gender) class relations of men within those modes of reproduction. Changes in the organization and practice of reproductive labour included changes in (1) the volume and distribution of such labour between women and men in the private domain; (2) the qualitative form of that private domain labour; (3) the volume and distribution of such labour in the public domains; (4) the qualitative form and impact of that public domain labour.

Reproduction isn't just a 'something' or a 'process of some-things' which may or may not be organized in specific organizations. It is a social process in any social situation, organized or not. And thus an important aspect of the organization or organizations is the control of reproductive process in the organization – this is indeed one of the prime, though not necessarily conscious, activities of management and professions. Control of reproductive process has become more intense, sophisticated, and complex with the historical growth and technologizing of organizations, of all sorts.

Perhaps the simplest way to summarize the character of changes in modes of reproduction in the late nineteenth and early twentieth centuries is in terms of *fragmentation and diversification* between its different elements, particularly procreation and sexuality. These included historical elaborations in the control of paternity, and the development and availability of new forms of contraception on a wider scale.

Various forms of contraception (some of them invoking what we would call magic) have been practised since at least 1850 BC (when apparently a vaginal plug of honey and crocodile dung was recommended – Miles 1988, p. 204). Throughout the nineteenth century there was a steady stream of propaganda and controversy around the control of birth. By the 1820s, methods such as the sheath, the sponge, and withdrawal were both advocated and condemned. Interestingly, the sheath was originally developed to protect men from venereal disease rather than women from pregnancy. By the 1840s there was some knowledge of the rhythm method, with the accumulation of information on the ovulation cycle (Weeks 1989, p. 46). Perhaps the most significant single technical change was the vulcanization of rubber in the 1840s. This was followed by the modification of caps originally made in iron and silver, and then the patenting of the douche syringe in the 1870s (Miles 1988, p. 214). These and other innovations soon met major oppositions from legal, medical, and religious quarters.

The introduction of contraception has to be placed in the context of the power of the Victorian medical profession. Medical men and associated professionals were prime actors in the construction of 'womanhood' and female/feminine sexuality, particularly so in terms of procreation, procreative sexuality, and the overwhelming significance of reproductive organs. The medical profession, a male bastion in itself, insistently excluded women, and spoke for both genders.[4] The definition and conceptualization of 'female sexuality' on the basis of 'masculine parameters' (Irigaray 1985) is exacerbated by such public domain dominations. Rosalind Miles (1988, p. 215) continues the story of contraception as follows:

> Medical men . . . trapped as they were in their own parallel struggle to make their profession respectable, drew back in horror from this 'vice perversion of nature'. Sex for its own sake, with the deliberate intention to avoid conception, was no more than 'conjugal onanism',[5] and every 'choked germ' constituted 'indirect infanticide'. 'But like all crimes, it is not and it cannot be practised with impunity', thundered the Jeremiah of the British Medical Association, Dr. C. H. F. Routh:
>
> > . . . chronic metritis . . . leucorrhoea . . . menorrhagia . . . and haematocele . . . hysteralgia and hyperaesthesia . . . cancer in an aggravated form . . . ovarian dropsy . . . absolute sterility, mania leading to suicide and the most repulsive nymphomania are thereby induced . . .[6]

. . . In 1877 the British campaigner Annie Besant was sentenced to prison; she escaped gaol, but lost custody of her daughter as an 'unfit' mother. Ten years later, a British doctor, H. A. Allbutt, was struck off the professional register for writing about birth control in *The Wife's Handbook* [in 1889].

The first birth control clinic was opened in 1882 by Aletta Jacobs, Holland's first woman doctor. The late nineteenth century was a time of intense pamphleteering on the subject (Banks & Banks 1964), with *men often taking leading roles on both sides of the argument*. By the early twentieth century the middle classes, particularly the professional middle class, were successfully limiting family size. Though church and some medical opposition continued, by the 1920s many of the taboos against contraception had been effectively lifted. Sexuality and procreation (in the latter case, if only in its avoidance) were matters of the public domains. While some feminists were active in the promotion of birth control, liberal, humanist, and progressive men were also influential in bringing these issues from the private bed into public and corporate organization and decision-making.

With the broadening introduction of birth control, the subsequent *diversification* of public patriarchies has been characterized by a progressive *separation* of sexuality and procreation, for men at least, and their further separation from the structuring of nurture (through the professions and welfare institutions) and violence (through the development of the state). These separations remain fundamental features of the elaboration of public patriarchies. They are both social structural and institutional developments; they also involve definite psychological effects for men – in the separation of (hetero)sexuality and biological reproduction.

This separation of sexuality and procreation, realized for heterosexual men in the late nineteenth century, has to be understood in relation to the established historical separation of sexuality and procreation for 'homosexuals'. Interestingly, the late nineteenth century also saw 'a deepening hostility towards homosexuality, alongside the emergence of new definitions of homosexuality and the homosexual' (Weeks 1977, p. 2). In considering these contradictory movements, feminist and gay histories of homosexuality have moved 'decisively away from the conception . . . that history of masculinity is the story of modulation, through time, of a more or less fixed entity' (Carrigan, Connell & Lee 1985, p. 589). This is particularly clear in the work of Jeffrey Weeks, working in Foucauldian mode on the complex interrelations of relevant medical, psychiatric, sexological, and political definitions and movements (e.g. Weeks 1977). A slightly different perspective on gay history is provided by John D'Emilio (1983, p. 144):

> By the second half of the nineteenth century, [the] situation was noticeably changing as the capitalist system of free labor took hold. Only when *individuals* began to make their living through wage labor, instead of as parts of an interdependent family unit, was it possible for homosexual desire to coalesce into a personal identity – an identity based on the ability to remain outside the heterosexual family and to construct a personal life based on attraction to one's own sex. By the end of the century, a class of men and women existed who recognized their erotic interest in their own sex, saw it as a trait that set them apart from the majority, and sought others like themselves. These early gay lives came from a wide social spectrum. . .

D'Emilio's approach is structurally based and encompasses the structural creation of space(s), spatial, social, and metaphorical, within which different masculinities and sexualities of men may be changed and enacted.

More recently, Marny Hall (1989, p. 126)[7] has argued for the complex interrelation of homosexuality and heterosexuality during this period:

> The same social and economic paroxysms that transformed the agrarian family into the highly gendered and private domestic arrangement of the late nineteenth century, also spawned the category of 'homosexuality'. . . . Indeed, by serving as repository for all the impulses which conflicted with the new emphasis on gender differences and sexual 'normalcy', the homosexual with its indeterminate gender and abnormal sex practices, buttressed the new family.

In such ways feminist, lesbian, and gay scholarship on 'homo-sexuality' points to the deconstruction of heterosexuality and

heterosexual men. The sexual dynamics of homosexuality paradoxically maintained changing forms of heterosexuality, and
changing development of heterosexual men and heterosexual
masculinities. The movements to public patriarchies are as much
a series of developments of heterosexuality and homosexuality as
of the economy. This is most apparent in the 'progressions' of law
(see pp. 119–26), and the establishment of mass media display of
heterosexual images in the public domains (see Ch. 8). Less
visible, but no less important, were the changing forms of
sexuality within heterosexual marriage, with slow movements to
companionate and supposedly 'egalitarian' heterosexuality, in
ideologies if far less so in social practice.[8] Late nineteenth- and
early twentieth-century sexual 'progressivism' was most explicit
and self-conscious amongst middle- and upper-class 'sex radicals'.
More generally, the emergence of the 'New Woman', politically
and sexually liberated or potentially so, and the 'odd woman' or
'redundant woman', seen as surplus in numbers to men,
unattached, and not necessarily interested in men, posed clear
challenges to men, politically and sexually. This particularly challenged men's sense of being at the centre of things – producing a
kind of 'sexual anarchy'.[9]

Fathers, professions, and the state

Discussions of 'the economy' and of sexuality and procreation
have already highlighted the place of 'the family'. In this section,
I want to focus more specifically on the significance of change in
men as fathers for an understanding of public patriarchies. One
basic problem of charting movements towards public patriarchies
in terms of the family and the father is that the *form* of private
patriarchies has itself been historically and culturally highly
variable. Domestic, family, generational, and community forms
have varied, so that the 'ideal-typical' private patriarchal family
appears, disappears, and reappears in a very uneven way – and
certainly so before the 'advent' of capitalism. Indeed, *different*
versions of the private patriarchal family appear in such widely
separable instances as feudal society, sixteenth-century bourgeois
society, Victorian middle-class society, and Edwardian working-
class society. While the patriarchal nuclear family was codified, in

property, among the upper and propertied class in pre-capitalist times, working-class family forms remained extremely varied and 'disrupted' in the nineteenth century (e.g. Gillis 1985). Accordingly, it is inaccurate simply to equate the patriarchal nuclear family with bourgeois or petit bourgeois family forms.

Throughout the eighteenth and nineteenth centuries, major changes certainly occurred in both the role and power of the father, and family form more generally. For example, childrearing manuals in the eighteenth century were directed towards the father as reader, albeit a father of relatively affluent class position. By the end of the nineteenth century, childrearing manuals were directed towards the mother, and indeed mothers across a broader economic class range (Matthews 1987). This is not of course to say that the power of the father had decreased, merely that its form may have changed and begun to operate *in a less direct way*, via the authority of the mother. For example, there was a considerable social movement for the promotion of women's domesticity, with much greater stress on marriage etiquette and (modern) methods of homekeeping than was previously the case. The power of the father in the late nineteenth century was becoming more symbolic, though no less (materially) real. The father could be used as a symbolic threat *and* as real material practices and punishments in specific instances.

The power of the father also operated indirectly in another way, via the state, the professions, schools, youth and other social movements for boys and young men. The late Victorian 'flight from' or 'revolt against domesticity' of some middle-class men and fathers can be understood partly in this way. Whereas Samuel Smiles wrote in 1871 that 'Home is the first and most important school of character' (p. 31), Robert Baden-Powell in 1908 in *Scouting for Boys* urged that 'manliness can only be taught by men, and not by those who are half men, half women' (p. 226; see Tosh 1991). This period was significant in the creation of new categories of 'youth' and 'adolescents', in relation to the public recognition of the 'boy labour problem', and particularly the problematic 'character' of working-class young men (Hendrick 1990).

Rearrangements of power in families thus occurred in the context of changing relations of the private and public domains, and changing age/class/gender/ethnic relations. From the middle of the last century, an increasing number of visitors, that is, organizational agents, came to the 'private domain' of the family. These included police, public health and sanitary inspectors, child health officers, health visitors, community nurses, social workers, and school board men. These purveyors of organization–client relations were representatives of organizations and agencies particularly, though not exclusively, in the growing state sector.

The beginnings of the modern welfare state were found both in the voluntary and philanthropic sectors, as in the Charity Organisation Society founded in 1869, and in the increasing responsibility of local and central government administration, as in the establishment of the public health system through the 1875 Act. That period saw the rise of visiting and inspecting of homes and indeed factories, the monitoring of mothering along clear economic class and gender lines, and, in the case of the National Society for the Prevention of Cruelty to Children and various local anti-cruelty societies, especially the London Society, which preceded it, the establishment of an inspectorate of families, and especially of mothers, by men. Visitors – *outsiders* of both their 'parent' organizations and the homes they visited – had a variable effect on and relationship to family form and paternal power/ authority. In one sense they may have assisted in the breaking down of the power of the father. They tended to be seen by the mother, as the knower of the private (at the front of the house), while the father was absent, leaving, or retiring to the back of the house.[10] Visiting was a major means by which state, and other, organizations maintained indirect power and influence over and within the family. On the other hand, the process of visiting as part of the action of state and other agencies was a vital means of reinforcement of the power of the father, in law and in regulation – the conversion of informal, albeit in many cases absolutist, power to formal, albeit relativist, power.

The place of professional, and especially medical, power is particularly important here. Though the 1876 Russell Gurney Act in theory removed restrictions on the granting of qualifications on the grounds of sex, in practice the professions generally continued as male bastions. The growing modern professions excluded women, minimized their entry, or kept them to lower-status occupations, like midwifery; in so doing, the authority of professional men was in tension with that of the 'private' father, often simultaneously reinforcing it in specific ways and undermining it in a general way.

A slightly different emphasis in approach to public patriarchies is through the focus on the modern state. Increased state intervention in the family can be dated from the mid-eighteenth century, with the 1753 Hardwicke Act depriving betrothal of legal status, and closing legal, if not practical, access to clandestine marriage. State intervention in childcare in the eighteenth century included the placing of unwanted 'bastard' babies in the workhouse. From there, infants were often farmed out to local nurses who in turn allowed them through neglect to die in large numbers (Rose 1986, p. 3). Thus, although state intervention was present, it was dispersed and minimalist; one might almost call it statist laissez-faire. The men of the state merely sponsored the minimal, initial management of these young lives, which could then be subsequently left to the whims of social neglect and the forces of physiological deterioration. Men may have been watching over this process, but in only the most negligent way. In the British case, especially rapid change in the transfer of local and private domain powers to state law occurred in the 1830s. Within a few years the 1833 Factory Act regulated child labour; the Education Act of the same year began government grants for education; shortly after came the Poor Law Amendment Act, enabling family break-up in the workhouse, and subsequently the instigation of marriage regulation; loss of women's swearing of paternity; mothers' child custody rights; and state registration of births. From 1839 the rights of fathers over legitimate children were no longer seen as absolute, even though women and children remained the property of the husband/father until 1857.

From 1844 the Doctrine of Substituted Judgement was applicable so that courts of law could act as a substitute for parental authority in specific cases. A particularly interesting feature of increasing state intervention in the construction of 'the child' was the legal stipulation of what was a child in the first place, as a baby. This is especially important in the judicial and medical discourses on the unborn or newly born child – a question of great importance with greater state interest in infant death. First this was clarified in a number of individual cases in the 1830s:

- In *Poulton* ([1832] 5 C. & P. 329) a child became a 'reasonable creature in being' when it had been wholly expelled from its mother's body and was alive. There was some lack of clarity whether the child's life must be independent of its mother.

[111]

- In *Crutchley* and in *Brain* ([1834] 6 C. & P. 349) it was said not to be necessary to establish that the umbilical cord had been severed as long as the child had breathed. (Also see *Enoch* [1833] 5 C. & P. 539.)
- In *Crutchley* ([1837] 7 C. & P. 874) it was established that the child should have a circulation independent of its mother (see Stone & Johnson 1987, pp. 2–3).

The 1861 Offences Against the Person Act codified the law more fully, and brought together specific sections on killing the unborn child as well as a more general overhaul of types of violence. Legal interventions were further extended in 1868 through the Poor Law Amendment Act, from assault and murder to the questions of 'neglect' to children (see pp. 121–2).

Another facet of state intervention in the lives of babies and young children was the question of baby food. From the 1860s branded baby foods were available to the more well-off classes at least, and opiates and other soothers were more widely available. This latter practice was hardly restricted by the Poisons and Pharmacy Act of 1868, or even the Food and Drugs Act of 1875. Indeed, a large number of babies died from the application or over-application of baby soothers such as potassium bromides. In the late nineteenth century babies were still often kept quiet by the use of a variety of applications and medications. It was not until 1920 and the passing of the Dangerous Drugs Act that opiates like laudanum became available only on doctors' prescription, so that the 'dosing' of babies became illegal and unfashionable (Rose 1986, pp. 11–12). Men's action there was thus then more proactive, more concerned with setting the conditions of motherhood, rather than with maintaining a minimal 'net' of care (through which many babies could fall), as in the eighteenth century.

Meanwhile, by the late nineteenth century more 'children' were taken out of the employed workforce and placed in the schoolforce instead – at least some were, some of the time. The 1870 (Forster) Education Act introduced *permissive* board schooling up to 10 years, and effectively brought large numbers of poor working-class children into the purview of the state; compulsory attendance was enacted in 1876, the school leaving age was extended to 11 in 1893 and to 12 in 1899, and in 1902 the (Balfour) Education Act moved the state into secondary education and its increased standardization through local authorities. Bearing in mind that these innovations occurred before the advent of women's suffrage, it seems likely that the education of girls is more readily understandable as a means of reproducing gender divisions, including motherhood and women's office labour, than of promoting women's citizenship (Lewis 1986; Brehony 1985); even though the imitation of boys' education and single-sex schooling for girls may also contradictorily challenge men's hegemony.

From the 1890s onwards there was strong reinforcement of the division between the man as breadwinner and the woman as childcarer, especially for families headed by skilled workers. It was in this context that the 1891 Custody of Children Act introduced the concept of 'unfit parenthood', usually in effect meaning motherhood. The 1907 Notification of Births Act facilitated early visiting by health visitors. More specialist childcare interventions fed into the broader infant welfare movement. Notions of women's domesticity were encouraged by municipal and voluntary clinics; national insurance, unemployment benefit, and pension reforms contributed to the control of types of work open to women and limited women's access to cash benefits; and subsequently the First World War produced a more systematic approach to childbirth and child welfare, and the inculcation of middle-class methods of childrearing among the working classes, culminating in the Maternity and Child Welfare Act, 1918. This permitted local authorities to provide salaried midwives, health visitors, infant welfare centres, day nurseries, and food supplements for needy infants and mothers.[11] Whilst confirming the creation of the 'child', such change also meant the child could be spoken for, by others, and so denied a voice (Hearn 1988a).

Movements to public patriarchies were dialectical, contradictory, historical. They involved changing power locations and concentrations from the private to the public domains. The ideology of the patriarchal nuclear family became more widely established across the economic classes, whilst state intervention undermined the families', the mothers', and the fathers' autonomies. Public domain powers, particularly in the professions and the state, but also in capitalist organizations, were instrumental in the establishment of this sponsored familialism. This undermining of the power of fathers as private patriarchies, particularly through professional and state power, was thus combined with the consolidation, and perhaps diffusion, of the patriarchal nuclear family (what is sometimes misleadingly called the 'bourgeois family'). This was especially so in the relatively affluent working classes, the families of the 'aristocracies' of labouring men underwritten by the 'family wage'. Meanwhile the state and state men took a more active part in the definition and control of mothers' (parental) rights and lives.[12]

Though the impact of the state, and indeed men in the state, on women and men in families increased in the last thirty years of the nineteenth century, a more pronounced change occurred during and after the Boer War. The state (that is, state men) recognized motherhood or women as mothers as a public domain issue, rather than as the preserve of the private domains or of men as fathers and husbands. Indeed, because of the apparent relative autonomy of the relationship of women/mothers and men/state, men in the private domains came to be defined less as fathers and more as husbands. Simultaneously the relationship of women/ mothers and men/state was itself paralleled by the relationship of private men and public men. The state at the turn of the century was developing relatively separate arms of interventions towards women as mothers, and men as workers and soldiers. These separations in the state are reproduced to an extent in the separations of women and men in the private domains. The state was sponsoring the means to be uninvolved in active fathering or active parenting – and instead was assisting the creation of the detached father and the status of husband. Public domain powers, which constitute public patriarchies, thus facilitate, control, and effect particular social forms *within private domains*, including historically specific microcosms of public patriarchies in the form of the nuclear family.

All these and other changes increasingly brought and have continued to bring the private powers of men, especially as individual fathers, into the public domains, in some cases to be overruled by men there. Once in the public domains, such private and public powers could and can themselves be challenged by women and men, in the sense that they are located in a *public* discourse. Motherhood itself was politicized; marriage was underpinned and determined by state law; the father was no longer absolute; and indirectly 'men' also became a politicized topic. Personal, private, and sexual lives were more exposed to increasing numbers of state organizational agents acting upon men, especially as fathers. These agents included the police, public health and sanitary inspectors, child health and child cruelty officers, health visitors, district nurses, midwives, school board men, and social workers, each occupation characteristically clearly gendered. Some of these, such as the 'cruelty men' and the 'board men', were themselves typically men, who in turn were to participate in an effective reduction of the power of individual fathers, especially amongst the working classes, as well as having their own private and sexual lives (H. Ferguson 1989; also see Hearn 1987a, p. 95). Men thus did become dependent clients or 'visitees' in some cases, although often the process of change was less direct, reinforcing established gender roles, with the mother assumed to be the prime agent of the private domain and the father a relative absentee.

These transformations provided the base for the more generally recognized transformation of the modern state. In that sense, nineteenth-century family and child welfare reforms produced the modern liberal welfare state, with national insurance and other reforms for working men following the Liberals' landslide victory in January 1906. The establishment of the modern state at the end of the last century and beginning of this further brought the welfare state, the economic state, and the military state.

(Hetero)sexuality, private violence, and the state

The pace of change around sexuality and violence was particularly rapid towards the end of the nineteenth century. In some cases this was concerned with increasing state intervention into sexual and other domains previously beyond direct state control, with an immensely complex series of implications for the enactment of masculinities. So what are the major ways in which state development connects with men's sexualities and violences during the period 1870–1920?[13] I deliberately say 'connects with' rather than 'causally determines', as one of the lessons of much recent feminist and other critical gender scholarship emphasizes the multi-faceted and complex nature of social change in that period (e.g. Mort 1985; also see Bland, McCabe & Mort 1978). Indeed, much of what follows concerns the mutual occurrence and mutual reinforcement of social phenomena at specific historical conjunctures. Inevitably state organizations and men's sexualities were subject to common historical forces, including enduring patriarchalism, developing feminism, and widespread concern about the 'population problem' or the 'population question' (Soloway 1982).

Feminism was clearly a major force in the transformation of the state at the end of the last century, especially from the 1880s (Durham 1985). While many feminists from middle-class and upper-class backgrounds saw the state 'as an instrument for enacting their own class specific demands . . . many others rapidly became aware that the state itself was patriarchal' (Mort 1985, p. 219). Christabel Pankhurst, precursing Catharine MacKinnon, considered 'the state was composed of men who not only denied women the vote but also tacitly condoned male immorality and sexual violence' (ibid.). Pankhurst had a similarly clear view of men's sexuality as the basis of societal problems: 'What a man . . . really means is that women are created primarily for sex gratification of men and secondly for the bearing of children if he happens to want them' (Pankhurst 1913, pp. 19–20).[14]

Recognition of the 'population problem' came from a combination of interests in the purity lobby,[15] from medics and eugenicists, as well as from the demands of war and militarization, and fears of international competition and insufficient 'national efficiency', particularly in comparison with Germany, Japan, and the United States (Bland 1982). The 'problem' entailed national concerns about the quality and purity of 'the race', the health of children, the 'fitness' of mothers, the physical state of men as workers and soldiers (in the Boer War and the First World War), and the appropriate measures for the mentally deficient and feeble-minded (Simmons 1978; Barker 1983). With the onset of the Boer War, the reality of men's ill-health was revealed, as many recruits failed to meet the basic requirements for fighting. Thus economic and military considerations coalesced with a number of concerns around child health in schools; the relationship of sexuality, moral purity, and physical purity; the relationship of sexuality, racial purity, and physical wellbeing; support for maternalism, eugenics, and population planning.

Although these were not solely sexual questions, they were focused on the 'correct' use of the healthy body including sexual activities, albeit in ways different for men than for women.

Sexuality and health were both often seen within a 'racial' evolutionary framework; eugenicists, such as Karl Pearson, advocated sterilization for the weak and male avoidance of 'dissipatory' sexualities. Margaret Stacey (1988, p. 73) sums up this ideology as follows:

> Men were 'driven' by strong sexual urges. They required an outlet for these. Hence the necessity of the occupation of prostitution; it went along with monogamy and was needed to sustain it . . . masturbation and night emissions were not only morally wrong, they were also medically pathological. Treatises from medical men such as Acton (1862) made this plain. . . . Men were expected to exercise strong self-control over these urges. . . . However, the temptations which they experienced were enormous and could be resisted only with the help of women. Thus it was the women's fault if men were overcome, and the particular sin of the prostitute was to tempt them.[16]

Jane Lewis (1984, p. 127) succinctly states: 'male virility could not be denied and within evolutionary thought was believed to be crucial to the progress of race and nation.' Accordingly, 'natural urges' and 'self control' (the will) went hand in hand (cf. Hollway 1984). Masturbation was seen as a particularly dangerous 'dissipation', and frequently associated with homosexuality (Weeks 1977, 1989). Less visible were the attendant 'hidden anxieties' (L. Hall 1991) felt by individual men within this ideological context. Furthermore, as with contraception and despite contradictions, the 'population problem' placed men in control of public domain discussion of the (re)production of people. These themes were influential in the development of the state in some rather contradictory ways.

First, the period 1870–1920 was one of major, almost massive, change in the interrelationship of the state and men's sexuality. Municipal and central government increasingly became administrative centres of power at the expense of voluntary and philanthropic organizations. The 1885 Criminal Law Amendment Act offered a spurious compromise between state organizations and purity groups, but in the event the resources and machinery for an equal partnership were not forthcoming and the state was extended further in the control of 'vice'. State corporatism also facilitated the modernist paradox of increased awareness of the self and yet overwhelming of the individual, including men's sexual selves as state members and state clients. These state transformations were noticeably accelerated in the late nineteenth-century liberal municipalism, the Liberal reforms of 1906–11, the beginnings of a welfare state, and the centralizations of First World War and post-war reconstruction. The 'population problem', with its racial–sexual subtext, was significant in moves to a more corporate governmental machinery, as in the interdepartmental Committees on Physical Deterioration (1903) and the Medical Inspection and Feeding of Children Attending Public Elementary Schools (1905).

Secondly, such changes were, in a profound sense, faltering, gradual, diffuse, and irregular. This was partly a reflection of the general development of state organizations at that time. Indeed, the 'state' consisted of rather unfamiliar and locally variable collections of councils, boards, committees, royal commissions, legal apparatus, inspectorates, and visitors, as well as a vigorous interplay of political actors, including lawyers, property owners, medics, purity lobbyists, and feminists. Each part of state machinery had its own particular generic and, indeed, sexual structure. This unevenness applied all the more so in the politics of morality and sexuality.

For example, the royal commission, the prime unit of 'neutral' deliberation, was typically intensely male dominated. Edward VII, in 1909, was specifically opposed to female membership of the Royal Commission on Divorce and Matrimonial Causes (which reported in 1912) because 'the nature of the subject is one which cannot be discussed openly, and in all its aspects, in any delicacy, or even decency, before ladies'.[17] In the event, just two women became members, and even its limited recommendations for new grounds for divorce were not enacted till 1937. Meanwhile, another part of the state machinery, the police, was involved, increasingly from 1907, in surveillance and control of suffragettes, including at times their violent control. Brian Harrison (1982, p. 63) comments: 'Police and anti-suffragist manhandling made window-breaking seem attractive as a way of ensuring rapid arrest and consequent relative security.'

Increasingly in the late nineteenth and early twentieth centuries, the state (that is, men in the state) was subjected to demands and pressures from women, not just in terms of the formal obtaining of suffrage, but also in all manner of other social and political services. State men, especially middle-class state men, were located as *receivers* of the demands and opinions of women, especially middle-class women, as in the Royal Commission on Divorce of 1909 (Minor 1979). Other distinctive parts of the state included the law, the police, and the military.

Two particular types of legal interventions can be identified: those addressing marriage and the family;[18] and those on prostitution and other 'dangerous sexualities' (Mort 1987).

The reform of the legal treatment of men's violence to women within marriage in 1878 followed shortly after the Cruelty to Animals Act of 1876 had itself extended to all animals the provisions of the Cruelty to Animals Act 1849, which had made it illegal to 'cruelly beat, ill-treat, over-drive, abuse or torture' any *domestic* animal (c.92, s.2) (James 1986, p. 601). Prior to 1878, the 'rule of thumb', whereby husbands were not permitted to use a stick broader than a thumb, was operative in the courts. According to Bacon's Abridgement of 1736 a husband might beat his wife (but not in a violent or cruel manner) and confine her. Blackstone, writing some thirty years later, maintained that the practice had become obsolete in polite society but not among 'the lower rank of people' (Bromley & Lowe 1987, p. 148).

Marital criminal proceedings were also made near impossible by the 1853 Criminal Procedure Amendment Act, which made communications between husbands and wives beyond the jurisdiction of the courts, and made spouses not competent to give evidence for or against each other. However, this was soon followed by a whole range of contradictory Acts, including particularly interestingly the 1869 Act regarding breach of promise and the 1877 Act regarding nuisance on a public highway.

The 1857 Matrimonial Causes Act allowed divorce on *one* act of adultery of a wife, whilst she could not even rely on a series of associations unless the adultery was aggravated (Bromley & Lowe 1987, p. 171). This inequality remained in place until the Matrimonial Causes Act, 1923. Whereas with the private patriarchies of most of the nineteenth century men were able to routinely abuse wives, by 1878 the Matrimonial Causes Act allowed women to use cruelty as grounds for divorce. Magistrates were given powers to grant swift and cheap separation orders to women who could prove a *specific* incident of physical assault. State law, if only in word, had made an inroad into men's domestic violence to women, and recognized a division between violence and sexuality.

The Married Women's Property Act of 1882 introduced rights for women to keep property they owned, in marriage or acquired later,[19] even though no criminal proceedings could be taken against a husband whilst the wife was cohabiting.

The 1886 Maintenance of Wives Act empowered magistrates in local courts to grant and enforce maintenance orders of no more than £2 per week. In 1891 the husbands lost their 'rights' forcibly to imprison their wife in the matrimonial home to obtain their 'conjugal rights'.[20] The 1895 Summary Jurisdiction (Married Women) Act made it easier for women to gain protection of the court following persistent physical cruelty (rather than a specific physical assault). Furthermore, the 1895 Act allowed the possibility of separation orders for women on grounds of husband's imprisonment for more than two months.[21] Even though by the end of the nineteenth century married women's and married men's property rights were equalized, in practice little had been done to undermine men's authority over women. Men's domination was backed up by the state, and women's position on marital disputes, divorce, and maintenance was still weak. Julia Brophy and Carol Smart (1982, p. 210) have summarized this situation as follows:

> She had no right to leave her husband without his permission and if she did he could physically restrain her. She had no right to maintenance if she could not prove her husband had committed a matrimonial offence . . . he could divorce her on a single act of adultery whilst she had to establish adultery combined with another matrimonial offence. . . . Any challenge by a wife to his authority, or to the principle of sexual monogamy resulted in the courts refusing to grant her maintenance. The magistrates courts . . . treated adultery as an absolute bar to maintenance for wives.

(Also see Harrison & Mort 1980.)

Even after these reforms, including the right of husbands to apply for separation orders in 1902, divorces were few (about 600 per year). It was not until 1910, when the suffragettes took up the cause of assaults on wives, that women were no longer the legitimate victims of men's violence in marriage (Otter 1986, p. 108).

The extension of general criminal law on violence into the field of wilful child neglect was begun in 1868 with the Poor Law Amendment Act. However, although this specified the offence of neglect of children under 14 and included provisions against likely serious injury in the future, it did not provide for detection of such offenders or for the *removal* of children from the family. At an 1882 meeting of the Liverpool Society for the Prevention of Cruelty to Animals the suggestion was made to form a parallel society to protect children, and this was instituted in 1883. In 1889 the Poor Law Amendment Act gave the guardians parental powers over children in their control for all except religious upbringing, and in the same year the Prevention of Cruelty to and Protection of Children Act (the first 'Children's Charter') 'made it a misdemeanour for *anyone* over sixteen who had custody, control or charge of a boy under fourteen or a girl under sixteen *wilfully* to ill-treat, neglect or abandon the child in a manner likely to cause *unnecessary suffering* or injury to health' (Eekelaar 1978, p. 68).

The 1908 Children's Act repealed twenty-one whole Acts and parts of seventeen other Acts. It acted as a landmark in codifying and consolidating legislation on children. Of the six parts of the Act, the first two concerned with Infant Life Protection and Prevention of Cruelty to Children and Young Persons were especially important. The former instituted registration of any child under 7 received in the care of any person. This applied if the child was handed on to another person, or if the person receiving the child moved home. If the child died, it was made compulsory to report this within forty-eight hours. To effect this, local authorities were required to appoint infant life protection visitors, who might under certain conditions be voluntary workers. These were to visit the infants and their homes, to offer help, advice, and encouragement to foster parents, and if necessary to seek an order from the local authority or a justice to remove the child to a place of safety. Prior to this, registration of one child had not been required, so it was possible for a 'baby farmer' to receive one at a time, and watch over its demise, or to pass it on to another person, without any state recourse. Even the starvation and neglect of such single children usually went unmonitored and without state intervention as such houses were not subject to inspection.

[121]

The part of the Act dealing with the Prevention of Cruelty to Children and Young Persons placed a heavy emphasis on parental responsibility towards children. Cruelty was punishable by a fine up to £100 and/or imprisonment up to two years. Cruelty included not just physical cruelty but also failure to provide adequate food, clothing, lodging, or medical attention, or indeed, if being unable to provide these, failure to procure them by resorting to statutory relief for the poor.

Moreover, these arrangements were institutionalized not directly through the state, state workers, and men in the state, but indirectly through the incorporation of the National Society for the Prevention of Cruelty to Children, a charitable society, into the confines of the state. The public were urged to give information about the neglect or ill-treatment of children, and about children living in immoral surroundings, to the Society or to the police. Children could then be removed to a safe place with other carers, whether relatives or not.

Other matters of protection dealt with by the Act included the problems of the death of children through 'overlaying' by their parents, in most cases fathers (this became an offence where the child was under 3 and the adult was under the influence of drink); burning and scalding (parents were required to provide properly fitting fireguards where there were children under 7); juvenile smoking (it became illegal to sell cigarettes to any child apparently under the age of 16); pawning by children (illegal to take pawns from a child under 14); the children of vagrants (they were now required to have a certain minimum amount of schooling, equivalent to approximately 100 days a year); alcoholic drinking by children (illegal to give children under 5 alcoholic drink, except on medical advice; and illegal to allow children under 14 into licensed premises); the safety of children at entertainments; and the condition of schoolchildren (this empowered local authorities to insist that children were not sent to school in a filthy or verminous condition, and if necessary to clean them themselves) (Allen & Morton 1961). The child was officially 'spoken for'.

As far as the law around 'dangerous sexualities' (Mort 1987) was concerned, the most famous and most controversial laws of the time were the Contagious Diseases Acts. Under the CD Acts of the 1860s, a combination of men (as police, medics, and justices) were able to enforce three months' detention in certain hospitals on women considered by them to be prostitutes in certain naval ports and garrison towns, under threat of imprisonment and hard labour. Although these Acts may appear to be specifically about women and sexual procurement, they were in fact (not very implicitly) about men's sexuality rather than women's sexuality – it is just that it was not seen as appropriate to control men, for example by curfew, in order to control their sexuality (perhaps thought uncontrollable). These Acts in fact enabled speech to be conducted on men's sexuality. They are also about men's sexuality in a different way, as a documentary statement on the sexuality of a 'different group' of men, the enacters and implementers of the Acts as state organizational agents.

Meanwhile, arguments against state intervention in this arena came from a variety of quarters. Josephine Butler, the purity feminist, campaigned on the basis of the rewards of moral voluntarism, and the deleterious results of individuals not experiencing the effects of their own behaviour through state protection. George Russell suggested in the House of Commons debate on prostitution (20 April 1883) that the CD Acts 'all but close the paths of regeneration against these women . . . we stamp them with the signet of the state, which marks them as the common prey of animal desire'[22] (presumably of certain men). Following extensive campaigns by feminists and some men, the Acts were suspended in 1883 and repealed in 1886, superficially suggesting a withdrawal of state intervention in sexual matters. However, the Criminal Law Amendment Act, 1885, had raised the age of consent from 13 to 16, increased penalties for brothel keepers and, with the Labouchère Amendment, outlawed male homosexuality, institutionalizing a heterosexual state dominance that persists.

Another focus of state attention was the legal construction of rape, as processed through the courts of law, operated and managed by men. Jennifer Temkin has observed: 'Historically, the law of rape was concerned particularly with the theft of virginity, reflecting a preoccupation with the protection of virgins from rape, abduction and forced marriage' (1987, p. 26). In 1285 the Second Statute of Westminster made rape a capital offence. Also in the Middle Ages it was usual to assume that women had to raise a hue and cry if they were to proceed with a complaint of rape. In recent centuries, much legal practice has followed from the seventeenth-century survey of rape conducted by Sir Matthew Hale, including particularly significantly the legal 'justification for the marital rape exception'. The legal prosecution of rape was impeded in another way until relatively recently – namely, by the assumption by men that conception indicated consent by the woman. Dr Samuel Farr, writing in 1812 in *Elements of Medical Jurisprudence*, a text compiled for coroners and courts of law, suggests:

> without an excitation of lust, or the enjoyment of pleasure in the venereal act, no conception can probably take place. So if an absolute rape were to be perpetrated, it is not likely she would become pregnant.[23]

This test stood in tension with the need for swift complaint.

However, by the 1880s, and in keeping with controversies elsewhere on the public protection of children, the 'feeble-minded',[24] and others, legal construction of rape was becoming a more complex and scientistic matter – though this movement by no means necessarily eased the process of prosecution of the rapist. Rather, it moved it to the intersection of psychiatric, legal, medical, welfare, humanist, and above all public discourses. Rape was a public issue in all its intricacies. In dealing with the consent of children, young persons, and the mentally subnormal, consent was generally taken to imply some knowledge of the type of act – even though the *degree* of knowledge was disputed.

In *Dee* ([1884] 15 Cox C.C. 579) the issue of consent was highlighted, and the case was made that consent could be given only by a 'reasoning being' rather than by a mentally deficient person. Palles C.B. considered: 'consent is the act of man [*sic*], in his character of a rational and intelligent being, not in that of an animal. It must proceed . . . from the will sufficiently enlightened by the intellect . . . .' In contrast, in *Fletcher* ([1886] L.R.l. C.C.R. 39) the three judges expressed the view that, if the 16-year-old mentally deficient woman acted out of 'animal instinct', she would nevertheless be regarded as having consented. By 1911 in *Dimes* (7 Cr. App. R. 43) we see the application of forensic medicine to the assumption of the necessity for evidence of violence in rape (beyond its own inherent sexual violence). Accordingly, 'the jury was directed that the prosecution had to establish that the defendant had acted violently and against the will of the prosecutrix' (Temkin 1987, p. 62). In this case the judge emphasized that no evidence was forthcoming of bruising of the victim's thighs or of any other sign of struggle. Woman's speech was superseded by public evidence, as against the private evidence of her own body formerly.

Two other examples of the development of the indirect, impersonal, and thus social and public nature of men's assessment of rape were in the development of the 'recent complaint exception' and the suppression of the name and address of witnesses. In the first case, it was acknowledged in 1905 (*Osborne*, 1 K.B. 551) that the complainant may give evidence that at the earliest available opportunity she voluntarily and without prompting reported the rape to a third party. In the latter, in 1913 (*Gordon*, Cr. App. R. 237) the common law discretion of the court to suppress the name and address of a witness, where to reveal them would hinder the course of justice, was invoked. In both these cases the movement from the speech of the woman complainant to the procedure of the court might be said to make rape more public, and a little easier to prosecute.

Family law, sexuality law, and law against violence came together in the processing of the Incest Bill. The first version was introduced in 1899, and it was finally enacted in 1908. This was not so much a reflection of the popularity of eugenic perspectives at the time (Wolfram 1983), as a matter of concern at the sexual exploitation of children by parents (Bailey & Blackburn 1979).

While state law may be an obvious focus of attention, it can be seen that it has to be treated with some caution as a determining factor. According to Mort (1985, p. 210), the state rarely initiated moves to criminalize sexual 'immoralities'. Furthermore, with regard to sexuality, there was no major expansion in direct state functions, state functionaries, or incorporation of intellectuals into the state in this period; instead, law around sexuality was often the outcome of protracted political relations, particularly between feminists, purity groups, and others, to which state agents reacted cautiously and usually patriarchally (Mort 1985, pp. 210, 222). In addition to state legal intervention directly attending to men's sexuality and violence, there was a recurrent *moral* theme in other reports and parliamentary Acts (Bland, McCabe & Mort 1978, pp. 106–7). Moreover, it is not possible to abstract sexuality and violence from the social construction of gender relations, so that laws, policies, and state policies in such areas as childcare, health, and education are all relevant.

[125]

Thus in state development around sexuality and violence, not only were there numerous laws, but there were numerous 'legal truths' – in both legal interpretations and use of the laws (Wickham 1987). The CD Acts were suspended, then repealed; other Acts were put in place, increasing control of some men by other men. Diverse Acts and laws operated in diverse conjunction. *Certain men controlled 'other' men*, with other men acting as intermediaries, for example the police, medics, and justices. Often Acts were not fully enforced (or were used largely pre-emptively, for example the Labouchère Amendment and Obscenity Acts). Private patriarchies were 'rolled back' by the state law of public patriarchies, though very unevenly. At the heart of this complexity of masculinities, is the contradiction of *law and patriarchy*: law as the father, the man, even the phallus, and the problem that even law that appears to further certain women's interests (e.g. married women's) or to constrain certain men's is still a reinforcement of law and the state as men-dominated. The movement from the law of the father to the law(s) of the state is a crucial historical change. By the end of the last century, the state or parts of the state enacted laws that, at least partially, dethroned the father. Though the state is 'child' to the father, the 'child' state seeks to kill the father.

These legal changes, not surprisingly, have contradictory significances for men and masculinities:

- they reinforce the law of legitimation;
- they purport to override the power of the father/family;
- they are enacted by some men on others;
- they assist in reinforcing the power of men in public;
- they operate in diverse ways and in diverse conjunctions, even in random interconnections;
- they form part of the change in the form of law – from the definition of the private domains as that beyond the rule of public domain law to the public domains overriding of the private *in law* by men;
- they continue the ideology that family law and law around gender is not really law at all.[25]

The state and public violence: polity, police, military, and monarchy

A number of historians have argued that from the late 1860s the British state underwent fundamental change – what A. V. Dicey (1914) called the shift from utilitarian reform to extensive state intervention. Commenting on this, Eric Midwinter suggests 'Dicey was right by accident: namely, [prior to 1860] the state intervened in theory, but it failed to work out in practice' (1968, p. 44). More important, as the century went on the scale and the awareness of problems increased. In place of Dicey's formula, Midwinter offers the shift from 'the preventive principle' to collectivism and consolidation. In the later years of the last century, there were also more specific changes in government, including the movement from appointed boards to ministerial government (Willson 1955), and increasingly the central government facilitation of local government policy and municipalism. In focusing on the modernizing of the state and public violence, two major arenas of transformation are the creation of the enfranchised male polity, and the expansion of the state military apparatus, almost exclusively managed and staffed by men. Two closely aligned developments were the modernizations of the police and of the monarchy.

The escalation of industrial society in the late eighteenth and early nineteenth centuries brought the urban mass – not just in the accumulation of houses, but in the occupation of streets. The abstract urban mass found its concrete social form in the urban crowd. Though women were prominent in some urban protests (Thomis and Grimmett 1982), religious, political, and industrial meetings and gatherings were most usually dominated, peopled, *manned* by men. This was particularly so in those gatherings, organized or less organized, where violence occurred – for example, in London (the Gordon riots, 1780), Birmingham (the Priestley riots, 1791), Bristol (Reform Crisis, 1831), South Wales (the Rebecca riots, 1839–44), London (the Hyde Park disturbances, 1855; Garibaldi visit, 1864; Reform League demonstrations, 1866 and 1867; socialist gatherings, 1886 and 1887), Southsea (1874; Field 1980), Featherstone (Ackton Hall Colliery strike, 1893), and Northern Ireland (1857–87; Stevenson 1978). Sometimes the mass of men was met with the violence of state men in the persons of the military and the police – for example, at the Peterloo massacre in Manchester in 1819, the Luddite riots at York in 1817 and elsewhere, and the Sunday Trading Association in Hyde Park in 1855. As so often, men were fighting men.

Men on the street and the men of the developing police forces were counterposed in an uneasy tension during this period. On the one hand, there was clearly a development of a more organized, more controlled state response to civil disorder; on the other, there were also a number of retrospective state inquiries into 'excessive' police intervention and other police incompetencies, especially at the end of the century (for example, in 1886 and 1893).

The expansions of the urban mass and the urban middle classes facilitated the reform of parliamentary franchise in the nineteenth century – and the faltering movement from an *ancien régime* of the landed aristocracy that had still held sway in the eighteenth century. What was at stake was extension of voting rights to increased numbers of *men*. Class-defined franchise, voting defined through property and land holding, was in fact the class definition of men by way of property. Enfranchisement was a matter of property relations, facilitated by succession, and inheritance in marriage through the lineage of men.[26] The First Reform Act of 1832 and then the Second Reform Act of 1867 extended voting to greater numbers of men by reducing the value of the property, in the form of buildings and/or land, to be held. The electorate of men was increased further in 1869, with the compounding of rates otherwise not paid for personally (Beales 1969, p. 243). The history of franchise in Britain is up to this point the history of some men allowing other men the possibility of voting. This was not a smooth process – it was a mixture of bourgeois men's political pressures, and the range of largely proletarian men's political pressures, direct and indirect in formal political organization, incipient trade unionism and socialism, chartism, as well as public assembly and indeed violent rioting.

In 1872 Walter Bagehot, the constitutional historian, wrote in the new edition of *The English Constitution* of 1867 made necessary by the Second Reform Act that 'both our political parties will bid for the support of the working-man'. He viewed this with some disquiet, as a potentially divisive innovation (Bagehot 1928, p. 269). Indeed, the period from 1867 to 1918 was a rather peculiar one. It can be seen as a *brief episode* of *men's relative democracy* (or viriocracy: government by adult males) standing between the earlier inequities in men's suffrage and the movement towards women's suffrage after the First World War. It can thus be seen as an interlude, characterized by complex, public political coalitions of men, interrelating with other public patriarchal institutions (such as monopoly capitalism, the elaboration of law, and state institutions), *between other political forms of men's rule*.

This period can also be seen as the beginnings of the very creation of *the modern public*, in its various guises – the citizenry, the mass (or masses), the electorate; all in fact *collectivities of certain men*. Modern electoral methods and modern (British two) party political organization both date from 1867. The Representation of the People Act of that year (1868 in Scotland) extended borough franchise to householders, subject to a one-year residential qualification and the payment of rates, and to lodgers occupying lodgings worth £10 a year, also subject to the one-year residential qualification. It also created an occupation franchise in the counties for those occupying land worth £12 a year and a property franchise for those with lands worth £5 a year (Hanham 1968, p. 35). The 1872 Ballot Act made voting secret and in 1883 the Corrupt Practices Act eased the proof for conviction of electoral bribes or similar pressures on (men) electors. The latter also lowered the limits on candidates' expenditure. Expenditure per head at the 1885 general election was less than a quarter of what it had been in 1880 (O'Leary 1962).

These procedural reforms were mirrored in the development of national party organizations of men. Partly this is to do with the rise in the number of contested rather than unopposed elections. The parties changed from loose parliamentary coalitions to more organized national federations of local associations, with the foundation in 1867 of the National Union of Conservative and Constitutional Working Men's Associations (soon renamed as the Conservative National Union) and the National Liberal Federation in 1877. In 1870 the Conservative Central Office was established – though much of the latter years of the last century was characterized by a laxity in national organization that would now be laughable. Party democratization of men had begun, albeit in a limited way.

The 1879–80 election campaign was notable for the movement to modern electioneering, pioneered by Gladstone himself, with the 'whistle stop' campaigning by train, and the greater use of media and photography in the press and photo call. The 1880 election was also the first time a government with a clear majority (Disraeli's Conservatives) had been overturned by the electorate (in favour of Gladstone's Liberals) at a single election. National 'democracy' of men electors had, for once, more direct influence than the 'democracy' of parliamentary men.

Members of Parliament were granted payment for the first time in 1911, and the movement to the professionalization of politics, at least at the national scale, thus received a definite consolidation. A small group of men had in effect become the paid custodians of the political life of the mass electorate of men. Parliamentary work also changed from being a part-time occupation from February to August to something approaching a full-time job.

These innovations accounted for the creation of the 'male' polity, that is, a(n almost) universal polity of men, for all men householders, regardless of property ownership, in 1884. Under the Representation of the People Act of that year, a uniform householder and lodger franchise was created in every borough and county in the United Kingdom, based on the franchise granted for the English borough in 1867. It also provided for an occupation franchise for those with lands or tenements worth £10 a year (Hanham 1968, p. 35). Thus, by the end of the century the urban crowd had been tamed to the extent that it was no longer the prime means to *mass* political change by men. Crowds became more regimented and controlled, sometimes through the organization of the newly developing trade unions, sometimes with the increased monitoring of the police. The 1889 Dock Strike was the archetype of this new respectable crowding, with the rise of the 'New Unionism', the labour aristocracy, and respectable manliness in time and space.

Political debate in the public domains was very largely by men and of men. Party organization was of men; trade union organizations spoke of 'men' even when they meant women too; 'public figures' were generally men;[27] and men's political discourse generally invoked 'men' in an unashamedly unproblematic way.[28] In the nineteenth century, affairs of the public domains, especially those of formal discourses there, were dominantly about men. Either men or working men or gentlemen were explicitly referred to (even often when women were included), or people were genderless but men were meant. Public affairs were men's affairs.

Inevitably, Acts of Parliament (for example, the 1875 Employers and Workmen Act and the 1905 Unemployed Workmen Bill) were about 'men' too.

These 'male principles' remained dominant with the revived organization of the Liberals at the end of the century. As Gladstone pronounced in June 1886 in a speech at Liverpool:

> I am thankful to say that there are men wearing coronets on their heads who are as good, as sound, as genuine Liberals as any working man who hears me at this moment. Still, as a general rule, it cannot be pretended that we are supported by the dukes, or by the squires, or by the established clergy, or by any other body of very respectable persons.
>
> (*The Times*, 29 June 1886)[29]

The domination of men was hardly eased with the formation of the Independent Labour Party in Bradford in 1893. Despite the involvement of women in trade union and socialist causes, formal and particularly national Labour organization (through the Labour Representation Committee) was largely men's work, even though local unionism and local strikes were sometimes organized by women. Furthermore, in the early years of this century, the political position of the trade unions was precarious. Even so, while the Taff Vale decision of July 1901 threatened their whole existence, within a year of the judgment affiliation to the Labour Representation Committee had risen from 356,000 to 861,000. With this level of trade union membership their significance within the political scene should not be overestimated (see Briggs 1964, p. 65). Trade union membership increased from just over 2 million in 1901 (12.4 per cent of the employed population) to 3,139,000 in 1911 (17.1 per cent) and 6,663,000 in 1921 (34.3 per cent) (*Historical Abstract of British Labour Statistics* 1971). Growth came from both the expansion of 'New Unionism' among un-skilled workers and the impact of the First World War. The pre-First World War years were a period of high strike levels – of the dockers, seamen, railway workers, and miners, amongst others; while in 1908 there were 380 strikes, in 1913 there were 1,450.

The speech of men dominated even the more radical sections of the labour movement. Following the Osborne Judgment of 1910, hostility towards the owning classes increased further, and

[131]

syndicalist activism for 'the elimination of the employer' and against nationalization developed in coal mining and was feared by many, including Labour politicians, as threatening revolution. A South Wales publication announced 'Every fight for, and victory won by the men, will inevitably assist them in arriving at a clearer conception of the responsibilities and duties before them'. It continued that, with the overthrow of wage slavery, 'mankind shall . . . have leisure and inclination to really live as men, and not as the beast, which perish' (Unofficial Reform Committee 1912).

Meanwhile, the movements for women's suffrage, of both suffragists and suffragettes, were making uneven progress. Despite the dominant opposition from men (B. Harrison 1978), a small number of men were supportive (Strauss 1983; D. Morgan 1992). Susan Kingsley Kent (1987) has pointed out how women's demands for suffrage interrelated with a whole range of other political issues around work, sexuality, and other matters in the public domains. Judith Walkowitz (1980) has clarified the overlap and continuity between the campaign for women's suffrage and that against the CD Acts, for feminists and some men.[30] The First World War brought an abrupt shift in dominant national priorities, even though some women continued to organize nationally and internationally around pacifism and ending the war. Women's national suffrage was not granted in its entirety until 1928, following the initial national suffrage (Representation of the People) Act of 1918, in the wake of post-First World War optimism. This gave the vote to all men at 21 and all women at 30. However, unmarried women had received the vote in borough elections under the 1869 Municipal Franchise Act, and had the vote at the local elections for the newly created county and borough councils in 1888. Even so, men's domination of local government was near complete in the 1870s. For example, it was not until 1875 that the first woman Poor Law guardian was elected. Following the 1888 reform of county council elections, two women were elected to the first London County Council in 1889, by which time there were twenty-six women Poor Law guardians in total (*Englishwoman's Review* 1889). In 1894 both unmarried and married women were granted (*by men*) the vote for the new urban and rural district councils, and indeed could stand for election for these councils. This latter right was extended by the 1907 Qualification of Women Act, according to which women were allowed also to stand as councillors of the county councils and county boroughs and to become mayors. Such genderings of the local state were also spatial. The 1888 Local Government Act threatened municipal (men's) autonomy in relation to county and national administration. However, in the event, the Local Government Board created sixty-one (rather than ten) county boroughs, and thus solidified specific localized municipal masculinities or masculine municipalisms that are partly still with us.

A particularly important aspect of local–national state relations for the formation of public men has been the modernization of policing. John Stevenson (1978, p. 156) summarizes the early modern development of the policing as follows:

> In the eighteenth century the government had only the parochial authorities and the army with which to keep public order. But the need for greater flexibility and prevention turned attention towards the need for an effective police force to handle popular disorder. A nucleus of professional police was built up in London at the Bow Street office and the seven police officers set up under the Middlesex Justices' Act of 1792.[31] But in the rest of the country the army and auxiliary forces such as the Yeomanry and militia remained of importance until the introduction of professional police forces modelled on the Metropolitan Police.[32] This force was set up in 1829 and was soon copied in most other boroughs in the British Isles. Rural police forces were set up from 1840 and the armed forces were able to assume a supporting role in relation to civil disorder. Thus increasingly from this period, the government was concerned to establish and regulate the function of the police in relation to the various forms of civil disorder present in the nineteenth century.

Policing has itself always been gendered, and no less so in criminal work. 'Crime' is being increasingly recognized by feminist criminology as very much the speciality of men (e.g. Allen 1989), and this introduces a recasting of historical analyses of crime as also usually about men. In the policing of crime, one set of men work against, and sometimes with, another set of men.

The modernization of the police, and the development of a

proto-national system of policing, has its roots in the nineteenth century. A variety of Luddite, socialist, and Chartist threats, from the post-Napoleonic Wars period onwards, were countered by the gathering of intelligence from local police forces (including plain clothes officers), the Factory Inspectorate, Lord-Lieutenants, magistrates, and concerned citizens (Bunyan 1977), and its passage onto the Home Office.

During Gladstone's first premiership (1868–74), the Irish Question loomed large, and his own attempts to resolve the problem, not least because of the demands of military expenditure there, proved inconclusive. Indeed, the reforming First Irish Land Act of 1870 led to increased hostility, bringing the response of the 1871 Coercion Act, which granted the police increased powers of arrest and imprisonment. However, more violent efforts were made in the 1880s with the beginning of a series of dynamite bombings in 1883, including three in the London Underground. The Explosives Substances Act was quickly passed in 1883, giving the police wider powers of arrest for offences of this type, and late in 1883 the Political Branch, soon renamed the Special Irish Branch, was formed from the CID in Scotland Yard. The Branch consisted of twelve men, all Irish by birth, headed by a Scotsman, Inspector Littlechild. In 1884 the Fenians were successful in blowing up the offices of the Special Irish Branch itself, though a number of other attempts, most notably the blowing up of Nelson's Column, were unsuccessful. The bombings ceased in January 1885, and in 1886 the Branch was involved in the arrest of five Irish MPs, wanted by the Royal Irish Constabulary for incitement to sedition. In 1888 the word 'Irish' was removed from its title (Bunyan 1977, pp. 104–5).

An interesting feature of the modernization of the police at the end of the last century was the introduction in the 1890 Police Act of police pensions, following a number of unsuccessful attempts in the 1880s. Up to that time, only about 10 per cent of policemen received pensions, even though they contributed $2^1/2$ per cent of their pay to pension funds. From 1890 discretion of the police authority was replaced by a national system, adding a much sought after stability from the point of view of both officers and chief constables, themselves created only in 1886. The second 1886 Parliamentary Select Committee (I.U.P. Police 10) agreed and recommended the creation of chief constables. Jennifer Hart (1978, p. 202) reports on this innovation:

whilst it made the very sensible comment that 'the real efficiency of a force greatly depends on the way in which promotion is administered', it also inconsistently considered the chief constables should be 'gentlemen of good standing, and, as a general rule, officers who have seen service in the Army or Navy . . . such men would be treated with respect and regarded with confidence by the force.'

Such social prerequisites, however contradictory, stood in contrast to the 'bodies of barely literate and often drunken ex-labourers with a rapidly changing membership that constituted many nineteenth century forces' (p. 209).

Nineteenth-century modernization of the police was paralleled by the reform of the military towards a more bureaucratic and more professionalized institution, as a central feature in the consolidation of the modern nation state. Modern reform began with the regime of Edward Cardwell as Secretary of State for War from 1868 to 1874. These changes included in 1869 the institution of the Commander-in-Chief with direct responsibility for tendering strategic advice to the Secretary of State; and in 1873 the establishment of an Intelligence Department in the War Office with responsibility for topographical and statistical information. The latter years of the century were characterized by a mixture of gradual reform, complacency, and internal division in military reorganization. The Boer War proved to be another stimulus to military reform, and, following the 1902 Committee of Inquiry into Military Intelligence and the 1903 Esher Committee on the organization of the War Office, the General Staff concept was instituted in 1904. Although some reforms to the management of the General Staff were made, especially after Richard Burdon Haldane's appointment as Secretary of State for War in 1906, when it came to the test of the Great War the organization proved not fully effective, not least because of the domination of political, non-military decision-making. It wasn't until December 1915, following several major failures, that the General Staff was revivified with more autonomy and power granted to it from the War Cabinet (see Gooch 1974; Kennedy 1980). Here we find the early establishment of the modern, professional army, the means of mass public destruction, relatively autonomous from political government, and organized along the lines of 'Scientific Management'.

The Great War and the associated war machines had major

effects on many aspects of the gendered construction of public life. For example, it also strongly influenced the development of national planning, partly on the basis that the methods of war could be carried over into 'peacetime'. The huge institutions of monopoly capitalism could not be relied upon to control national resources and industry effectively. Initial moves in bringing science and national planning into government followed from concern at British overdependence on German chemicals and industries. The Advisory Committee on Scientific and Industrial Research (1915) and the Haldane Committee (1918) were the beginnings of a new major governmental responsibility, culminating in the Committee of Civil Research (1925) and the Economic Advisory Committee (1930), which ensured central overview of economic, scientific, and statistical research in relation to state policy (Gummett 1980). The state was thus further expanded as a supposedly 'neutral/neutered' overseer of national affairs.

Finally, of special significance in Britain at least is public men's relation to the monarchy. There is no more absolute signifier of patriarchal hierarchy than monarchy. Though in the British case women can become queens, male children amazingly do still take 'precedence' over female children.

Though Prince Albert had been buried nine years by 1870, 'Victoria stayed in a seclusion that was absolute except when foreign potentates arrived, royal princesses were married, or heroes from the wars came to be decorated' (Bott 1931, p. 71). By the mid-1880s this invisibility was catching the public's imagination, aided by stories of her homely and selfless kindness in private. The Jubilee celebrations of 1887 brought this phase to a close. Even then Victoria herself did not wear State robes, so providing a simple and outstanding contrast with the splendours of the royalties, militaries, and other powerful people, usually men, on show. The next ten years up to the Diamond Jubilee of 1897 saw more public appearances and 'meeting the people' by Victoria – and consequent acclaim of the monarch as both grand and personal. This phase of the late 1880s and early 1890s did much to invent the modern 'traditions', rituals, and pageants of the monarchy, at which 'ordinary people' could see and perhaps hear the monarch, and powerful men could display themselves.

In the twentieth century, and even more so in the reign of the current monarch (Elizabeth Windsor), the monarchy has become further institutionalized, regularized, bureaucratized, personalized, and normalized. It no longer appears as an independent absolute – it is now a normalized/bureaucratized absolute.[33] It is family, community, nation, 'race'; past, present, future. Its abolition in the UK is rarely proposed, not even on the Left, even though it embodies one of the most long-standing grand patriarchal narratives. The Divine Right has been long superseded by the Rule of Parliament, but the monarch is still the Sovereign. Abolishing sovereigns is a suitable way of interrupting the sovereign power of public men. It remains a psychoanalytic, cultural, economic element of the imaginary and the publicly patriarchal order.

Organizations, streets, and movements

Throughout this chapter the 'public domain' has been shown to be a variety of public domains. In addition to the relations analysed, a further distinction may be usefully made between organizations and streets, as spaces not clearly belonging to a single organization. Both organizations and streets are gendered social institutions – where men often control women, resources, each other, in the first case; and where men can often 'move freely', and women less freely, in the second. In the remaining chapters my emphasis will, for several reasons, be mainly on organizations. This is in recognition partly of the greater institutional power of organizations, and the fact that even streets (and other 'open spaces') are usually owned, controlled, watched over, and monitored by organizations; partly of the magnitude of changes in organizations with the movement towards public patriarchies; and partly of the greater amount of information available on organizations compared with streets. An adequate history of streets under patriarchies, including relations of special use, sociality, sexuality, violence, and movement, remains to be written, although there is now a considerable social history of the crowd, the mob, and several other features.

The organization and organizations are bastions of the power of men. The street may appear as a *public* place – supposedly all can go there. But of course to see the street in this way is to deny the complex ways in which streets are themselves bastions of men's power, sometimes men's violence. What is also important is *potential power* on and over the street, most usually maintained by the police and the military. This involves variable, sometimes regular, sometimes irregular, forms of surveillance of the street, of which electronic monitoring of traffic and travel movement are significant parts. Such surveillances have their own genderings: for example, the monitoring of the highway is an exercise in (certain) men's power. Then of course there is the display of organized, perhaps national, strength in celebrations, demonstrations, and official events, and also, at times of 'civil disturbance', 'civil disorder', and even 'civil war', through paramilitary control of time and space (Jefferson 1987). These internal and 'local' militarizations may sometimes be the bases to the superstructures of organizations, just as the private domains and reproduction are bases to the public domains and production.

These powers of men are, however, not always exerted by national or military forces. They also persist in the ordinary power of groups of men, such as young men, which John Remy (1990) has called the frat. These can comprise relatively small groups of men who take on the assumed right to control, take territory, exert force, do violences, and perhaps kill – ordinary street gangs; men on Saturday night outings; men at football gatherings; as well as, more dramatically, men on the streets of Northern Ireland, Lebanon, Sri Lanka, and many other sites of men's violence and civil war.

Contestation of space and territory, and space in time (for example, at certain times of night or day), is directed not just against women. It may be directed against other men, as relative peers, as with inter-gang rivalry. It may also be exerted as forms of resistance, say by black men or young men, or black young men, against the powers of more powerful other men and importantly more powerful organizations of men like the national or local police (Westwood 1990). Other groups of men may exert their power through what may appear as peaceful occupation of space; for example, the control, use, and defence of sporting space like golf courses, cricket pitches, and sports fields. Other men may temporarily occupy space to seek changes in the public domains themselves; for example, demonstrations for rights sought within the context of national domination.

The street is place, site, throughway, medium, territory – all of which may present complex interplays of danger and relative safety to different people, with women most usually at risk from men, as well as different types of men (young men, black men, gay men) sometimes being in danger from other men, or even from each other in some cases, such as with groups or gangs of young men. These differential dangers to and safeties of women and men, and different types of women and men, are at the *root of responses* such as 'reclaim the night', black, anti-racist, lesbian pride, and gay pride demonstrations *on the street*. Similarly oppositional practices against dominant forms of organizations include the creation of women's organizations, networks, 'non-organizations', and anti-organizational practices.

Finally, there is the changing form of *movements* between organizations, through streets, and between streets and organizations, within public patriarchies. The separation of the paid workplace, other organizations, and the home, in both space and time, has been an important part of patriarchal, capitalist, imperialist, and urban change, with its uneven and unstable character over and above the living norms and aspirations of individuals, households, classes, and collectivities. These separations – in space, time, *and in men and masculinities* – were intensified with the growth of transport and of commuting, by train, bus, trolley bus, and tram. Public men and public masculinities were not only able to move more rapidly; they were also more discontinuous, more compartmentalized, more separated. Public men's collective power and potential power was increased, yet the individual public man was momentary – a sign of the times.

CHAPTER 7

Organizations of men (1): size, structures, and hierarchies

In the previous chapter I outlined some major historical shifts in the relations of the public domains and private domains, and their significance for public men and public masculinities. In this chapter, rather than focus on the social and spatial spread of public domains, I am more concerned with the internal structures of institutions and organizations themselves. The movement to public patriarchies is thus not an abstract process: it develops through particular social institutions, most significantly through organizations. The forms that organizations take are major features of the form of public patriarchies; in turn organizations construct and are dominantly constructed by public men and public masculinities. This applies in both the formal structuring and social processes of organizational life. This is to be seen in the immense change in the size, shape, power, hierarchy, and complexity of the *organizations* of the public domains over the last hundred years or more – in economic organizations, capitalist and corporate, national and multinational; state and government; the military and military industries; international agencies of all types; science; education; religion; the professions; the sex industries; crime; covert, surveillance, and 'security' industries; retail and distribution; information processing, communications, telecommunications and transportation; clubs and cultural associations.

Public patriarchies and organizations

Contemporary organizations exist within public patriarchies, and are the most visible public patriarchal social form in the public domains. Contemporary organizations are generally publicly patriarchal in form and content, in structure and process. Thus we

[140]

may ask: what are the specific forms and structures of organizations that occur in public patriarchies? What organizational forms and structures are characteristic of public patriarchies?

As previously discussed (see pp. 52-68), various feminist scholars have explained the historical shifts to patriarchy and public patriarchy in different ways and located them at different historical times. While O'Brien sees patriarchy (in terms of the domination of the institution of paternity) as inherently about public domain domination of the private, others see the shifts to public patriarchy as relatively recent. This latter shift has been explained by reference to more particular developments, including the advent of wage labour (Ursel), monopoly capitalism (Brown), the modern state and the modern professions (Stacey and Davies), the post-war state (Borchorst and Siim), and the welfare state (Hernes).

Such theories have definite implications for organizational forms and structures. Not only do they suggest a different historical timing for the growth of organizations within public patriarchies, they also suggest different explanations of public patriarchies, and hence organizations therein. This combination of different timing and different explanations suggests that different organizational forms and structures are likely to follow. While there are differences in approach to public patriarchies, and hence differences in the kind of organizations that might be expected to be predominant within public patriarchies, there are similarities between most of these accounts. In particular, most seem to imply that organizations within public patriarchies are a *second-phase process*: within public patriarchies, *already existing* organizations undergo a second-phase transition to more structured or more complex forms. Furthermore, these transitions are themselves clearly and necessarily *gendered*. Thus, to summarize so far, we are concerned not just with patriarchal organizational structures, but with the transition to second-phase, publicly patriarchal organizational structures, and their implications for public men and public masculinities.

In analysing such complexities of public patriarchies, it is not enough just to state that there are many different social arenas in which men have become dominant in the public domains. What has to be done is *to show how particular aspects and arenas of public patriarchies, in this context particular organizations, work.* However, before looking at some of those arenas in more detail, there is a need to consider briefly some of the ways in which organization(s), domination, and the power of men may often mutually reinforce each other.

Power, domination, and the changing shape of organizations

Men's domination of both the public domains and organizations was immense throughout the nineteenth century. Men's power and domination persisted through the medium of organizations in the public domains, and through the domination of public domains, and therefore organizations, over private domains. Thus men's power, especially formal power, in organizations in the public domains has to be understood at (at least) two levels – within the organization concerned itself, and more generally in terms of the power and domination of (the organization(s) in) the public domains over the private domains (Hearn & Parkin 1986–7, 1992). For example, an adequate account of power, leadership, and management by men *in* organizations involves considering the *double* nature of that power – that is, specific power within specific organizations, usually formally hierarchical, and the general power of the public domains, within which organizations are located. This is partly a social structural matter, and partly a more subtle question of process, including men's domination of the agendas (at least the explicit agendas) of the public domains. Such domination operated then, as now, partly through the type of issues discussed, debated, and decided upon in public forums. Thus, in talking of men's powers, domination, and organization(s), I am necessarily referring to the relations of organizational domination in society to men's domination in society. In the modern world it has become increasingly difficult to separate out these two forms of domination. Men's domination was and is organizational and organized.

Furthermore, connections between men, power, and organization existed and exist not just in the form of the respective dominations, but in the notions and meanings of '*men*' and '*organization*' themselves, as their potential historical power increases through control of (corporate) resources of all sorts. Organizations were and are corporate bodies; men's power exists inextricably in relation to those corporate bodies. The connections between men, power, and organizations were and are also much more specific, and mutually reinforcing.[1]

In recognizing these various dominations by men, it is important not to underestimate the powerful importance of women and women's activity in organizations. First, even though exclusion of women from some organizations was absolute, organizations still existed as relations between women and men. Exclusions were both imposed, by men, and negotiated, between women and men, particularly in the minutiae of social relationships. This might be seen in the combination of further imposition and negotiation in the relationships of men and women, in both the public and private domains, that surrounded the lives of men in public life. For example, the wives of Members of Parliament in some cases had a relatively prominent public role in 'society', even though Parliament, London clubs, and their organizational sources of income remained exclusively or almost exclusively in arenas populated by men.

Secondly, there is the question of the distribution of women and men within organizations, and in particular men's domination of the *formal* positions of power within formal organizations. Although this has been the overwhelming pattern, women did of course obtain formal positions of power in particular organizational settings, including the following situations:

• in mixed-gender organizations, usually dominated by men; for example, women were prominent in the organization of industrial workers, through trade union and other means, the Bryant and May matchworkers' strike in 1888, and the Manningham Mills strike of 1891 that led to the formation of the Independent Labour Party in 1893;

• in organizations that were virtually all women or that represented other groups that were virtually all women; for example, the leaders of the developing professions of nursing, health visiting, and midwifery (Donnison 1977);

• in women's organizations themselves, with their own varying forms of gender and sexual ideology and consciousness. Some such organizations were oriented more to overcoming the public domain exclusion of women by pressuring men and men's organizations for inclusion; others were oriented more to the transformation of the public domains by the establishment of women's organizations providing communities, education, services, and facilities for women paralleling those of men (Vicinus 1985).

Thirdly, there is the large-scale presence and enormous activity of women in (certain sectors of) the public domains. The presence and power of women was most obvious in paid work. As already noted (p. 66), women, and of course children too, worked in very large numbers in the paid industrial workforce, in the public domains, from the earliest days of the Industrial Revolution (Pinchbeck 1981). In some industrial sectors, women and children were the largest group of workers; for example, in cotton textiles in the early nineteenth century. Restrictions on children's labour (especially but not solely in terms of numbers of hours worked per day) were introduced from 1819 and on women's labour from 1841 to the First World War through the series of Factory Acts and related Acts, such as the Mines and Collieries Act of 1842. While a quarter of married women were employed in 'extraneous occupations' in 1851, by 1901 the figure had declined to one in eight (Klein 1965). It was not until after 1850 that the campaign for reducing men's working day to 10 hours was initiated.

These broad patterns of association between power, domination, organization(s), and men in the nineteenth century were both determined and contradictory, both profoundly fixed and subtly variable. They also entailed change in both form and content. Changes in organizational form included the elaboration of organizational structures and hierarchies. Such changes were important, though usually neglected, facets of change in public patriarchies. Changes in organizational content comprised organizational growth within different sectors, and developing definitions of organizational aims and purposes. In specific situations these distinctions may not be clear cut: form and content may closely interrelate.

Among these organizational changes which have been significant in the production of public men and public masculinities, we may note the following:

- the movement of more activities and experiences into the realms of the public domains, partly through the professionalization, rationalization, and bureaucratization of people work;
- the creation of new organizations in the public domains;
- change in the unevenness of the relative size and power of

[144]

organizations – in different sectors, industries, services, state forms, and so on. The relative growth of organizations is related to their differential location in relation to reproduction and production;

- the increasing size of many organizations;
- the vertical and horizontal integration and consolidation of organizations into multi-organizations;
- the growth of hierarchy, more bureaucratic structures, and more specialist management and managerial functions in many organizations. This movement also includes the development of the social separation of both owners and controllers, and controllers and workers; and, in turn, the creation of workers' own organizations, with their own hierarchy and bureaucratization;
- the increasing internal complexity of organizations, in structure, task, technology, and social process;
- change in organizational ideologies and ideologies in organizations.

Absolute (and relative) growth in the size of organizations has been and remains closely tied to the growth of hierarchy and increasing complexity in organizations. The growth, hierarchization, and increasing complexity of organizations all feed men's, or rather certain men's, command of power and resources. The command of power and resources is both a means to men's collective power and a means to the power of individual men in specific organizational niches. In saying this it is important to consider that formal organizational structures (perhaps like organizations themselves) are *abstractions*. While these clearly comprise definite relations of power, authority, divisions of labour, and communication within organizations, the *notion(s)* of formal organizational structure, as in the organizational chart (on the manager's wall), are themselves an abstraction – most likely an abstraction of the manager's mind and practice, *him*self (*sic*) set within definite social relations (see Addelson 1982, p. 183) – and as such are open to critique. These themes and theses were and remain highly gendered: they do not result from agendered operations of the 'neutral' organizations that they may be presented as or said to be.

The remainder of this chapter examines some examples of organizational work and organizational structures in public patriarchies. These instances – people work and professions; office work and bureaucracies; and managerial work and managements – are all *gendered*. They are not mutually exclusive, rather they are broad major types of publicly patriarchal organizations.[2] These different types of organizational work are also forms of reproductive labour; they provide the basis for different kinds of organizations, even though clearly specific organizations may combine a number of different types of work.

People work and professional organizations

Organizations of professionals: associations of men

The *fundamental forms* of (human) life and (human) labour – birth, nurture, sexuality, violence – that compose the reproduction and reproductive character (or reproducibility) of human social life, and indeed compose what is called productive economic labour, underwent a major transformation in the movement towards public patriarchies. These fundamental forms of life and labour became dominantly transformed into organizational substance. People work[3] was increasingly organizational work.

The most obvious way in which this took place was through the growth of people organizations – in the professions, the state, and professionally dominated organizations. It also applied in the transformation of the institutions of capitalism – production, consumption, exchange, the market, and capital themselves. These organizations can be more fully understood as instances and relations of reproduction in the public domains – that is, of birth, nurture, sexuality, violence. For example, the buying of labour on the capitalist market is also a form of violence to persons, is sometimes direct violence, as in factory discipline, and is underpinned by violence, as in imperialism. There remains a need to draw together current thinking and theory on the nature of labour, and the nature of other activities such as care, love, and violence.

In a long-term historical perspective there has been both absolute growth in public domain activities and institutions, and related shifts in bringing more realms of life within the purview and concern of public domain institutions. These are not just matters of quantitative change; they are also matters of qualitative change. As realms of life, activities, and institutions grow, they also come to be organized differently, to operate through different organizational processes, and to be open to greater elaboration. They create their own specialist workers and specialist managers. Thus we now have specialists in the management and labouring of what were once seen as private activities.

The nature of people work, and indeed reproductive work more generally, is reproductive; it is qualitative in form and process; it is subject to its own reproducibility. It is not just a matter of its finite quantity, finite completion, or finite control. The bringing of people work increasingly into organizations and the professions is partly a question of control; but control is not its totality, even though movements to public domains facilitate control.

We are thus concerned here with a complex set of shifts not just from private domains to public domains, and from women's relative autonomous labour to men's management of women's labour both in private and in public; but also in the qualitative nature and control of people work.

The historical transformation of tasks formerly completed by women in the private domains into the public domains necessarily involves movements of activity from home to organizations. The professions, professional organizations, and related organizations of people work and welfare work were major actors, individual and collective, in these movements of private domain experiences into the public domains. A focus on people work in the medical and other professions, and its transformation at the end of the last century, cannot easily be separated from other changes – in work, technology, offices, service industries, bureaucracies, and management. The growth of the state can be understood, at least in part, in terms of the socialization of reproduction (in its broadest sense), including the professionalization of violence through the modern professional military.

Whilst associations of men are ancient, the late nineteenth-century professionalization of reproductive and people work was a major impetus to the further formation and expansion of associations of men. First, the actual process of professionalization proceeded partly through the activities of men in men's associations – associations that often excluded women. Secondly, professionalization of people work involved the creation of new associations of men, as well as the expansion of men's existing

[147]

associations. Thirdly, the increasing organization of reproductive and people work in and through the professions, the state, and the capitalist sectors of the economy had definite effects on the powers and cooperation of men in the private domains as fathers and husbands. This provided definite incentives for some men to form their own associations for trade and union organization. Professionalization, state expansion, and capitalist control of reproduction were paralleled by the rise of unionization and other economic and political associations of men in the public domains.

The late nineteenth century also brought a number of contradictory developments in the professions. On the one hand, many of the professions underwent a definite phase of consolidation – and in particular the development from relatively 'one-gentleman' bands to larger professional organizations. On the other, there were the beginnings of women's re-entry into professional domains of medicine, teaching, and law, through small numbers of women operating within what were formerly men's enclaves, or women creating their own organizations for professional education and professional practice.

Professionalized organizations: the challenge of schooling

In addition to the growth of associations of professional men, some professionals, women and men, were routinely located in relatively large-scale direct work with clients and customers within professionalized organizations. The most obvious example of such people organization was schooling, which underwent a considerable expansion after 1870. Like many other professionalized organizations, their work was on and with people, in this case young people, usually organized separately for girls or boys. Their ostensible task was education, just as the ostensible task of medical organizations is caring and curing. However, in the schools and other education organizations of the time the task of education, as now, also involved containing, enacted through profoundly hierarchical structures and ideologies. Boys' schools were also examples of usually small-scale associations of men and young men.

During the 1870s the number of teachers in inspected schools in England and Wales more than doubled, and their numbers continued to increase by a further third between 1880 and 1888. The expansion of teaching offered new opportunities for both women and men, including working-class men. By 1888 two-thirds of teaching posts were filled by women (Hamilton 1883, 1890). This produced the interesting intersection of small-scale men's associations and women's further specialization around reproductive and people work, especially in early education. These contradictions were further complicated in professionally led organizations, where part of the professional ideology included setting the profession itself aloof from or against bureaucratic norms. Thus the professional mode may bring new kinds of power, and sometimes tyranny, with respect to the control and autonomy of professionals themselves, other workers, and clients.

Total institutions: creations of men
Another type of people organization which expanded considerably in the late nineteenth century, and particularly so at the hands of men, was the total institution. State power and commercial power, including the power of imperialism and colonialism, not only provided the mechanisms for institutional and organizational growth; they also provided for the creation of whole new organizations and institutions, in the form of separate total institutions, charged with specific objectives and rationales, and deliberately set aside from society.

Some of these total institutions were of course expansions of previously existing institutions (for example, asylums); others were new creations (for example, the labour settlements). Many segregated women and men, as, for example, in the workhouse. In some, men controlled other men; in others, men controlled others – women, young people, children. In virtually every case, total institutions embodied major social divisions – of class, gender, age, ethnicity – both in their creation and in their internal structuring and peopling. They were a major form of Victorian social and demographic policy – a response to dire social problems, at once a means of optimistic social engineering (by élite men), and a testimony to moral pessimism and the desperate abandonment – men's 'logical' conclusion of classification of humans and human problems.

Office work and bureaucratic organizations

Mental and manual labours: separations and modernizations

Not only did the late nineteenth century see a movement of activities into the public domains, it also saw large-scale consolidations and differentiations in who did which types of work. While people work and reproductive work in the private domains *appear* as fundamentally manual work (even though they are and were also emotional labour and mental labour), in the public domains their amalgamation into larger 'units' creates the possibility of their transformation to mental labour performed or managed by professionals, that is, by men, initially at least. In this sense professionalization in patriarchies can be seen as an equivalent to managerialism in capitalism. On the other hand, both state and capitalist sectors were subject to other differentiations, including the increasing separation of *apparently* manual and mental labours – as represented by the factory and the office. Capitalist and, to an extent, state growth and consolidations created the possibility of institutional distinctions between the factory and the office, as well as their own partially autonomous hierarchies.

A number of historical accounts of office work (Braverman 1974; Anderson 1976; Davies 1982) indicate that until the end of the nineteenth century administration and administrative work were generally completed either as a specialist function in small-scale legal, account, and other offices, or as an aggregated part of the business in hand. This is especially so outside the Civil Service, which, as will be seen, had its own particular kinds of status hierarchies (see pp. 153–60).

At the mid-nineteenth century the office sector was still very little developed, with 91,000 men employed in such commercial occupations and virtually no women. The developing situation is conveniently summarized by Gregory Anderson (1976, p. 2):

> From mid-century . . . there was rapid expansion, the number of men in commercial occupations increasing to 130,000 in 1861, 449,000 in 1891 and 739,000 in 1911. Women were also increasingly employed in commercial occupations, the number rising from 2,000 in 1861 to 26,000 in 1891 and to 157,000 in 1911.

However, even in the 1870s office work was relatively little developed, was distributed in small units, such as counting houses and small parts of larger organizations, and was performed predominantly by men. In the extreme case we find from the 1871 Census for Great Britain that there were 29,242 men employed in the insurance, banking, finance, and business services sector, and apparently 1 woman so employed.[4] From the 1870s the social barriers against women's employment outside the factory were reduced. Employers showed increasing interest in the employment of women (particularly unmarried women) in offices, and increasing numbers were employed as clerks, typists, and telephonists. The typewriter was invented in 1873 by Remingtons, and from the beginning typewriting was almost exclusively a woman's occupation. The office was further transformed by a range of other new technologies – ticker tape, the light bulb, the telegraph, the telephone – many of them emanating from the Edison laboratory. By the end of the century the expansion of the administrative component of organizations brought on considerable expansion in the clerical function and in the demand for clerical workers. At the same time, the office and clerical work were becoming increasingly feminized,[5] not least through the impact of a more educated workforce of women (in terms of literacy and numeracy). Jane Lewis (1988, p. 31) summarizes these changes as follows:

> the increase in demand for clerks in the late nineteenth century and the possession of equivalent skills of young men and women emerging from the new state elementary schools, meant that men as employers would contemplate employing women who were of course a cheaper source of labour. But women were not hired *en masse* to replace male clerks. The process of feminization was slow. Moreover women were, from the outset, largely confined to their own grades and departments. Male employers and male trade unionists both wanted to minimise the competition between male and female workers.

Despite the relative autonomy of some offices, these changes must also be understood in relation to changes in the private domains. In particular, by the early twentieth century increasing numbers of middle-class women needed to enter employment because of their single status or lack of financial support by men, a situation exacerbated by an over-supply of governesses with the increasing educational attainment of middle-class women (Silverstone 1976; Lowe 1987, p. 17).

The expansion of the office and the feminization of the office were closely associated with each other; they represented major changes in gendered organizational structures. So what are the implications of this feminized expansion for men? In *Contested Terrain*, Richard Edwards (1979) argues that bureaucratic control developed first in office and so-called 'white collar' (or 'white blouse' – Anderson 1988) organizations. In suggesting this, Edwards sees an historical development from divisions deriving from class power or technological determinants to divisions based more fully in social or organizational distinctions themselves (1979, p. 135). In this sense, divisions within organizations, including gendered divisions under the control of men, became more autonomously determined, albeit within *organizational discourse*. This thesis is important for an understanding of men, particularly in relation to a broadly Foucauldian concept of power.

Although many men, both clerks and others, resisted (sometimes with great hostility) the growth of women's occupation of clerical jobs (or alternatively the clericalization of women), these developments also produced new gendered organizational strata in bureaucracies. The increasingly feminized office complicated both the horizontal and the vertical segregations (Hakim 1979) of organizations. Gender-typing of occupations was reinforced through the office, as were the gender relations of authority. Through the office some men may have had relatively less access to certain kinds of clerical jobs, but other men had more direct control over a new form of women's labour – nothing less than an 'administrative revolution' (Lowe 1987) had taken place.

The office, or more precisely the major and fundamental expansion of the office (to the point of normalization), was and is a significant site of men's domination of women and women's labour – clerical, administrative, gendered, sexual. The office can also be looked on as a site that brings together a mixture of manual work (e.g. typing, filing), mental work (calculation, planning), and people work (administration, social relationships). While the exact ways in which the gendered office changed and fitted into broader organizational structures clearly varied between organi-

[152]

zational sectors, offices were necessary major building blocks in the developing bureaucracies. The office literally provided the archetypal form of the general bureaucracy. This particular late nineteenth-century form of bureaucracy offered new possibilities for the location and action of men. Moreover, in more recent years, banks and similar offices have shifted from being remote repositories of money for the few to more customer-oriented 'shops' on the high street (Morgan 1992). This functional change has been paralleled by changes both in women's and men's participation and visibility on 'the front desk' and 'behind the scenes', and in dominant images, from black-suited serious men to those that are lighter, more colourful, even 'postmodern'. As such, office work and the developing modern bureaucracies were and are continuing to be significant elements of public patriarchies.

State bureaucracies

The separations and modernizations of offices and factories facilitated the growth of bureaucracies and bureaucratization. Bureaucracies can be understood as organizations in which the principles of office organization or the principles of rational and/or legal rules and authority are represented as dominant. I say here 'represented as dominant' because in many, and perhaps most, bureaucracies what is presented as 'rational–legal' may on closer examination be clearly 'charismatic' or more likely 'traditional' – in the sense that much of the authority of bureaucrats rests not on rational rule-following but on the following of almost feudal authority. Either way, bureaucracies are built fundamentally on hierarchy. The organizations of public patriarchies are predominantly bureaucratic and hierarchical (see Ferguson 1984).

Alternatively, bureaucracies may be understood as mixtures of patriarchal and fratriarchal organizations – *organizational hybrids* in which men may meet with each other in fratriarchies yet relate to each other through the processes of patriarchal and hierarchical authority (see Remy 1990). Within bureaucracies, different sections and moreover different bureaucrats and bureaucratic men sit uncomfortably alongside each other, partly in individualistic competition and partly in an overall sense of corporate unity. A major example of the complexities and contradictions of bureaucratic organization is to be found in the historical change of the state.

The second half of the last century marked a major increase in state employment. For example, employment specifically in public administration increased from 67,000 (of whom 64,000 were men) in 1851 to 163,000 (of whom 146,000 were men) in 1891 (Mitchell & Deane 1962). This was dramatic enough, but government employment was nearly to double again in the period from 1891 and 1911, from over half a million to $1^1/_4$ million, and to increase by over 40 per cent further between 1911 and 1921 (to nearly 2 million).[6] Thus, although the First World War clearly accounted for major increases in government employment (most obviously in the armed forces), increases were in fact greater in central and local government than in the military. Even though the numbers of women were relatively small, the early twentieth century saw some rapid increases amongst them too.

State organizations not only grew but became more bureaucraticized and more modern in their methods. A fundamental feature of this growth of the state has been the increasing employment of men in central and local government. State bureaucracies gradually became one of the main sites for the spread of credentialism among men; through this and other means men, or at least some men, were 'modernized'. From the middle of the nineteenth century, work functions, payment, and promotion of civil servants were rigidly classified and as far as possible standardized between departments. Men were recruited to a particular department and could not be transferred to others (Cohen 1965, p. 124). Departmental heads were often distant and isolated, and clerks, placed in common gendered grades, were obliged to combine together in unions and associations to have their grievances heard; to an extent bureaucratization facilitated unionism (Anderson 1976, p. 112).

The basis of the modern Civil Service was laid in the Trevelyan–Northcote Report of 1854, in which proposals for merit to replace the then existing system of patronage were made. This was partly a matter of checking abuses, but it was also more significantly geared towards production of higher-quality personnel and the introduction of more modern methods of organization and bureaucracy. The following year the Civil Service Commission was established as an examination board. Qualifying examinations were introduced *for nominees* for some limited competitions in 1861 (no more than about one in eight). However, open competition was applied in only twenty-nine situations between 1855 and 1862 (Cohen 1965, pp. 119–20). From 1870, recruitment to the Civil Service was moved to so-called 'open competitive examinations' – that is, open to men. However, even then the new system was introduced unevenly, with, for example, all vacancies in the Foreign Office and the Home Office filled by patronage. The open (to men) system was more or less established in its entirety by 1890.

The case of the Post Office

Women's entry into the Civil Service can be dated to 1869 with the takeover of the Electric and International Telephone Company by the Post Office, which had been formed in 1861. The first hiring of a woman Civil Service clerk was by the Post Office in 1871, and relatively rapid expansion of women Post Office clerks followed. The Post Office continued to be the main employer of women within the Civil Service. In 1914, 90 per cent of the 65,000 women in the Civil Service were in the Post Office, which had grown to become one of the most important offices of the state.[7] By 1919 the total number of women in the Civil Service had risen to 170,000 spread through many departments.

There has been an extensive debate on gender relations in the Post Office during the late nineteenth and early twentieth centuries.[8] In the early years of the Post Office women worked mainly as telegraphists. This followed on their earlier involvement in telegraphy within the commercial companies. From the 1850s at least some men perceived women as ideally suited for the dexterous work of telegraphy. According to Maria Susan Rye in 1859, it was about 1853 that the chairman (*sic*) of the Electric and International Telegraph Company heard of a daughter of a railway station master who had ably completed all of her father's telegraph business. This suggested to him the idea of training and employing women to do this kind of work in the company as a whole. The company (i.e. the men managers and owners) were 'perfectly satisfied that the girls [*sic*] are not only more teachable, more attentive, and quicker-eyed than the men clerks formerly employed, but . . . also . . . more trustworthy, more easily managed, and . . . sooner satisfied with lower wages'.[9] Such a statement probably says more about men than it does about women. It was thus that telegraphy was seen as suitable for women by some men. Indeed by 1871 no fewer than 539 women were employed in the main telegraph office in London alone, while the district branches were 'worked by a staff almost wholly composed of young and generally well-bred women' (Bott 1931, p. 65).

In the early years of the Post Office, telegraphists, as with many other civil servants, were appointed following nominations – that is, nomination by men, in that case either the Postmaster-General or local postmasters. Nomination was supplemented by qualifying examination, which was subsequently replaced by competitive examination. Successful appointees then entered telegraph school for several months' training, undertaken without pay until 1905 (Holcombe 1973, p. 165). The Post Office was also the first government department to employ women in clerical work. This innovatory policy followed close on the taking on of women telegraphists in 1869.

The Post Office is an example of a complex form of bureaucratization in which both women and men were major participants. Women were represented in relatively high numbers in the Post Office, certainly relative to many other state and commercial sectors.[10] In addition, in some ways there was a relatively low overall level of 'gender-typing' of tasks in the Post Office. Most grades were formally open to both women and men; only the London-based sorters' grade and the grades of urban postman were officially reserved for men. Elsewhere women and men completed identical duties. On the other hand, within these global distributions of women and men, there were more detailed differences between women and men: men were often formally paid more, as was the norm then; and duties were often performed by women in different offices and on different shifts. This is even though experiments with the mixing of women and men began in the Post Office as early as 1871 (Holcombe 1973, pp. 165–6). In 1876 the Marriage Bar was introduced for all women, except for the categories of subpostmistresses, 'charwomen', and women factory employees. This was officially because of the lower status of these workers, but 'in reality because the recruitment of replacements was so difficult' (Grint 1988, p. 89). The telephone was made available to the public in 1879 and in most cases daytime telephone operators were women, with men specializing in night duty work (Holcombe 1973, p. 166). Thus from the 1880s gender-typing was reinforced alongside the relatively high level of women's participation.

In 1881 a new pay scheme was introduced by Henry Fawcett

for the Post Office, in an attempt to produce a more uniform and equal treatment of all postal clerks. However, the scheme was never fully implemented, and telegraph clerks came to be regarded as inferior to sorting clerks. For example, the Reports of the Committees on Post Office Wages indicated that in 1904, out of twelve supervisory appointments for men clerks at Manchester Post Office, only two were telegraph-based, and that indeed in 1913 some men telegraphists had no promotion after thirty years' service (Anderson 1976, p. 113).

Meanwhile men Post Office clerks had their own grievances against other men. In August 1899 *The Post Clerks' Herald* reported:

> Our real grievance is with the way we are governed, with the worries of postal life, the snubs, the petty tyrannies and the little injustices. The treatment, fit for a child, meted out to men, as being told: 'You have made a mistake and you must stay in two hours as a punishment.' There are noble men in the Post Office who have black records which under a proper government would have been stainless. This it is that like a cancer eats away all the content and leaves a festering sore behind. In the Post Office there is no friendship between the governors and the governed.[11]

The form of bureaucratization in the Post Office was one in which men included women *within* the occupational and organizational structure rather than excluding them completely (as with some professions) or simply confining them to 'women's' occupations.[12] In the Post Office we find a bureaucracy developing through the interplay of pressure to both segregation and integration of women and men. Although equal pay was awarded for specific age groups on particular grades in 1921, it was not established for almost all women until 1961.

The Civil Service context

If we turn back to the broader questions of the development of the Civil Service, we also find there distinct separations of women and men – by occupation, grade, physical distances, and indeed age. For example, from 1870 there was a new category of un-established clerk – the boy clerk – reserved for young men of 14 to 18 years old who were not yet part of the establishment, and in 1881 a new grade of women clerks was created.

[157]

Women generally occupied clerical and typing grades, which were 'watertight compartments', strictly separate from comparable men's grades. Women could not obtain promotion to higher grades, but were restricted to supervising within their own grades (Holcombe 1973, p. 176). Thus women often supervised women, and men supervised men and women. The hierarchies of women were, however, usually flatter, in the sense that women supervisors were responsible for larger numbers of workers than men supervisors (ibid., p. 178) – about three times as many in the Post Office (Grint 1988, p. 94). Thus the Civil Service was also very much a site of both unities and divisions between men – with men separated off into separate grades with relatively steep hierarchies. Men, in theory at least, could rise from grade to grade until they reached the Higher or First Division, the highest grade (Holcombe 1973, p. 176).

The Civil Service is also particularly significant as the canopy within which common grades were created by men for men across departments. The Lower Division clerks and the copyists were the first grades to straddle the whole of the Civil Service and it was there that the first professional associations or trade unions were formed. The men copyists, known simply as 'writers' after 1871, were employed to do the mass of routine copying work before the advent of mechanical means. The nature and conditions of the work caused numerous grievances between these men and their superordinates. The eventual 'resolution' of this complex interplay of unities and divisions amongst men was to be the development of the typewriter. Sir Algernon West, head of the Inland Revenue, was prominent in promoting both the use of typewriters and the employment of women. By 1888 he had all important letters typed; however, there was still only one 'female typewriter' at the Foreign Office; the Admiralty had a machine but no woman to operate it (Cohen 1965, pp. 151–2). It was not until 1894 that the status 'woman typist' became an established Civil Service grade. Even in 1914 there were only a few hundred such women typists concentrated in about half of the departments.

The basic division amongst men in the established Civil Service was between the Higher Division (which became the First Division), recruited from university graduates and destined for the top level of government, and the Lower Division (which became the Second Division), recruited from men with an 'ordinary commercial education' to perform the more routine clerical duties. From 1876 Lower Division clerks were gradually introduced into all offices. By 1888 there were 3,000 of them, and they had organized themselves into an association (Cohen 1965, p. 141). Sir R. E. Webley, the Permanent Secretary to the Treasury, complained about their combination to improve their working conditions. In his evidence to the Royal (Ridley) Commission of 1888 (Second Report of the Royal Commission 1888, p. 17) he reported: 'These men act practically like one man, and bring all their political influence to bear in a manner of which we have seen the effect.' As to the quality of their work there was, officially at least, nothing but praise (1888, p. xiv). However, this distinction was further elaborated, with the increasing amounts of mechanical work within the Second Division leading to the creation in 1896 of a new lower-paid clerical grade of male 'assistant clerk'; and the inevitable overlap between First and Second Divisions led to the creation of male 'supplementary' or 'intermediate' clerks (Holcombe 1973, p. 173).

The MacDonnell Commissioners, reporting in 1912–13, still considered that women should not be eligible for open competitions; that where women were employed they should be separated from men; and that the Marriage Bar, whereby women were required to resign on marriage, should be retained (Cohen 1965, p. 65). The First World War and the Sex Disqualification (Removal) Act 1919 changed this to an extent, though not conclusively (Walby 1986, p. 157). Indeed, the Marriage Bar, the organizational authorization of 'celibacy', was not completely removed till 1946 (see p. 156).

Thus men were clearly very capable of dominating other men as well as women. Men maintained control of the Civil Service by confining women to lower grades and by placing women in specialist occupations, for example school inspectors for 'women's subjects'. This was reinforced by divisions between men, as noted in the examples above. This gendered grading was itself designed, managed, and accomplished by particular men, even though individual senior men civil servants, such as Fawcett and West, were progressive in their own terms and within their own contexts. The strict division of men and women was part of men's power and sense of themselves, even if women were often willing actors in this process (see Lewis 1988). For one thing, clerical work and other work for the state was relatively attractive compared with factory work, especially for middle-class women (Davies 1982). Additionally, men had a special place in the higher levels of the Treasury in controlling the personnel, establishment, and structure of the Civil Service, including the general belief that the appropriate position for women was subordinate (Zimmeck 1988, p. 89).

While it may be unwarranted to see bureaucratic ways and means as *essentially 'male'*, the connections between bureaucracies and masculinities are *socially and historically intense*. The modernization of bureaucratic rules and procedures certainly reinforced the power of men in most instances.

Managerial work and managerial organizations

Changes in professional and state organizations, and the reorganization of men's power there, have been closely paralleled by changes in capitalist and managerial work. Just as professions may be seen as the organization of people work, and state bureaucracies as the socialization of reproduction, similarly 'economic' categories of people are also (or even fundamentally) reproductive categories (pp. 94, 146). Capitalist work is itself reproductive work: reproduction is subordinated to the power and demands of capital and capitalists. Similarly, capitalist work is also people work subordinated to the machine, production line, financial investment, or profit-making process.

As with the two previous sections I am concerned here with historical change in both a particular kind of work – in this case managerial work – and particular kinds of organizations and organizational forms – in this case managements. Managerial work can be thought of as a specialist kind of work that often, though not always, involves elements of people work and office work. In particular, managerial work is people work and office work with corporate authority and control of resources. That authority and control may be as a relatively autonomous manager of, say, a single factory, or as a member of an occupational stratum called 'management'. Thus, in focusing on historical changes in managerial work and managements, and their implications for the construction of public men and public masculinities, I shall look, first, at the management of factories, and, secondly, at the growth of the occupation of management, managerial organizations, and managerialism.

The management of factories

Nineteenth-century factories were often organized far less rigidly than contemporary factories.[13] Additionally, there was a vast range of forms of factory organization operating in the middle years of the nineteenth century, varying by industry, region, religion, size of factory, degree of stability and change, technology and industrial process, as well as different social relations and relationships. Much hinged on the nature of the interrelation of gender with technical and technological arrangements. Of special importance was the nature of the reciprocally defining relationships of the 'master' and (his) 'men'. These may have been 'feudal', 'conflictual', 'paternalist(ic)'; 'familiar'; based on family, locality, economic necessity; or some combination of all three. The development of more fervent unionism in the late 1860s was a special factor, but it would be unwise to overstate its general impact on the organization of men in factories, or their sense of economic class solidarity. This developed partly from a sense of place and partly from the gradual formation of more organized forms of bargaining in wages and conditions – a process facilitated by the *reciprocal* organizations of workers and capitalists. For example, the National Federation of Associated Employers of Labour was supported by many of the leading employers of Lancashire and the West Riding, and became directly involved in parliamentary lobbying on the labour laws of the early 1870s (Joyce 1980, p. 170). This was not so much in opposition to unionism, as a response to it. In his testimony to the Labour Law Commissioners in 1875, the Federation's chairman, R. R. Jackson of Blackburn, praised the responsible behaviour of trade unionists in his area, and the amicable relations of master and men (Labour Law Commissioners 1875, pp. 123–4).

A particular controversy has been the possible impact of factory size on class organization (see Foster 1974). This debate in our context could be extended to consider the implications for labouring men's sense of solidarity with each other, both as manual workers and as men. While large size (itself associated more with certain industries and certain regions) generally allows greater numbers of people to meet and to share social experiences, it is mistaken to see this as the prime basis of the formation of class consciousness or social solidarity, amongst men or women (see Giddens 1981, pp. 202–7). Patrick Joyce (1980, p. 161) notes, for example, that large employers were often more popular than small employers, where familiarity sometimes bred contempt. This suggests comparison with French historical studies which argue for an increase in class consciousness at each end of the scale, in both large and small factories (Hamilton 1967).

Partly because of these complexities, and possible inconsistencies (cf. Foster 1974), Joyce (1980) suggests that a more important distinction in factory culture was between the 'feudal', often larger and more distant, and the 'familiar', often smaller and more immediate, even though even this broad contrast should not be overstated. In the extreme case, Beatrice Webb (1971, p. 180) recognized in the mid-1880s the relative absence of class feeling in the familiar structure of Bacup: 'class feeling hardly exists because there is no capitalist class; those mills which are not companies being owned by quite small men of working class origins and connected with working people.' In other small familiar factories, workers may be involved in a mixture of experiences, of both equality and deference, with owners.

In the pre-bureaucratic factory, control by owners over workers was maintained by a variety and often a combination of means, some coercive, some accommodating. In some situations employers were aloof and magisterial, to be looked up to by workers; in some, it was the sons of the owners who acted as the managerial 'middle men', keeping the shop until their time came to move onward and upward; in others, control was enacted by managers as 'the connecting link between the firms and the actual workers' (Beckett 1892, p. 12). As Joyce (1980, p. 162) remarks: 'control over factory authority was the mark of the most successful paternalist regimes.' Samuel Morley, a large and prominent employer in the 1880s, used his managers to achieve 'the fullest and freest fraternity' with the hands. He also counteracted the effects of increasing size of operations by creating a system of junior partnerships 'to accrete the firm's experience around his own person' (ibid.). These various forms of control involved a definite chain of command, the perpetuation of male authority and the authority of men, and, particularly significantly, a means of transmission of authority across generations, whether by the patriarchal line or the regeneration of managers.

In some of the smaller firms and mills of the late nineteenth century, control was maintained and confirmed in much more subtle, albeit paternalistic, ways. Joseph Wilson, a Bradford employer of 250 workers, made various social and cultural provisions, including his 'Annual Gathering', 'Yearly Letter', tea-evenings at his home, personal birthday cards for workers, use of first names, as well as a detailed knowledge and interest in the personal lives of his workers (Wilson n.d.). Other industrialists taught their illiterate workers basic literacy. As the son of mill-owners, Sir Gerald Hurst notes that in his own childhood in the 1880s and 1890s family household wants were supplied by the relatives of his father's workpeople: 'There was . . . a sense of personal intimacy and of common interests between master and man. The later growth of amalgamations and large "combines" destroyed this sense' (Hurst 1942, p. 5).

Principles of duty and honour also often figured in the building of industrial business. Max Weber's (1930) *The Protestant Ethic and the Spirit of Capitalism* should perhaps have been entitled *The Masculine Ethic* or *Protestant Masculinity and the Spirit of Capitalism*. Masculinity was affirmed in management through a mixture of denial, earthly works, achievement, and salvation. External works complemented internal denial: masculinity was a combination of doing and not-doing.

These various complex associations of age, economic class, status, gendered identity, generation, and masculinities were subject to major change with the mechanizations, automations, bureaucratizations, and managerialisms of the late nineteenth century. The transformation of factories entailed movements from relatively loosely organized arrangements, based on steam power and machine technology, to more rigid sets of structures organized increasingly on electric power and automated technology. Dan Clawson (1980) has specifically argued that this movement from a relatively craft-based system to modern methods of production was both an explanation for the establishment of bureaucratization, and a means of greater control by capitalists over the productive process and the workers who maintained that process. In this sense, bureaucratization of factories is one of the many ways in which a difficult and sometimes spurious consensus is maintained over outright conflict – conflict that would be inconvenient, in the short term at least, to all concerned (see Burawoy 1979).

[163]

An obvious question that follows is the implication of these organized managerial masculinities for working-class men and masculinities, and indeed for middle-class men and masculinities. Men within different economic classes have generally defined themselves and others primarily through activities in the public domains, as workers, trade unionists, workmates, managers, owners, with clear implications for the construction of masculinities. Masculinities have often been assumed to be formed, to exist, and to be expressed in public domain activities, especially paid work and its associated 'class cultures of men'.[14]

Under normal working conditions, outside times of rapid change and crisis, working-class masculinities appear to be relatively stable, constructed in the *immediate* conditions of the organized workplaces rather than in the mediated conditions of social relations of reproduction and production. Under crisis conditions, for example during trade depression or strikes, men's external experiences appear more important in displaying working-class masculinities. Working-class men have tended to work in workgroups with other men, under direct supervision from other men, in difficult and sometimes dangerous working conditions, engaging in direct physical, manual, and machine labour. Accordingly, working-class masculinities can be seen as valuing such practices as group solidarity with other men, physical toughness, resistance to both authority and danger, and facility with machines.[15]

In contrast, middle-class men have tended more often to work in relative isolation from other men, under less direct supervision from other men, and indeed perhaps supervising women and other men, in more comfortable working conditions, engaging in mental labour. Middle-class masculinities can be seen as valuing such practices as independence from other men, social facilities and interpersonal skills, the embodiment of authority, and the search for comfort. Such practices and valuations of practices parallel what have sometimes been called 'traditional working-class' and 'traditional middle-class' perspectives, or, more accurately, traditional working-class and middle-class *masculinities*.

Managements and managerialism
The expansion of the management function in state, capitalist, and other organizations in the late nineteenth century was accomplished through and in turn brought into being the creation of

management as identifiable and separable collectivities of men. While all societies have their managers in some sense, what is special about late nineteenth-century developments is the formation and consolidation of a distinct, some might say 'professional', occupational grouping of managers, who made management their defining activity and occupation. In this sense, managers and managements since the late nineteenth century have been *primarily* managers, and thus quite different from monarchs, clergy, politicians, capitalists, academics, and other public men who have been managing, as a secondary activity, for centuries.

The institutional rise of (modern) management as a distinct activity is seen most clearly in the progressive separation and differentiation of ownership and control of industry and commerce, and the progressive separation and differentiation of control and labour. Furthermore, particular men, located within particular elaborated organizational hierarchies, came together in a variety of local and national management associations. In 1911 the Sales Managers' national association was established; in 1915 that of the Office Managers; and in 1920 the Industrial Administrators came together (this was later to become the British Institute of Management). At the same time, 'management' itself became recognized as a distinct area of 'academic' study, with the initiation in 1919 of three ventures: the teaching of industrial administration at Manchester Technical College; the setting up of the Oxford management conference; and the creation of a school at Cambridge under C. S. Myers leading to a number of publications on management (Child 1969).

These innovations were followed by a more general movement towards the establishment of management as an economic class grouping, very largely of men, and the ideology, or ideologies, of 'managerialism', according to which the power and expertise of management take on a special importance for the plight of society 'as a whole'. The progression towards the increased formalization of managers and of managerialism, that is, of men managers and male managerialism, was a matter both of 'improvements' in techniques of work and organization, and of the social legitimation of managerial authority (Child 1969). This ideological thesis clearly has major political implications, particularly for a reformulation of economic class analysis, whether within Marxist (Burnham 1941) or liberal variants of the malestream.

Management theory, especially 'Classical Theory' and

'Scientific Management', has generally sought, and continues to seek, universalizable prescriptions for organizing – like modern-day Baconian strategies for modern men. Not only were such methods designed for the expanding, more complex organizations of the late nineteenth and early twentieth centuries, but they also acted as a possible supposedly neutral (that is, male) organizing principle (a transcendental male signifier) against and in relation to which 'others' (as the Other(s))[16] – especially women, black people, ethnic minority people – could be organized by white men of the managerial class. This applied in different ways in different societies at different times – to women entering white blouse occupations in increasing numbers, to the organization of European immigrants to the New World at the turn of the century, to the accommodation of 'all-comers', as long as they were moderately organizable to corporate life – a form of apparently democratic, yet hierarchical, non-democracy.

Management and managerialism, along with bureaucracies and bureaucratization, can be understood as places and processes of men's domination of women's labour, men's conversion of women and women's labour to signs of the supposedly rational–legal organizational process. Furthermore, many organizational functions, particularly management, provide major opportunities for people work, both in themselves and in their control of and relation to others' people work and their emotions (see Hearn 1987a, Ch. 8).

In focusing on the United States experience, Peter Filene (1986) suggests that change in the corporate 'order' brought complex challenges to men, especially middle-class men. Masculinity was no longer enacted simply through doing direct manual labour, mental toil, or fatherly acts, but *at a distance*, especially in relatively distanced, emotionally controlled corporate work. He outlines how such early twentieth-century 'manliness' was enacted in complexity: 'Behind their sternness lies the further meaning of "character"': 'without control, his sexual appetites would make a beast of him . . . [y]et control must not go too far, must not tame his manhood away' (p. 70). In the parlance of ethnography, masculinity had to be 'done'.[17]

In these and other ways, *men managers* and *men managements* are significant social groupings in public patriarchies, both in the structural organization of tasks (the social relations of reproduction/production), and in the immediate supervision of tasks (the technical relations of reproduction/production).[18] The social structural and technical relations are further implemented *in particular ways*, including, for example, the enactment of different 'styles', that is gendered styles, of management and leadership. Sometimes styles are labelled autocratic, democratic, liberal, or even 'macho'.[19]

With men's historical domination of management, where the vast majority of organizations have been and are managed by men, the very notions of 'manager' and 'management' have particular gendered significance: 'managers' and 'managements' represent men, or perhaps more precisely the cultural 'male'. Similarly, every manager who is a man has a signification in terms of men's domination, whatever his own particular intentions, even his possibly benevolent practices. This kind of interpretation of men/ management is part a matter of social meaning; it is also partly a question of their access or potential access to networks of men's power and male power, and the possibility, perhaps probability, of their benefiting from such networks regardless of what they do.

An interesting and important exception to the general association of 'men'/'maleness'/'masculinity' and management lies in personnel management, and its subordination to other managements, usually of men. Karen Legge (1987) has traced the origin of personnel management from the activity of 'welfare workers', largely 'gender-typed' for women, in the pre-First World War factories. In 1927, 95 per cent of the members of the Institute of Personnel Management were women. The occupation was at this time subordinated, defined as secondary and marginal relative to the 'main tasks' of management. Its recent higher profile has been the medium and outcome of changing industrial relations, and with it the large-scale influx of men. By 1970 more than 80 per cent of IPM members were men. Thus management is itself a site, or set of sites, for gender divisions, relations, and subordinations within it and between its sectors (Collinson & Hearn 1990, 1992).

Rationality, neutrality, and the processing of information

Much of what I have talked about in this chapter has concerned large modern organizations and their formal structures. In this final section I want to shift the discussion towards the question of *process*, that is, organizational processes, by considering the issue of *information-processing* as a prelude to the discussions of the next chapter. In particular, organizational processes of information and information-processing are themselves forms of power, with the increasing impact of new technologies for the production and circulation of information. 'The 'Information Society', the 'information organization', and the 'informationization' or 'informization' thesis can all be seen as variants on the rationalization theses of Weber and others, and similarly relevant to the construction of men and masculinities.[20] Though not spelt out by Weber, the rationalization thesis seems to have at least three major implications for men and masculinities:

(1) it is mostly men who manage the introduction of rational method;
(2) men and masculinities will be affected by the progressive introduction of rational method;
(3) what is understood by rational method will be reciprocally related to men and masculinities.

In many respects, 'informization' raises implications for men that are parallel to, if rather more complicated than, those around rationality and masculinity. Thus we may note:

• the involvement of men in implementing the control and circulation of information;
• the impact of information and its circulation on the construction of men and masculinities; and
• the way what counts as information is reciprocally related to men and masculinities.

These extra complications include, first, the inherent variability and disaggregated nature of information, unlike the singularity, or tendency to singularity, of rational method; secondly, the fact that much of the circulation of information is done by women workers, such as keyboard operators, even though the control of such information may remain with men; and thirdly, the quality of *potential* use that information has. Information is a form of value of *non-immediacy*, which in turn may reinforce many aspects of public men's power and dominant public masculinities in organizations. As information circulates in greater quantity, yet with less general (public) access, the control of that information becomes more important. And where control and power are important issues, so too is often the presence of men.[21]

The development of a processual approach to organizations draws together a number of strands: the growth of tertiary (service) and quaternary (information) sectors; the inadequacies of overly narrow approaches to labour process; the increasing use of and reference to visual and other images in organizations. Together these and other processes contribute to the increasing complexity of organizations and organizational dynamics – and simultaneously their reduction to sign.

CHAPTER 8

Organizations of men (2): processes, sexualities, and images

This chapter examines *processual* change in public patriarchies, particularly *qualitative* change in organizations and the construction of public men and public masculinities. Processual, qualitative change in organizations is discursive and reproductive – the pluralizing of discourse, and the reproduction of organization (Burrell & Hearn 1989). Such processes, reproductions, and discourses are generically and sexually encoded (Grosz 1987). Accordingly, this chapter will focus on the connections between qualitative changes in organizations and changes in sexuality, particularly men's sexualities, in the public domains.

In looking at men in this way I draw on the concepts of organization sexuality (Hearn & Parkin 1987) as a fundamental aspect of the reproduction of organization, and the sexuality of organization (Hearn *et al.* 1989). Organization sexuality refers to the *simultaneous* enactment of organization and of sexuality. One does not precede the other; both coexist and refer to the other, reproducing each other and themselves. The dominant form of organization sexuality in most organizations involves domination by men and men's sexualities.

As already discussed, the period 1870–1920 – the period of the development and intensification of monopoly capitalism, public patriarchies, modern imperialism, and much more – involved quantitative change in the number and size of organizations, their corporate size and power, their increasing power, and the reproduction of masculinities. It also saw major changes in patterns of consumption, distribution, retailing, mass media, the form and intensity of movement and communication, and representation and imagery. These are therefore also matters of qualitative change in organizations.[1]

Relevant specific developments of *both* organizations and

(men's) sexualities during this period included the extension of state intervention in the family, child welfare, homosexuality, and prostitution; the growth of the film industry and other mass media organizations, and the accompanying media stars, mass popular pornography, use of sexuality in advertising and public relations, and 'girlie calendars'; the advent of typing office technology and the female secretary, and her particular significance in male fantasy; the expansion of sexology, the academic, medical, and clinical study of sex, the sex hygienist movement, and the more popular sex manuals; the popularization of sex scandals; the recognition of sexual harassment as a workplace issue; the rise of censorship, and a vast range of public 'moral panics' and 'outrages'.

The increasing power of these public domain processes upon the person, in technology, imagery, law, and so on, contributed to modern forms of men's sexualities – in public, in organizations, in men's psyches. The bombardment of the individual by the sexualization of everything, and especially of (every) woman (MacKinnon 1979; Haug 1987), has become one element in the making of 'modern masculinities'. Together these changes form part of a broad movement towards public patriarchies, not as forces external to men, but rather (re)produced by men. Thus the construction of the *modern* experience for men entails a developing relationship of modernism, masculinities, and men's sexualities,[2] consciousness of that sense of modern masculinities and men's sexualities, the ability to look at the 'male' self (see Afterword), at other men, and at women, at a distance – in short, an increasing normalization in the interplays of organizations and sexualities.

Through these historical processes, sexualities are increasingly *matters* of public domain discourse. Men's sexualities were both subject to (objects of) more direct public domain control, and subjects of their own public domain discourses. The private was placed more fully into the public, and in so doing the *possibility* of control of private oppression was more than compensated by the *actuality* of public oppression.

Three main kinds of connections between organizational processes and men's sexualities are now examined: first, the conceptualizing of *internal organizational processes* as men's (hetero) sexualities; secondly, the specific significance of various *fragmentations of sexualities*, including the retailing and consumption of the

[171]

visual in distribution, the mass media, and travel; and, thirdly, the understanding of *the very forms of men's organizations* as inter-relating sexual fragmentations and unities. In describing these complex, often fragmented interrelations of organizations and sexualities, it is necessary to reflect this in the very organization of this chapter.

Organization (hetero)sexualities

The connections between organizations (that is, publicly patri-archal organizations) and sexualities (that is, men's sexualities) are many. In contrast with the mythology of much public discourse, organizations are intensely sexualized, and men's sexualities are intensely organized. Some of these links between organizations and sexuality have already been outlined – including the changing interrelations of the elements and facets of public patriarchies, most obviously in the changing relations of the public and private domains; the growth of state and capitalist interventions; and the growth of organizations themselves. These historical changes do not, however, convey the processual and qualitative nature of the connection between organizations and sexualities – the kind of connections summed up in the phrases 'organization sexuality' and 'the sexuality of organization'. In these perspectives, organi-zations are not *imposed upon* sexuality, and sexuality does not *infiltrate* organizations; rather organizations and sexualities occur and recur simultaneously, mutually defining and reciprocally reinforcing each other. The dominant and dominating form of sexuality was and is heterosexuality, and particularly men's heterosexuality, even though the detailed structuring of that heterosexuality in the public domains has changed. Organization sexuality is both consumption, consumption of itself, and pro-duction, production of itself. For these reasons it is necessary to address the reciprocal construction of (capitalist) organization and men's sexualities more directly. These qualitative developments occurred partly in and through the changing relations of capitalist production and reproduction. Sexuality was inevitably affected both by the general nature of capitalist relations and by specific changes in technology. In Marxist terms, sexuality, like humanity, was alienated. Furthermore, as already discussed, capitalist enterprises usually were and remain patriarchal, in effect little patriarchies of their own. Such supposedly direct connections between economic relations and sexual relations do not fully capture the subtlety of qualitative change at that time.

In order to follow this processual approach, it may be helpful to move back a little to what preceded the transformations and experiences of the late nineteenth century. These events acted as the historical contexts to the movements to public patriarchies, not as some primordial hierarchy, but as linked processes of change. Both state organizations and capitalist organizations have long been sites of men's sexuality. However, the intensification of capitalist industrialization was certainly accompanied by increasing concerns with sexuality within and around capitalist enterprises. An early example of an attempt to exclude sexuality from the workplace was the sacking in 1772 of the head accounts clerk by Josiah Wedgwood on the grounds of embezzlement, extravagance, and sexual misdemeanours (McKendrick *et al.* 1983, p. 61). Considerable debate on the dangers of sexuality ensued, for example, in the passing of the 1833 Factory Acts, which themselves need to be placed in the wider context of state intervention in education and the family in the 1830s (see pp. 111–12).

The growth of state and capitalist organizations was not just a means of 'intervention', of dominating women and men in the private domains, it was also itself an arena of social relations, of social–sexual processes. Whereas in the early days of capitalist development there had been mixed-gender and indeed mixed-age workplaces, by the 1830s and 1840s this was beginning to be challenged and changed.

Sylvia Walby (1986, p. 115) approaches this phase in terms of the patriarchal nature of dominant discourse, and especially 'the male bourgeoisie's hypocritical stance on female sexuality'. She continues (pp. 115–16):

> Publicly, these men adhered to the condemnation of non-marital sexuality, particularly for women. In so far as conditions in paid work were held to encourage female sexual activity then they were especially condemned. The factories were believed to encourage sexual contact between the female operatives and the male operatives and masters. The wages enabled women to buy drink and consequent drunkenness was also held to encourage 'immorality' . . . .

[173]

The conditions in the mines particularly horrified the Commissioners who investigated them in 1840–2. The presence of men and women together working in near darkness was held to be an invitation for all sorts of immoral practices. The commission was obsessed with the sexual conduct of the colliery women. . . . Behaviours such as drunkenness, immodesty and profanity were also held to indicate the likelihood of promiscuity. The Commissioners focused on this aspect of women's work underground to the neglect of other aspects such as physical suffering. There are continual references to the state of undress that the male and female workers are to be found in.

The creation of mixed-gender workplaces in the mines and elsewhere appeared to raise problems for men around fear of women and women's sexuality. This also interfered with men's homosocial workgroups, and probably also provided sites for differential sexual harassment. The Parliamentary Papers of 1842 (Vol. XV, p. 24) describe the situation as follows:

In great numbers of the coal-pits of this district the men work in a state of perfect nakedness and are in this state assisted in their labour by females of all ages, from girls of six years old to women of twenty-one, these females themselves being quite naked from the waist down.[3]

In their discussion of the same period, Susan Atkins and Brenda Hoggett (1984, pp. 12–13) draw attention to the even greater concern that was expressed towards 'the greater immorality of married women who, it was alleged, left their homes and families, neglected their domestic duties and forced their menfolk to seek the comforts of public houses, thus subjecting the next generation to "all the evils" of a disorderly and ill regulated family'.[4] They go on to explain that '[t]hroughout the century both male and female workers felt it necessary to give evidence to rebut . . . such assertions of immorality. Yet it seems to have persisted in the public imagination. In the Report of the Royal Commission on Labour in 1893 the Lady Commissioners were still discussing the employment of married women in these terms' (Atkins & Hoggett 1984, pp. 200–1).

Mid-nineteenth-century movements towards 'separate spheres'

[174]

for women and men were uneven, incomplete, contested, and rent by contradictions. The 'separate spheres' thesis can be easily overstated, not least because the extent of separation in employment was highly related to economic class and the use of the marriage bar in employment was variable (see pp. 144, 156). Even so, this period can be characterized by a greater development of homosocial workgroups than was previously the case. This facilitated the establishment of highly ambiguous homosocial/homophobic organizational cultures amongst men, which in some cases harnessed homosexual or homoerotic desire in collective endeavour (see pp. 205–7). From the 1860s there were also counter-movements against this with the entry of women into specific areas of employment, including professional, office, retail, and other service work. Statements such as that made at the Trade Union Congress in 1877 that 'It is the duty of men and husbands to bring about a condition of things when wives should be in their proper sphere at home instead of being dragged into competition of livelihood with the great and strong men of the world'[5] should be understood as set in the context of opposition to women's organizing not as unfettered proclamations. The organization of women and public consciousness of women as women were rapidly growing through women's separate organization, trade union and workplace organizing, the increasing activity of some middle-class women, and the beginnings of modern feminism.

The limited entry of some women into public domain organizations alongside, or usually subordinated to, men was thus both a well-established and a novel feature. This is particularly significant for the understanding of the place of the sexual in the modern office, and in cultural life more generally. Of special interest here is the occurrence of sexual harassment, which is often at high levels when women enter what are traditionally men's domains and occupations.[6]

A detailed account of such events has been provided by Cindy Sondik Aron (1987) in her remarkable study of United States federal government offices in Washington, DC from 1860 to 1900. In 1864, only three years after women had been appointed as clerks in the Treasury Department, a special congressional committee was instituted to investigate 'certain charges against the Treasury Department'. This reported that some men supervisors had sexually harassed and propositioned women clerks. This fed into men's contemporary fears of both the corrupting influence of sexually immoral women (as whores?), and the corruption of sexually innocent women (as virgins?) both by other women and by men.[7] These fears were spelt out by John Ellis (1869) in his book, *The Sights and Secrets of the National Capital*, according to the logic that it was government employment that corrupted women: 'The acceptance of a Government Clerkship by a woman is her first step on the road to ruin.' The question of the potential and actual immorality of women clerks remained a popular, and often scandalous, issue for men journalists, writers, and others in the public domains in the late nineteenth century. This appeared to have special poignancy in the Washington case, perhaps by way of the assumed contrast for men between the serious weight of the men's world of federal government and the 'sexual danger' of and to women. There are two more general points to be drawn out here: first, there is for men the continuing interrelation of asexuality (in this case of federal government itself) and sexuality – asexuality as sexuality;[8] second, there is the assumption of women *entering*, as sexual, the supposedly pre-fixed, 'normal' world of men. According to Aron (1987, p. 169):

> These working women posed an enormous challenge to the Victorian middle class because they threatened to invalidate the standards by which middle-class society judged a woman's character. . . . Where male and female spheres remained distinct, society [men?] could easily distinguish the 'good' from the 'bad'. Respectable ladies exercised great care, especially when outside their homes, churches, or schoolrooms, to follow rules of decorum that guaranteed their reputation as virtuous women. But those women who left their sphere, flouted the rules, and placed themselves in compromising situations . . .

Thus the understanding of sexual dynamics in these offices has to be placed in the wider interrelations of the public and private domains. Though further reports were made of sexual harassment in the 1870s and 1880s, major attempts were made to maintain 'the highest standards of sexual morality' and sexual etiquette, especially on the part of women. Men, who were generally considered to be subject to uncontrollable sexual urges, were allowed more latitude, but even they could be punished, to the point of dismissal, for sexual misconduct, particularly adultery.

[176]

The rapid expansion of women Post Office clerks after 1871 raised the problem of how to accommodate women and men workers. The place of women clerks and other women workers was also certainly contested here in the eyes and practices of men (Walby 1986, pp. 144–55), with women sometimes seen as sexually vulnerable (Anderson 1976, p. 39), at others as *sources* of sexualization.[9]

> [I]n 1872 the Post Office experimented in employing male and female staff and putting them in the same room. 'It was considered to be a hazardous experiment' wrote a senior official at the time, 'but we have never had reason to regret having tried it . . . it raises the tone of the male staff by confining them during many hours of the day to a decency of conversation and demeanour which is not always to be found where men alone are employed.'
>
> (Delgado 1979, p. 39)

This 'civil' approach was in contrast to those organizations where it was forbidden for women and men to use the same lavatories. In 1889 a 'progressive' government department employing two women put them in an upper floor room and had a separate women's lavatory installed so they would be completely free 'from any danger or interference'. Other strategies of men in the Civil Service included locking a number of women in a room and serving meals to them through a hatch in the wall (Delgado 1979, p. 39).

During the 1870s and 1880s men in effect constructed new organizational rules to structure sexuality in the office. In some ways this can be seen as an extension of men's bureaucratic control over the sexual, with supervisors and managers able to determine arrangements and sanctions. However, by the 1890s sexual dynamics were at the same time becoming more informal and more complex, with 'a large gray area where innuendo, flirtation, and bantering became the norm . . . behavior between men and women which would have once been regarded as improper was by the 1890s, often seen as innocent. The line between good natured, "innocent" flirtation and impropriety had become muddled and difficult to determine' (Aron 1987, p. 174). This was particularly apparent from a Congress investigation into the Pensions Bureau in 1892 following news of corruption and

[177]

scandal, in which a number of highly ambiguous incidents were reported, on the borderline between the friendly and the sexual, with very different interpretations by the women and men concerned. Such a working environment was 'less formal and more relaxed, but still fraught with the potential for sexual exploitation and manipulation' (p. 178).

While it is very difficult to reconstruct definite levels of sexual harassment, it is possible to attend to its organizational recognition and naming. A particularly interesting series of incidents in 1891–2 at the Evans and Berry Weavers, Nelson, Lancashire, has been researched by Lesley Fowler (1985). Controversy was high about the use by the men overlookers of the 'slate and board' system, in which the mainly women weavers' productivity was chalked up for all to see, along with sometimes derogatory comments such as 'won't be here much longer' and 'must try harder'. The system was hated by the weavers and anger at resistance from the employers to its abolition became intermingled with complaints about sexual harassment, 'immoral language and conduct' by one of the overlookers, Houghton Greenwood. A strike followed from December 1891 to March 1892, with widespread support from Nelson and elsewhere. Attempts at arbitration were initially thwarted, but eventually the overlooker agreed to submit to an independent Committee of three local clergymen. The inquiry's final award read as follows:

> As rumours of a very odious character respecting Houghton Greenwood are in circulation it is necessary and only just to him to state that no charge of actual adultery has been made against him, and that there was nothing in the evidence to show that such a charge could have been made. The offences complained of by the Weavers' Committee were not of so serious a character; they accused him exclusively of language and conduct tending to immorality. After most carefully and thoughtfully weighing up all the evidence brought before us on both sides, during an investigation extending over four days we are reluctantly compelled to come to the conclusion that Houghton Greenwood has been guilty, first of making immoral proposals to a married woman, and secondly, of using indecent language to other females. . . . It was with the deepest regret that we learned during the inquiry that the offences of which we have been compelled to adjudge

[178]

Houghton Greenwood guilty, are not uncommon among men who have the oversight of the female operatives in other mills, and as ministers of religion, we most earnestly appeal to the employers of labour to practically recognise their duty in this matter and to seriously consider how essential it is to the happiness and well being of those under their charge as well as to their own credit to make the moral conduct of their workpeople a subject of nearer concern and of greater importance. We also wish to state that in our opinion the action of the Weavers Union in endeavouring to guard the morals of the workpeople is highly commendable . . .

What subsequently happened to the overlooker is unclear, yet the significance of the episode lies in the recognition, first, that 'the offences . . . are not uncommon among men who have the oversight of the female operatives', and, second, that public intervention in such an issue, and its future prevention, was legitimate. Recognition of sexual harassment and intervention against it go hand in hand in the same public discourse.[10]

By the early twentieth century, popular literature published stories of the experiences of women who had migrated to the cities to find work and had found sexual harassment instead or as well. In such ways, sexual harassment in the workplace sits alongside interventions in 'child saving', against 'white slavery', and associated welfare movements and media genres. Such public displays were sexual twice over – in the act and in the representation.

The sexual dynamics of many organizations were by the end of the last century intensely ambiguous – both formal and desexualized, and informal and sexualized; mixed-gender/heterosexual and homosocial; involving routine sexual harassment, and sometimes recognizing such behaviour as illegitimate. These conditions and contradictions have provided material for the development of men's sexualities, modern and fragmented. Not only may men portray women as asexual (virgin)/sexual (whore?), but men's sexualities may be founded on both the inclusion of women in heterosexual domination, and the exclusion of women from men's homosocial groups and homosexual subtexts (R. Wood 1987). These interplays of organizational processes and men's sexualities were thus far from monolithic. They were both

[179]

structured and fragmented; separated through the differential impacts of labour powers, exchange values, and use values. Furthermore, the turn of the century also brought increasing specialization in sexual organizations, including the industrialization of the brothel, and the increasing creation of sexualized, or parasexualized (that is, where sexuality is 'deployed but contained, carefully channelled rather than discharged'), organizational cultures and representations. This entails not just the growth of 'sexual organizations', that is, organizations with sexual goals, services, or clients, but also developments in the type and meaning of sexuality, including its separation off as manipulatable (in some cases, though not necessarily, as a commodity) and manageable (Bailey 1990). Accordingly, a minority of men specialized in the management and marketing of pleasure and leisure, and thus the negotiation and control of the sexualities and sexual display of a larger number of both women and men, for consumption by a still larger number.

Visual fragmentations, fragmenting sexualities

Further, more subtle modes of fragmentations in organizational processes and men's sexualities derived from the selling and buying of the visual; the expansion of the mass media; and travel and transport. The interrelations of these fragmentations inevitably reproduced further fragmentations.

The selling and buying of the visual

Processual, and indeed sexual, transformation of organizations cannot be understood without attention to the visual. Not only was the late nineteenth century the period of the growth of the service sector and the organizational consolidation of consumption, it was also the period of the increasing interrelation of consumption and the visual. Consumption was increasingly organized through the visual and the visual itself was consumed. The visual was connective and pervasive: scenes were seen. Public discourse included the changing reproduction of visual knowledge, publication, image manufacture. This was and is predominantly organized and managed by men; it was and largely remains knowledge and imagery between men, even when, perhaps especially when, it is of women. Public discourse, like the malestream, is dominantly 'male discourse'. The reproduction of 'public men' is partly in discourse and image, particularly sexual imagery, and in turn these can have an immense impact on men's sense of ourselves, our masculinities. In that way, masculinities are ideology. Major sites that will be examined to explore these issues include retailing, advertising, and, in the next section, photography and film.

Retailing
Retailing, wholesale, distribution, consumption, and service organizations were transformed from their typically small-scale, often one-man structure in the mid-nineteenth century (Holcombe 1973, pp. 104–5) to more consolidated patterns in the late nineteenth century. This often entailed relatively few men managers or proprietors having authority and supervision over relatively large numbers of women. These changes have a further significance for the relations between women and men, because of women's special place *as customers*. Growth in the *scale* of distribution combined with gradually increasing numbers of women working in shops and similar establishments.[11]

Accordingly, it is important to note that

[Employment] protection was only very slowly extended to traditionally female areas of work and those where women predominated. It seems as though the *'family type'* conditions which existed – for instance, for domestic servants and living-in shop workers – were felt to be protection enough. Yet women in these occupations appear to have been more at risk from sexual harassment and subsequent loss of livelihood.
(Atkins & Hoggett 1984, p. 13; my emphasis)

A series of Shop Acts and related Acts were passed between the 1886 Shops Act, instituting a maximum of 74 hours work per week, including mealtimes for young persons under 18, and the 1913 Act, which introduced a maximum of 64 hours excluding mealtimes. It was not until the 1963 Offices, Shops and Railways Premises Act that shop workers gained the same conditions as factory workers.

Meanwhile, changes in the form of retailing included the growth of the multiples and chain stores, the co-operative

[181]

societies, and the department stores (W. Fraser 1981). The department store developed gradually from the 1830s with the expansion, particularly in London, of linen, drapery, and clothing
retailing, initially for the middle-class, and particularly women
middle-class, clientele. The significant feature of Kendal, Milnes
and Faulkner's Watts' Bazaar (Manchester), Emerson Bainbridge's
(Newcastle), Anderson's Royal Polytechnic (Glasgow), Duncan
McLaren's (Edinburgh), William Whiteley's ('The Universal
Provider', Westbourne Grove, London), was that a wider variety
of materials, garments, other products, and even funeral services,
were offered under the same roof. Davis Lewis's began in
Liverpool in 1856, branched out to Manchester in 1880 and
Birmingham in 1885. Lewis's, 'The Friends of the People', also
encouraged browsing, so much so that a court action was brought
against them for encouraging crowds to gather, and so causing a
nuisance. In 1884 the first Marks and Spencers 1d Arcade was
opened in Manchester. Gordon Selfridge, an American, who had
worked at Marshall Field's store in Chicago, opened his Oxford
Street store to a blaze of publicity in 1909. By this time variety,
quality, and reasonableness of price were not enough – seats, lifts,
escalators, restaurants, and rest rooms were also necessaries. Like
Lewis, Selfridge encouraged browsing – the visual economy was
on a rapid rise; the aim, in the words of Selfridge, was 'to
reproduce the subdued and disciplined atmosphere of the gentleman's mansion' (Adburgham 1964, p. 238). These were places
where senses of sight, smell, and touch were appealed to in a more
total experience than applied in simple acts of buying.

At about the same time the first supermarkets were being
established in the United States. The self-service Frank Munsey's
Mohican Stores were opened in 1896, and in 1910 the Alpha Beta
operation was opened and converted to self-service in 1912
(Markin 1963). Also in 1912 the Atlantic and Pacific Tea
Company began the first large group of 'economy stores' based on
the cash-and-carry principle and depending on rapid turnover at
low markup. In 1916 the retailing innovator, Clarence Sanders,
developed the Piggly-Wiggly Store, his first self-service grocery
outlet, in Memphis, Tennessee (Brand 1965, p. 1). Other similar
establishments followed in Texas, Los Angeles, and Massachusetts
in the early 1920s.

The significance of changes in retailing and selling in the
United States has been documented for women by Susan Porter

Benson (1986) and for men by Jurgen Kocka (1980). Kocka has attended to the way that the jobs of 'sales clerk' and 'salesman' often carried for men a sense of superior status over manual workers, and the prospect of moving on to become store owners and 'businessmen'. Early twentieth-century self-help and advice books for 'salesmen' emphasized individualism and competition, using masculinized metaphors such as the aggressive 'fighter'.

Thus what is significant in retailing in this period is not just the increasing numbers of women employed, the changing relations of women and men, the development of new organizational forms and structures which men create, and within which men act, but also the creation of a dominant visual retail culture. The superstore, supermarkets, and the rest are part and parcel of contemporary life – the hypermarket, the shopping mall, and the out-of-town centre are now overtaking them. The point is that the movement to public patriarchies includes new positionings of men, new forms of authority, harassment, and imagery partly over and in relation to women shop workers and customers.[12]

Advertising
Retailing was of course facilitated by advertising and related forms of promotion of products. The earliest institutional developments were made in the United States, with the growth of mass production, non-local impersonal selling, and the means of communication, physical and visual. The first advertising agency was opened in Philadelphia in 1841 by Volney B. Palmer, and by 1845 he had opened further offices in Boston, New York, and temporarily in Baltimore (Hower 1949; Mandell 1968). This was at about the same time as the rise of pictorial journalism, primarily through woodcuts. In 1867 Carlton and Smith (subsequently the J. Walter Thompson Company) and other agencies began annual contracts with their publications. By the end of the century, we see the beginnings of agencies which had a reputation for *creative* work for their clients.

Late Victorian newspaper advertising was designed by men and, though restrained by current standards, showed clear signs of the use of women as 'mass' sex objects – perhaps most obviously in the advertising of corsets, underwear, soaps, and toiletries – but also as 'support figures' in the advertising of health products. An advert for 'Vogeler's Cures' – 'The Created Blood Purifier and Strength Restorer known to pharmacy and medicine' (*Illustrated*

London News, 25 February 1896)[13] – shows a statuesque woman, scantily clad in see-through robes, one breast bared, holding the elixir in one hand aloft before 'The Fountain of Health'. Similarly two adverts for Mr C. B. Harness' Electropathic Belt – 'exceedingly comfortable to wear, [giving] wonderful support and vitality to the internal organs of the body, [improving] the figure' – use supportive women in flowing garments, with breasts exposed or nearly so (*Illustrated London News*, 31 May 1891 and 16 May 1890). The later advert had moved from the showing of the top of a breast loose within the robe to an exposed breast with nipple.[14]

Many of these adverts used neoclassical, firm, erect, statuesque, often scantily dressed figures. Very similar to the Vogeler advert was that for 'Arctic Lamps' (*The Queen*, 30 October 1887), which featured a woman clad in a fur robe with only arms and lower legs exposed, holding the said lamp aloft and accompanied by a polar bear. Arctic lamps are 'Recommended by the leading society papers as the daintiest and most artistic form of lighting'. Other adverts used continental European, especially French, references, from the Moulin Rouge, the Folies-Bergère, and the like.[15]

End of the century advertising was more explicit still. For example, Edwards 'Harlene' for the Hair depicted a mermaid with breasts exposed (*ILN*, 11 November 1883), and Women Made Beautiful by Diano: 'Develop the Bust; fills all hollow places' (*ILN*, 12 May 1900).

Early twentieth-century advertising developed further through the adaptation of behavioural science, especially psychological techniques of persuasion. Walter Dill Scott's (1913) *The Psychology of Advertising* was one of the first of these contributions, and this was followed by a number of semi-academic books on the psychology of desire, usually labelled 'appeals', 'urges', or 'wants'. For example, Starch (1923) listed forty-five such 'appeals' in 1923, followed by Woolf's (1925) eighteen and Poffenberger's (1925) twelve. Such texts and their more recent successors have been explicit about the use, abuse, and exploitation of 'sex desire' in advertising. In this social context, it can hardly be surprising that consumption, particularly conspicuous and surplus consumption, may carry sexual meanings: consumption as sexuality.

Mass media and mass culture

Institutional expansions of the public domains were not only in the realm of capital, state, or public politics, but also matters of word-production, news, journalism, image-production, image-circulation, public domain mass culture.[16] A vital component of public patriarchies has been the establishment of mass media, organizationally dominated by men, and able to produce and circulate images (of both women and men) nationally and internationally. Less directly through the struggles and contests around such images, and particularly through the intervention of censorship, there was created what Annette Kuhn (1988) calls with respect to film 'a new public sphere'. Similarly, we might usefully think of the creation of a number of 'new public spheres' around different kinds of images.

Attention to the cultural realm also suggests some different reasons for looking at the question of men in public patriarchies at all. Cultural change has created the conditions for self-reflection for men, not just the 'intelligentsia' but on a much wider scale. Three linked examples of this process are photography, film, and psychoanalysis (see pp. 221–2). In contrast to, say, the control of sexuality by the father within private patriarchy, these developments brought back the subjective and the sexual firmly into the public domains, there to be contested and challenged.

A powerful way of conceptualizing qualitative change in the mass media in this period is through the lens of modernism. Eugene Lunn (1985, pp. 34–7) has conveniently characterized the 'unifying' features of modernism, particularly in the cultural realm, in the following way:

- aesthetic self-consciousness or self-reflexiveness;
- simultaneity, juxtaposition, or 'montage';
- paradox, ambiguity, and uncertainty;
- 'dehumanization' and the demise of the integrated individual subject or personality.

Seen in this context, 'men' and 'masculinities', as represented,[17] were fragmentary, and thus opposable by some of us, or parts of us. Part of the power of the visual is that the visual is contentious, contested, and contestable.

Photography

The increasing power of the visual was both institutional and apparent in specific visual artefacts – the photo and, a little later, the film. This has a special significance for the symbolic and visual power of the father in relation to the public and private spheres (see Ch. 6), especially the changing use and power of images in both working-class and middle-class families. Since the Reformation there had been clear religious reasons for Protestants to avoid the use of religious images as icons of the spiritual, and for some Protestant sects, most notably the Quakers, even images of family members were considered unworthy or worse. From about the mid-nineteenth century, such attitudes to family imagery began to break down, partly through the invention of photography, initially in the 1820s, and its development, especially from the 1840s onwards by Fox Talbot and others. From the 1860s, photographic printing on paper brought photography to others than the well off. The rise of family photography, of child photos, of photos in death followed.

Eric Rhode (1976, p. 21) cites a report from the *MacMillan Magazine* in September 1871 that working-class families took to the new medium with enthusiasm:

> Anyone who knows what the worth of family affection is among the lower classes, and who has seen the array of little portraits stuck over a labourer's fireplace, still gathering into one the 'Home' that life is always parting – the boy that has 'gone to Canada', the 'girl out at service', the little one with the golden hair that sleeps under the daisies, the old grandfather in the country – will perhaps feel with me that in counteracting the tendencies, social and industrial, which every day are sapping the healthier family affections, the sixpenny photograph is doing more for the poor than all the philanthropists in the world.

Of special interest was the developing popularity of war photography. Fenton was sent to the Crimean War in 1856 with the first wartime camera unit. In the American Civil War of the 1860s, the first modern war, one of the first things that the new enlistee did was to have his photo taken by another man, and then subsequently *sent back* to relatives and friends. There is a very large archive of portraits of 'manly' images of soldiers with soldiers,

soldiers with wives, and so on. Combinations of these were sometimes bound into books. At that time the Stereoview was the equivalent of the television/video now. The Anteitam stalemate of September 1862 was not only a decisive moment of the Civil War struggle for and against slavery, it was also the material basis of very many photographs of carnage of men, which had their own particular and shocking impact on consciousness and compulsive attraction.[18] The photo thus showed two very different new models of men/masculinities: a posed, proud, and imagined one, and an unposed, desperate, and physical one. Men's compulsion to view ourselves and others had entered a new historical phase, characterized by much greater prevalence, diffusion, and diversity. Family images, especially with a father absent, would never be the same again. The capacity of photography for both spectacle and surveillance (Sontag 1978) was beginning to be realized.

The middle years of the century saw a huge increase in the use of the photo. In 1847 over half a million photographic plates were sold in Paris alone; in 1862 over 105 million photographs were produced in Great Britain (Rhode 1976, p. 9). The 1870s and 1880s were marked by a considerable growth in commercial photography, particularly with the production of hand-held cameras. The fleeting and fragmentary rather than the grand and heroic uses of photography were now being more fully realized. In 1888 there was the first use of photography to decide the winner of a horse race (by Ernest Marks at Plainfield, New Jersey); and in the same year there was a famous photo of Queen Victoria 'caught' smiling at Newport, Isle of Wight, an apparent rarity in public after the death of Prince Albert in 1861 (Ford and Harrison 1983, p. 12). By the end of the century, photography had become more popular still, with the introduction of film roll cameras, developing and printing services, and in 1900 the Kodak Brownie, producing its 2½" square snapshots.

Photographs were of course not just addressed to people and animals; most obviously they were also used in advertising, catalogues, and above all postcards. Product and place were displaced onto the photo – a place and space were displaced onto products; place became an artefact. 'It must be appreciated that in the middle of the eighteenth century few people had any idea of what the rest of the country looked like' (Henderson 1974, p. 13); and even in the middle of the nineteenth century knowledge of other places was very limited. The postcard photo made place available as if *in vitro*. Place could be observed, moved, rearranged, and placed in albums, along with other places. From the 1860s there is also the beginnings of the novelty and toy market using photos in transfer prints, which subsequently developed into the souvenir trade. Place could now be placed on vases, jugs, cups, saucers, egg cups, cruets, bowls, plates, teapots, candlesticks, paperweights, and novelty figures. Space was dispersed and decentred, or at least centred only through the seer and the collector, themselves made fragmentary in the photo. Photography brought massive new possibilities for the parading of men, imaging men, in the public domains (including the modified publicness of living room, made public through the icon of the outside world) – both in established set positions as father, soldier, owner (*he* who is powerful and who is photographed) and in new fleeting, fragments of masculinities, 'taken' in a moment, held by others (in the eye of the camera) and lost. The photograph is the new public patriarch, *master* (*sic*) of the moment – giving power to the photographer, yet taking power from the photograph *to the image*, as it becomes available for circulation in the public domains.

Film[19]

The use of technologically aided projection of pictures has a long history. The invention of the magic lantern is generally attributed to Kircher, who wrote about the process in 1646, though very likely it was known earlier (McKechnie n.d., p. 176). Throughout the Victorian era a host of methods for providing 'moving pictures' – the Stroboscope, the Zeotrope, and so on – were popular (Reader 1979, p. 3). In 1872 Eadweard Muybridge took the first real photographs of an object in motion (McKechnie n.d., pp. 176–7), and shortly after[20] he devised a system for the multiple use of cameras to photograph a racehorse travelling at speed. This use of a number of exposures slightly separated in time and space was originated to settle a bet for the Governor of California. A row of twelve cameras made exposures 1/2000 of a second apart, giving a succession of pictures that could then be projected as movements. Amongst a series of pioneers, such as Etienne Marey, William Friese-Greene, and (Louis) Augustin Le Prince, it has generally been acknowledged that Thomas Edison leapt ahead with the Kinetoscope, a peep-show with a continuous film loop, in 1889 (like 'What the Butler Saw' machines), to accompany his newly invented phonograph. Recent research by Christopher Rawlence (1990) suggests that Le Prince, who was projecting film in 1888 and 1889, was a far more significant figure than formerly thought. The breakthrough of celluloid for film use may well have cost him his life when he went missing in France in 1890. The Kinetoscope had its first public showing in 1894 in New York. The projection of pictures in public, and thus to larger audiences, was begun by the Lumière family in March 1895 in Lyons, shortly followed by other forms of projector – Thomas Armat's vitascope in September 1895 (Washington), Max and Emil Skladanowsky's bioscope in November 1895 (Berlin), and Robert W. Paul's theatrograph in February 1895 (London). The first successful performance before a paying audience was by the Lumière family to thirty-three customers at the Grand Café, Paris, in December 1895. The first motion picture *show* in England was given by Trewey at the Regent Street Polytechnic in February 1896; and the first use of a music hall for this purpose was the Empire in March the same year (McKechnie n.d., p. 178). The first film show in the United States was Edison's at Koster and Bial's Music Hall, New York, in April 1896 (Brownlow 1973, p. 2; Wenden 1975, p. 10). Most of the initial subjects of these films were educational, documentary, or humorous, and indeed appear dull by current standards. Lumière's Empire programme of 1896 was in nine parts as follows:

Dinner Hour at the Factory Gate of M. Lumière at Lyons; The Landing Stage; Small Lifeboat; The Arrival of the Paris Express; A Practical Joke on the Governess; Trewey's Hat; Champs Elysées, Paris; The Fall of a Wall; and Bathing in the Mediterranean.

Though not exactly the height of sexuality, the programme significantly began and ended with leisure – the sight of bathing in the Med was an early realization of the power of sexuality in film. Also, the sight of a mass of women leaving the factory in Lumière's *Sortie des Usines*, available for *passive* viewing by men, may well have had a greater sexual interest than now.

The same period also brought the beginnings of the sexually focused film. In 1896 Edison produced *The Kiss*,[21] a discreet embrace of a middle-aged couple in a scene from 'The Widow Jones'. The following year, Biograph brought out *Fatima*, part of the act of a Coney Island bellydancer. The two films were relatively scandalous in their impact, and subsequently much imitated (Shipman 1982, p. 19). According to Wenden (1975, p. 117), '[t]he first demand for a censorship of material was lodged against *Dolorita in the Passion Dance* two weeks after its first public showing in 1896'.

By 1897 George Méliès had begun the first film studio near Paris, and by the following year there were over 1,000 films in the Lumière catalogue alone (Reader 1979, p. 5). Between 1896 and 1914 Méliès made literally hundreds of films.

Shortly after, in 1899, G. A. Smith produced *The Kiss in the Tunnel*, which included sequences of a train entering a tunnel, a man taking advantage of the darkness in the train compartment to kiss a woman, and the train leaving the tunnel. The film could be spliced to form a continuous loop, of In–Kiss–Out–In–Kiss–Out, etc., and this indeed is the form of the surviving copy (A. Lloyd 1984, p. 15). Movement and minimal plot were now combined with the sexual ritual/symbol. We can perhaps only speculate about the full succession of meanings brought about by change from the static embrace/kiss to the continuous repetition of sexual contact. However, the placing of the kiss in this dynamic though minimal narrative certainly suggests a number of intelligible meanings, including the sexual and phallic imagery of the train in the tunnel; the association of sexuality and darkness (under the covers); the fantasy of continuity, infinity, and insatiability; and, of course, the comparison of the darkened train and darkened cinema with their equivalent possibilities.

Méliès adapted the skills of pantomime, illusion, conjuring, magicianship, and trick photography to the production of film: 'people disappeared mysteriously, strange ghost-like apparitions emerged, animals changed into human beings and flew through the air . . . fast and slow motion, fade-outs, dissolves from one image to another, double or multiple exposure . . . ' (Wenden 1975, p. 17). The fantasy of theatre was granted a new *permanency* in/on film – theatre decor, curtain calls, and other devices were used, but the product was distinct. Méliès also indulged in other tricks of double exposure and superimposition on the theme of gender, just as a bus could suddenly turn into a hearse, so women suddenly turned into men (Rhode 1976, p. 34).

Film is important both historically and methodologically. The film brought qualitative change to the construction of masculinities and men's sexualities through its impact as a medium, through particular genres, and through particular examples, particular films. The innovation of film brought a mass of new images and much more. Following photography, it was a new social form that was able to provide a more total environment than static plates alone. Much early film was brought to people by the travelling 'showman' or through shows in buildings usually used for other purposes. In Yorkshire, England, it was not until 1907 that cinema halls were opened for exclusive showing of films. By 1914 there were 200 in that county (Benfield 1976, pp. 17–18). The space, the place, where films were shown was also a dark, near-total environment, often decorated as this century progressed *as woman*. The cinema was woman; it was also escape, addiction, and a site of distress, especially around sexuality. Much later, with the coming of talkies in 1926–7, an even more 'seductive' environment was possible (see J. Richards 1984), even though its acceptance was faltering at first. The film also contributed to the production of new elements which together, in combination and in contradiction, could produce masculinities. Films were and are both a direct means of showing men in public, and an indirect means of showing men by the portrayal of 'women' under the control and direction of men. Thus 'men' and 'masculinities' are displayed twice over – in image formation and in the direction of others, both women and men.

The early films provided relatively cheap alternative entertainment to the music hall, bar, and public house for working classes, both women and men. The growth of film needs to be understood not just in terms of class and gender relations but also in relation to changing ethnic relations. Many of the early films, for example D. W. Griffith's *Birth of a Nation*, appear directly intensely racist in their portrayal of immigrants. The British film *Alien Invasion* (1905) portrayed the arrival of Central European Jews at London Docks. An early film catalogue of this film suggested: 'Those are the people who oust the honest British toiler from his work and *this* the manner of their living.'[22] On the other hand, film can be seen as indirectly racist, as a means of giving basic information to immigrants on the white Anglo-Saxon, particularly American, way of life. Interestingly, East European Jewish immigrant men new to the United States played a prominent part in the film industry, particularly as directors and promoters. Their own immediate hardship was often in stark contrast to the American Dream, which some of them re-embraced in film, as if in an historical and structural overcompensation through a supreme act of will. Perhaps most famous of these men was Samuel Goldfish, who was to become Sam Goldwyn.

The early film-makers were not slow to realize the sexual potential of the film, and to develop its market potential to the masses. Early American films in the 1900s that developed sexual themes included *Wife Away, Hubby Will Play, Physical Games*, and *What The Butler Saw*. An early genre of more explicit blue movies was also produced in that period. Equally interesting were social conscience films of the silent era, in which the dangers of drink, promiscuity, and prostitution were portrayed. Much like the tabloid press of today, they engaged, often simultaneously and ambiguously, in both moral exhortation and exploitative display (Brownlow 1991). In 1907, Chicago introduced local censorship against the moral threat of films, and other American cities soon followed (Wenden 1975, pp. 23, 117–18). The following year all the nickelodeons in New York were closed down by the police, partly because of the sexual content of the films shown. In Britain, the 1909 Cinematograph Act began the system of local authority licences, although it was not until the 1920s that greater national uniformity in licensing was achieved via the Home Office recommendation of the use of the British Board of Film Censor certificates (Low 1971, pp. 55–8).[23]

Meanwhile the 1900s had seen the beginnings of both the star system and the pin-up. At first, film managements were unwilling to publicize the names of actors, fearing demands for higher wages. Public curiosity at such anonyms as 'The Biograph Girl' was eventually assuaged in the naming of Florence Lawrence and her successor, Mary Pickford (Wenden 1975, pp. 29–31) – to be succeeded by a whole series of other 'girls', 'pin-ups', and 'play-mates'. The female archetype of the girl angel of Pickford, Lilian Gish, and Mae Marsh contrasted with those of the 'femme fatale' of Theda Bara and later 'La Divine' of Greta Garbo and others. In 1903 the first use was made of a female pin-up on a company calendar by Brown Bigelow, and in 1913 the first female nude was portrayed on a commercial calendar. The pin-up represents a complex interplay of anonymity and stardom, of movement and stasis, of the fluent and the statuesque.[24]

The film star became an 'object of desire', attainable by seeing (following payments), either on the screen or in the fan and film magazines. *Photoplay* was launched in 1911. According to John Izod (1988, p. 45), such magazines 'first carry evidence from about 1916 that stars had significance in shaping Americans' emotional lives; and from about 1918 stars have clearly become objects of more than intense desire'. Such filmic desires fed into the popular appeal of consuming new releases at the first-run cinemas: the stars embodied not just consumption, but also cathexis and competition – the most famous, the most beautiful, the first seen. These cathectic rearrangements were paralleled in the expansion of the feature film, and the modernization and vertical restructuring of the film industry corporations. Corporate mergers, vertical integration, block-booking of cinemas, and star desire all went hand in hand (Izod 1988, pp. 46–7) – corporate economics was recognizable in the very look of the softly-lit, strangely glowing *face* of the star.

Through the 1900s films developed increasingly clear story lines. The earliest film shows were visual fragments, mixtures of bits of films, loops, and indeed breakdowns. By the end of the first decade of this century, visual narrative was more complete and more elaborate. In 1912 the feature film expanded from two or three to five reels, with *From the Manger to the Cross*. Serials became a favourite form, combining capitalist marketing and sexualized excitement in the problematic rescue of the heroine, as in the 1914 *Perils of Pauline* starring Pearl White.

Victorian heroism, in both ideals and practices, had arguably been superseded by the 1890s, with the loss of the frontier, imperial or natural, and the rise of large corporations and other public domain institutions.[25] In the context of this *apparent* anomie, a number of strategies were developed for the portrayal of men in film. The most obvious was the 'male sexual narrative' (Dyer 1985) of the 'male hero', reproducing an 'idealized' male (hetero)sexist ordering and interpretation of events in a continuous stream of movement, adventure, and excitement. Most usually this entailed and entails the chase, the entanglement, the climax, the world seen through the eyes of the 'heterosexual male'. It figured and still figures in sexual and romantic film, in crime and adventure genres, and in the early vice movies, themselves forerunners of modern pornography. For example, *Traffic in Souls* released in 1913 portrayed the white slavers' capture of immigrant 'girls', and the familiar chase and rescue of the 'pure' 'child' 'girl', and was hugely popular. While women were left for rescuing (virgin?) or showing as villainesses (whore?), men had a vast array of social and technological inventions to play with and within: the chase, the gang, the posse, the crash, the train, and the car; the car driving into walls and through buildings, the hero hanging on to moving trains or walking along the top of the train, the runaway train, and so on. These were used in both adventure and humorous films. There men may form primal male bonds and bands, chase other men, rescue women, or elope with them (perhaps by car, as in Hal Lloyd's *The Joy Rider*).

With the release of *Cripple Creek Bar-room* (1898) and *The Life of an American Cowboy* (1902) the western was established as a film genre, paralleling the western novel, for example Fenimore Cooper's *The Last of the Mohicans*. And in 1903 *The Great Train Robbery* was probably the first effectively organized piece of drama and film fiction, with the story of robbery, chase, and triumph of justice. The western combined both heterosexual male narrative and the homosexual subtext of homosocial groups of men.[26]

The city-dwelling anti-hero of Lloyd, Charlie Chaplin, and Buster Keaton was founded on anonymity, loneliness, clowning, and sexual ordinariness, even sexual coyness. Lloyd produced the character of Willie Work, and subsequently Lonesome Luke. In 1916 and 1917 he made nearly 100 films with variations on this character, such as *Lonesome Luke's Wild Women* and *Lonesome Luke's Lively Life*. The climax of the 'anonymous' male anti-hero/ victim was Buster Keaton in *Cops* (1922), in which he was chased by the city's entire police force. Against this was the romantic heroism of Douglas Fairbanks and Rudolf Valentino, themselves open to parody, as in Ben Turpin's *The Sheik of Araby* (1923), as well as the perpetuation of the tough male villain. These specific images were often heterosexually coupled, as in the romantic male hero and the very feminine female, embodied in Fairbanks and Pickford, married after her divorce from Owen Moore. In this sense film continued the theatrical tradition of famous couples. These images were also placed within the increasingly complex relation of content and form of the film narrative: with flashbacks, close-ups, intercutting, panning, night photography, dream sequences, lap-dissolves, tinting, irising, hooding, characterizations, descriptions of setting in which characters lived and worked, rapid alterations of action, and succession of incidents to create interest and tension (Dewey & O'Dell 1971; Wenden 1975) (as typified in the work of D. W. Griffiths).

In many respects, film, and to a much lesser extent photography, represents, is (the predicament of) men and masculinities in public patriarchies. It displays men and men's sexualities, reinforces men's power, simultaneously fragments men and men's power, makes them contentious and contested. Film is relevant for analysis and change of masculinities as a medium, in genres, and through particular films, and perhaps most obviously in the institutionalization of voyeurism. All these elements connect with the making of masculinities and men's sexualities. Modernism/postmodernism, masculinities/men's sexualities, and film itself are open to three-way *comparison* and three-way interrelationships. This perspective necessarily recognizes a number of diverse features of men in public patriarchies: the organizational and corporate colonization and control of the self by men and of men; fragmentation in imaging men/masculinities; the availability of universal, yet culturally changing, imaging of and by men; the extension of the relevance of cultural censorship; the creation of new forms of narrative; the existence of double takes, snapshots, frames frozen, of both reality in general and masculinities more particularly. The interrelations of these features certainly create paradoxes. Just as the most 'obvious' display by men in photography and film is the pin-up, so too it is the most obscure. 'Biograph girl' and Page 3 culture are the freezing of frames within the 'male sexual narrative' – a key into sexual fantasy that is known yet censored, displayed yet repressed, both consciously and unconsciously. Such displays are the display of women used by men *to display to men* – to say the silence of masculinities, the homosexual subtext of heterosexual narrative – the speaking of the unspeakable. These silent sayings also mask the real pain of women as sex objects in the production of these displays.

Time and space: travel and movement

Changing relations of the visual, service organizations and men's sexualities were intertwined with changing relations of time and space made possible by technological developments in transport and communications, movement and motion. The bicycle and the railway made mechanical mobility more normal and imaginable from the 1860s. The steam engine facilitated both commuting and holidaying: the first suburbs were created along the railways; and the first popular holiday resorts were established. For example, the expansion of Blackpool dates from the 1860s, with Raikes Hall and the Winter Gardens originally developed for the middle classes. In due course both became taken over by the working classes as they brought more lucrative returns, particularly with the creation of Bank holidays in 1871, and the staggering of annual holidays. Liquor licences were granted in the 1870s, and the 'otherness' of the resort was confirmed through exotic oriental architecture and decor in the entertainments. In 1879 the first woman 'human cannonball' performed there. From the 1880s switchback railways were introduced at Skegness and other East Coast resorts, followed by the modern roller coaster at Blackpool from 1907.

Subsequently, steam transport was supplemented by the internal combustion engine and by electric power. For example, in London the underground network of the Bakerloo (1863) and Circle (1884) lines was expanded by the Northern Line electrification of 1890. The movement to movement was confirmed at a number of different levels of experience, especially metropolitan experience. In 1899 a 'sliding staircase' was built as a central transept of the Crystal Palace in London, and in 1900 an early example of an escalator was included in the Paris Exhibition. In 1901 the first railway escalator, a kind of moving inclined platform, was constructed at Seaforth station on the Liverpool Overhead Railway. Interestingly this was dismantled in 1906 when the new Seaforth Sands station was built – one of the objections being that women's long and full skirts were frequently caught in the uncovered moving parts. An escalator proper was installed in a London station at Earls Court in 1911, and in the same year a halfpenny pleasure ride escalator was a feature of the Earls Court exhibition. Thus movement, travel, and electricity also brought dangers – in transport accidents, train crashes, fires from electric faults, cinema fires, even the invention of the electric chair, first used in August 1890. Electricity was speed and threat, the power of the unseen to produce the seen.

Late nineteenth-century modernism was partly concerned with the continuing sense of place, both geographically and organizationally, for example, in the creation of new places, suburbs, and separate institutions with specific locations in time and space. But at the same time it was also a period of transformation and 'melting' of time and space (see Berman 1983). The 'traditional' link between the spatial and the social, between physical place and social 'place', was historically disrupted, to what have now become breaking points (Meyrowitz 1986). Relative equivalences of social experience, time, space, and place were undermined by travel and indeed mass media.

The turn of the century also saw new contradictions between these fragmentations and new narratives. For example, there was an intense acceleration in the contradictions between the *universalizing* of time (and space) and the *particularizing* of time (and space), especially in the form of private time and private space, respectively (Kern 1983). Time and space could be simultaneously more global and abstract, more personal and intimate. Ways of talking of this could themselves be *global* and yet also *specific* to a particular organizational monoculture, such as that of the International Time Zone Systems. Even the global can be a (mythic) monocultural specificity.[27] The trans-temporal universal and the cult of the new could occur simultaneously.

A more specific kind of contradiction operated around the fragmentary and narrative nature of the visual. On the one hand, the growth of transport and media technologies contributes to these separations of time and space, space and place. On the other hand, the visual can be seen as a means, a literal medium, of connection between these separated realms of time and space, social place and spatial place. In the absence of any other connection, a picture, an image, an icon will do, be it a family portrait, a postcard, a picture of a 'star', or a souvenir from holiday. The visual (the connective visual) thus connects in the absence of other senses and perceptions of touch, smell, hearing, and so on. Accordingly, public and patriarchal imagery acts on and acts as these former equivalences of social experience, time, space, and place, however patriarchal they too may well have been (and no doubt were). What may be referred to as 'monopoly capitalism' for a shorthand is also publicly patriarchal in the construction of the visual – specifically as a *connective*, *narrative* social form, a glue of public patriarchies.

What have time and space, travel and movement, speed and image, to do with sexuality, men's sexualities? Well, quite a lot. I have already noted some of the ways of connecting industrial urbanization with the formulation of family, gender, and sexual practices and patterns. But the quality, process, and experience of sexuality entails much more than this. Men's sexualities, particularly those kinds of idealized and externalized sexuality that constitute such a powerful framework for men, become (are) modern; they are founded on speed and fragmentary, fleeting images. They entail separations of (sexual) experience, (sexual) time, and (sexual) place. Eroticization can be anywhere, anytime, and not just at the 'right' time and place (in fact, it's better not!). Men's modern sexualities are/invoke/seek that which is fast, smooth, sleek, slick, warm, phallic, plastic (invented in 1907), comfortable. They are/invoke/seek technologizations, measurements, scores (1 to 10?), perfection, ideal body shapes – of women and of men, for men's sexual selves exist in (the ideal of) others, body or not. For men, speed is sex(y). Men's modern sexualities are also inevitably visual, the connective visual, the glue of public patriarchies: they may be classical form, artificial, representation, showbiz, mask, make-up, celluloid, film – externalizations, externalizations of what? They can be anything, or any combination of contradictory elements – nature and culture; heterosexuality, homosexuality, narcissism, and other; hard, concrete, flow, milk, water, animal, fur, pets. They may be constructed 'especially for you', products to be consumed, speedy, 'rapido', electric, desire for the new – the contradiction of any elements and the connective visual. Through transport and media, direct sensual sex(uality), in which people's bodies are in contact, was increasingly separated off from visual sex(uality), in which 'sex' is seen and constructed in and through (the) gazes. This separation and fragmentation is sometimes presented as an apparent location of sensual sexuality in private domains and of visual sexuality in public domains. Sexuality, as in a passing glance, especially a glance where one of the actors was in motion, could be *at speed*. Sexuality could be the conjunction, or more likely *disjunction*, of sensual pleasure and distanced, separated looking. In contemporary terms, it is *the look* by men in cars at women pedestrians or men pedestrians at women in cars, of the man in the American football match crowd through binoculars at the women cheerleaders, at the Hollywood idol – the more distant, the more exotic, the more erotic, the 'better'.

Men's sexualities, fragmentations, and unities

One powerful logic of mass media representation might suggest that historical change in public patriarchies is a matter of increasing fragmentation of signs, masculinities, and men's sexualities. However, we have already seen how this would be an incomplete story – neglecting the interplay of fragmentation and narrative in film, time, the visual, and so on. The turn of the century and public patriarchies more generally are better characterized by contradictions of fragmentations and unities than by mere diversification. In this final section I shall look briefly at two further ways of understanding such contradictions in organizations: as myths of organizational monocultures, and as relations of desire between men.

Myths of organizational monocultures

The sexual dynamics of many organizations were intensely ambiguous. Alongside fragmentation, perhaps paradoxically made possible by this fragmentation, were and indeed are the significance of organizational monocultures, or more precisely the myths of monocultures.[28] For out of the various forms of fragmentations – cultural, spatial, temporal, photographic, filmic, symbolic, imaginary – men developed around the turn of the century new forms of men's cultures and new forms of organizational monocultures, typically intensely hierarchical. The most virulent and powerful forms of men's organizational monocultures were and are those that exclude women, and were/are homosocial and yet also typically heterosexual and homophobic.

In speaking of monocultures, specifically organizational monocultures, I am referring certainly not to any *substantive* unity of cause, system, or experience,[29] but rather to unities in *discourse*. To speak of 'organizational monocultures' is not to suggest monocausality; it is to relate to the dominant *presumption* of a single culture of cause, system, or experience, either *within* an organization or brought about by an organization upon the outside world. Thus, new organizational monocultures were another example of men doing what we have been doing for a long time – that is, trading in false universals. Masculinities might be thought of as examples of such tradings in false universals, as ideologies set within discourses.

[199]

Accordingly, new organizational monocultures developed apace at the end of the nineteenth and the beginning of the twentieth centuries – a vast array of new and spurious cultural unities. They were constructed – largely by men, often relatively powerful in their own arenas, and often led by white middle-class men – in art, culture, the media, politics, the corporations, management, the state, religion, charity, schools, youth movements, sport, the military, and beyond. Sometimes they comprised national organizations, sometimes local, like local sports clubs or scientific societies. Often they were 'men's clubs' or men's huts (Motherson 1979; Remy 1990), from whose fratriarchies women were excluded, and directly or indirectly abused.[30] Sometimes they involved men's organization of women. Monoculturalism was pursued in imperialism, morality, corporatism, militarism, and, more arguably, in cultural modernism, sometimes resurrecting pre-modernist notions or using anti-modernist motifs, as in classicism in art and olympianism in sport. Men, like capital in its flexibility and resourcefulness, were able to construct new *myths* of monocultures – facilitated by new technologies across time and space.

Men's cultural/organizational experiences were, and are, inevitably complicated and contradictory. Men construct and were (and often are) set within tensions between, first, various fragmentations of images and experiences, second, the elaboration of organizational monocultures, and, third, the peculiar occurrence of public domain sexualities. Within this three-way tension, the notion of organizational monoculture brings together apparent organizational asexuality and precarious unity of fragmentations. Men both *construct* these patterns for ourselves, for each other, and for women and children, and simultaneously *experience* these patterns as pre-existing and imposed by 'others'. Such others may of course be other men or even themselves/ ourselves.

These monocultures were and are not just organizational cultures of men, but also sexual cultures, centred in men, their spurious unities being carried off by the dominance and centring of men in discourse: men at the taken-for-granted centre of discourse. This sexualized discourse was constructed in two major, apparently contradictory but usually complementary, ways. First, men's monocultures may operate as heterosexual discourse, with men as the active pursuers within male sexual narrative – centre as subject. Second, men's monocultures may operate as homosocial discourse with men as the existent actors within homosexual subtext – centre as field. Typically and dominantly they carried (or were) both male heterosexual narrative and homosexual subtexts.

Organizational monocultures were new, frequently empty, and fantastic, yet concrete, institutional, powerful, sometimes violent, and deathly. They ranged from the ordinary everyday violences of public school regimes, with their fagging, bullying, and corporal punishment in the creation of 'gentlemen', to the First World War itself. I shall take just two examples to illustrate their complexity – the visual arts and the military – before concluding with a discussion of men's desire for men within organizations.

The visual arts

At first sight, organizational modernizations may appear at odds with the growth of cultural modernism in the visual arts.[31] Indeed the turn of the century is known for the overthrow of aesthetic traditions, from impressionism onwards, not least through the re-evaluation of art forced by photography. Yet this is far from an unbridled anarchism, and indeed the relationship of fragmentation and monoculture is especially complex in the creative arts. For example, late Victorian and Edwardian painting in England was dominated by classical revivalism. In Britain, Lord Leighton, George Frederick Watts, Sir Lawrence Alma-Tadema, Sir Edward Poynter, and John William Waterhouse dominated the Royal Academy from the 1860s until the First World War. They used classical, particularly Hellenic, figures, themes, and imagery in their depiction of classical myths and imaginary scenes – often involving tragedy, unhappiness, and despair, rather than high drama. Their inspiration was, or was said to be, aesthetic philosophy.

Their practice was the depiction of the nude, particularly the female nude, and, within that space, the repetitious representation of the *femme fatale*, such as Cassandra, Circe, and Helen of Troy. In this context,

Men mostly appear as victims – Hylas lured to his death by Waterhouse's red-haired nymphs, Demophoon pursued by Phyllis, the doomed figure of Orpheus, finally torn to pieces by frenzied bacchic women. Waterhouse typically painted

[201]

the head of Orpheus floating down a stream, watched by two pensive nymphs, thus recalling the story rather than confronting it. In this way the violence and bloodshed of classical myth is transmuted into a feeling of vague regret and nostalgia.

(C. Wood 1983, p. 26)

However, within Waterhouse's work there is considerable variety in his portrayal of the *femme fatale*, from the menacing Sirens, painted as birds with women's heads in 'Ulysses and the Sirens', to the doleful, girlish eyes of Hylas's nymphs, to the sad innocence of Echo in 'Echo and Narcissus'.[32] A broader question is how this particular structure of representation of women also displays men's sexualities – the portrayal of women as the means of the portrayal of men. It is in this sense that one can speak of a monoculture, even though the movement was diverse. There is also another sense in which Victorian classicism can be seen as a monoculture, that is, in terms of the supposed superiority of the classical over their own times, and the associated senses of nostalgia, and loss, that it symbolizes – a kind of myth of the myth.

In contrast to classical revivalism, and the aesthetic movement more generally, it is certainly possible to characterize much of the modern and modernist movements in film, painting, music, poetry, and other creative arts in the late nineteenth and early twentieth centuries as fragmentary. They brought *the new* – new languages, new colours, tones, lines, sequences, and composition. On the other hand, new unities were also created within particular fragmentary media or fragments of media, or straddling several media. At times, this took the form of new interpretations and amalgamations of fracturing, or potentially fracturing, social experiences; at other times, new monocultures were manufactured, as within film – new heroes, new *femmes fatales*, new genres, new corporations. For indeed, as elsewhere, these movements were generally led and populated by men. Even the modernist, avant-garde, symbolist, dadaist, futurist were generally men's movements – movements sometimes of very unconventional men, sometimes of men who were intensely masculinist in thought and deed, sometimes ambivalent men. Moreover, those fragments also created their own internationalist, and even nationalist, traditions, if not monocultures. They presaged in their violence and masculinism the coming of the First World War.

[202]

They both warned of the dangers of war and the end of tradition, and spoke lovingly for it, hastening its arrival.

A striking example of this is contained in the futurist movement; its Cinema Manifesto produced in 1916 by Filippo Marinetti was a stark statement of a powerful form of masculinism:[33]

> The cinema is an autonomous art. . . . It must become antigraceful, deforming, impressionistic, synthetic, dynamic, free-wording. . . . Painting + sculpture + plastic dynamism + words-in-freedom + composed noises + architecture + synthetic theatre = Futurist cinema.
>
> (Marinetti 1971, pp. 130–4)

Paradoxically, the environment sought was fragmented yet *total*.

Earlier, the first Futurist Manifesto, published in *Le Figaro* on 20 February 1909, had put forward ideals of fearlessness, rebelliousness, aggressiveness, patriotism, and the glorification of war (Lucie-Smith 1972, p. 485). The futurists brought not only 'frenetic energy' (ibid.), but also 'proto-fascism' (Lunn 1985, p. 249) – practice and symbol of the destruction to come. Ironically, with Marinetti's shift from art to politics, 'he passes', according to Frederick Karl (1985, p. 127), 'into history as the ally of Mussolini, the enemy of futurist art, the supporter of pseudo-Roman monumentalism' – a further instance of the movement from fragmentary to monocultural.[34]

These two apparently disparate traditions of classicism and modernism can also be linked through their common relation to *fin de siècle* ethics, in which rapid attempts may be made to make amends for intellectual and artistic monotony (H. Jackson 1976, p. 18),[35] or to combat feelings of what Max Nordau called 'imminent perdition and extinction'. The Twilight of the Gods can be seen as either a positive or a negative phenomenon (or indeed as both) – the fascination of the new that comes from the break with tradition or the threat of doom (also see Higgs 1987). The final phase of *Götterdämmerung* – the end of the beginning of public patriarchies – was of course the First World War itself.[36]

The military

The Twilight of the Gods certainly came with the Great War: 8 million soldiers were killed. The myth of noble military monoculture was literally exploded: 'It was a hideous embarrassment to the prevailing Meliorist myth which had the public consciousness for a century. It reversed the idea of Progress' (Fussell 1975, p. 8). It was also the arena for the fullest development of homosocial monoculture. The separation of the modern from the traditional, the new from the old, that characterizes modernism (Karl 1985) was reproduced in the distance and discontinuity of military men from other worlds, from previous personal experience (Leed 1979, Ch. 1), and largely from women. Men were immersed with men, in the awful male immersion. Men's sexualities were fragmented, complex, contradictory. Heterosexuality was certainly institutionalized, in letters home, in women as a means of exchange in talk between men, and in official brothels: 'blue lights' for officers, 'red lights' for 'men'. Homophobia certainly persisted, as did pockets of homosexuality[37] – although, according to Paul Fussell (1975, p. 272), probably very little actual homosexual sexual practice at the front. This leaves the general associations of sex and war, danger, anxiety, death, the blurring of practice and fantasy; the sexuality of the non-sexual. Such issues were distilled in the homoerotic tradition – 'a sublimated ("chaste") form of temporary homosexuality' – that pervaded military life, and also had a specific significance at the front line, where there was a special combination of fear, heightened physical consciousness, self-love, sexual loneliness, and self-sacrifice to the homosocial group or mass of other men. In the face of mortality and machines, front-line homoeroticism also brought a tender, pastoral sentimentality, sometimes overlain by officers' generalized affection for whole groups of men. A particularly poignant example of this is the memory of watching men (usually 'one's own') bathing naked – in this the 'quasi-erotic and the pathetic conjoin . . . to emphasize the stark contrast between the beautiful frail flesh and the alien metal that waits to violate it' (Fussell 1975, p. 299).

Perhaps at its root military homoeroticism is in the sexual space between erotic fragmentation and machine monoculture, the mutual affection and admiration that binds and threatens the military. It is as if being in these extreme adverse conditions forced certain dualities into sharper, sexual relief – beauty of the live body/ugliness of the dead body; flesh/metal; pastoral/machine; 'unlawful secret individual love'/'sanctioned public mass murder' (ibid., p. 271). These wartime conditions might reasonably be said to be special, even unique – yet homoeroticism in the sense used here is a much more generally applicable phenomenon.

Organizations as circuits and pyramids of desire between men

One of the dangers of focusing on the fragmented and (mono) cultural facets of public patriarchies is that the gender class power of men may be reduced to myth. Though organizational mono-cultures may in some senses be mythic, men's power and men's preference for men is material.[38] Indeed, the gender class of men can itself be usefully understood through men's preferential desire for each other and mutual recognition as sexually similar.[39] This deep structure of men's homoeroticism is organized rather differently in the private and public domains. In the private, this is primarily through (that is, with reference to) the suppression of desire in father–son relationships and brother–brother relationships and its sublimation elsewhere. Men's desire for men is obviously also present in all sorts of more explicit ways, including gay relationships.

In the public domains quite different patterns predominate, in the sense that the structuring of men's desire for men is contained within the street and/or organization. The street is superficially less formally structured; it is more a nebulous flow of desire between relative equals, but even there hierarchy presides, especially through state and other corporate relationships – most obviously the police and the military. The place of organizations in men's lives is often, even characteristically, contradictory. They may offer both status and meaning and threat and competition to men, as well as acting as *circuits* or *pyramids* of men's (suppressed) desire for men. Perhaps the archetypal example of this is the pub – a patriarchy on the street corner (Hey 1986). It may be a place where men are expected to 'keep their end up' – 'to give and take it', to buy rounds, to muck in, chip in, sup pints, become and be 'men'. It may be a place where, for these reasons, you can't relax, *and* a place that offers comfort and refuge, from other patriarchal institutions and roles, in both the family and organized places of work and employment. The pub is also a place where men can be served in public by women. With the transformation of the gin palace from the 1830s, the 'barmaid' became the representative woman, at the boundary of the public and the private, and often subject to occupational sexual harassment. This 'parasexual cultural prototype' was further elaborated with the expansion of men's leisure at the turn of the century (Bailey 1990). For men engaged in manual work the pub may offer a special consolation, and a means of resuming power. Men's manual work, like women's and, until the last century, children's and young people's, has often been, and for many still is, intolerably hard, stretching and stressing the body beyond reasonable limit – the physical pain of exploitation and oppression. The pub may be a place for reaffirming that labour power, and asserting power against exploiters, and against women, both those present and those women absent in the private domains.

In the light of all this, the sexual subtext of the pub, or the club, can be especially complex – a place to do, to talk, men's desire for men, with little interference from women, to engage one-to-one, and in the group, in 'cut and thrust', smoothing egos, rubbing shoulders, clasping, 'wo-hoh', in mutual projection, drinking drinks in ferment, orally satisfying, remembering milk, downing the phallic pint, with its seminal head, the mutual masturbation of setting them up, upright pints, in twos, threes and small groups, upstanding phalluses, a fairly basic and social scene. The 'normal' heterosexual men's pub is the way some men meet homosocially/homosexually.[40] The pub is for men a site of major cathectic relations, including the intimate interconnection of homosociality and heterosociality, which are for men rivalled only by those around the playing and watching of sport.

Organizational hierarchy is, in this context, far from just a matter of formal roles and responsibilities. It is also sexual, symbolic, and spatial. As such, organizations have and provide complex, sexual subtexts for/of men – as metaphorical bands of brothers, sons, lovers, warriors; as hierarchies of grandfathers, fathers, and sons; as feared strangers and Others; and much more in the manner of the lurid and the florid. Suits, black, grey, pin-striped, with ties, along with other organizational uniforms, become phalluses; bosses become father, and indeed mother, figures; dreams are dreamt and plots are hatched, sometimes in mocking humour, to deprive, behead, or kill them; they are admired and hated. Mutual projection may flourish. The private is brought into the public in massive, psychic dollops and proportions. Organizations and psyches interact in doomed dynamism: organizations, particularly hierarchical and managerial organizations, bring their own psychic destruction in the mastery and domination of men. This applies as much to things as to people: machinery, furniture, corridors, and the other organizational artefacts may all take on such special significances. Organizations provide massive public material for men's sexualities. This is most obviously so in heterosexual pursuit – the hunt, the chase, driven behaviour, both that which is explicitly sexual and that which is implicitly so in the male sexual narrative of organizational management, rationality, and goals. Importantly, this is a narrative that is both heterosexual and between men. Similarly, the placing of women in subordinate positions, for example as secretaries, is, like pin-ups, similarly heterosexual and homosexual – a form of talk between men.[41] Organizations also give ample opportunity for men's narcissism – self-love in a friendly and/or hostile climate. But most important a large amount of men's contact and discourse in public domains, particularly in organizations, is a deflection from, a sublimation of, or indeed a form of mutual masturbation. Gathering together, as managers and/or workmates, standing up, strutting, performing in public, orating, arguing, saying your piece, in the competitive world of men involves a symbolic waving around of the penis, and sometimes going the whole hog, 'wanking off', as a display of power to others, women and men, but most importantly men. Talk may be of cars, pubs, places, women, anything/anyone that is external(ized). The homosexuality of 'normal' heterosexuality is to be *seen* in such organizational structurings and processes. The whole sordid little show is a phallusy[42] – a desperate complex of moves by men to take the public stage by storm, to dominate the material world of reproduction. Men's dominant sexual mode of the public domains is homoerotic: the public domains are for men dominantly homoerotic.[43]

CHAPTER 9

Public men as persons: selves, psyches, and senses

Persons: individuals and collectivities

Changes in public men, public masculinities, public patriarchies, and public domains are social, economic, political, cultural; they are also matters of *the individual*. This chapter considers the changing significance of public patriarchies in terms of the creation of persons, selves, psyches, and senses. What counts as a 'person' is not any kind of given entity, just as what counts as 'personalities' also varies greatly (Hirst & Woolley 1982). There are no *essential* 'persons', 'selves', 'psyches', 'senses' – or indeed 'biographies' or 'bodies'. Instead, these are all the products of definite conditions of formation, specific technologies of the 'self'. As Gary Wickham (1990b) suggests: '. . . [t]he type of person formed in each instance of person formation is the type of person formed there, its conditions . . . are its conditions . . . .' Similarly, notions of 'men' as collectivities or as individuals are cultural constructions, aggregations of bits of lived material realities. There are no essential 'individuals' or 'types of individuals'. Like 'persons' more generally, they are historically and culturally specific: the type of individual formed in each instance of individual formation is the type of individual formed there.

Men may be analysed in terms of structural relations and agency, and men's collective practices within those structured relations and men's individual practices as forms of agency (Hearn 1987a). Likewise, 'men' are located within discursive practices, and the practices of men produce such discourses. 'Men' as individuals are thus simultaneously discourse on 'men' and practices of men.

There are numerous ways in which men within public patriarchies are produced as individuals. While the increasing power of public domain institutions has certainly increased the power of collectivities of men, paradoxically this has occurred through the simultaneous reproduction and representation of men as individuals. Thus men's collective power as fathers, husbands, workers, managers, owners, state workers, and so on, has increased, while at the same time men are represented as individuals – as the father, the husband, the worker, the manager, and so on. Indeed, the collective power of men operates partly by the construction of the power and practices of the individual, the individual man. Just as the power of capitalism lies partly in the construction of supposedly 'sovereign individuals' as 'free' entrepreneurs, workers, and consumers, so too does the power of public patriarchies lie partly in the construction of the supposedly 'sovereign individuals' of fathers, husbands, professionals, and state workers. Public patriarchies certainly construct a mirage of the independent individual man. Notions of men as individual, as 'persons', a 'man', and of 'men' as the collectivity of men are themselves culturally constructed within public patriarchies. This also applies to other more particular constructions of men as individuals (for example, the hero, the martyr, the pioneer) and as collectivities (for example, old men, young men, black men, white men).

In the movement towards public patriarchies, individuals and collectivities of men are subject to several contradictory processes – *publicization* (bringing their definition into the public domains); *consolidation* (of men's power as a gender class); *diversifications and fragmentations* (bringing variation between men); *disjunctions and fracturings* (in experience). Such formations are clearly not static: they are subject to various forces of change and rebellion. These forces include personal individualities; contradictions and conflicts between different individuals, between different forms of individuals, between collectivities, between different forms of collectivities, between individuals and the collectivities; relations and relationships between women and men, between men, and between infants, young people, and men; between reproductive consciousness and economic class; change also comes from 'accidents, chance, passion, petty malice, surprises, feverish agitation, unsteady victories, and power' (Davidson 1986, p. 224).

I shall now consider two main ways in which public men may be formed as 'individuals' – first as *selves* (which bring together behavioural and moral definitions of individuals), and then as *psyches* (which privilege internal definitions of individuals), using exemplifying materials from the late nineteenth and early twentieth centuries, from sport and schooling and from psychoanalysis and film, respectively. The chapter concludes by considering the formation of public men as 'individuals' in terms of the *senses* (that is, the cultural constructions of signs and perceptions that define individuals, selves, and psyches in the first place).

Public men as selves: souls and bodies

To see public men as selves is to refer to two, usually distinct, phenomena: the *general* category of the 'public self' of men in the public domains; and the *particular* 'public selves' of particular men. The former refers to the production of some generalized notion of typical, characteristic, preferred, or ideal public selves of men in the public domains, without any necessary reference to particular individuals, even though it may often speak of the importance of 'the individual'; it is about individuals and/or collectivities of men in general. Particular 'public selves' refer to the public selves of particular men. These two, the general and the particular, may of course interrelate and overlap in specific instances. Both general and particular public selves may be formed as or in terms of individuals or collectivities of men. In both cases, selves invoke behaviours and/or moralities that are presumed to carry and/or convey variable value.

The public selves of men, men's public selves, are a facet of men's participation in all aspects of the public domains and all public domain organizations. However, it appears that in certain public domain arenas the production and reproduction of general forms of 'public self', the *public self in general*, are a significant, or primarily ground, activity, or task. Perhaps the clearest example of this process is to be found in schooling, especially in the public schools. Public selves, 'manliness(es)', were reproduced there for middle-class and upper-class boys to become gentlemen. They were taught, *in theory at least*, not to be less gentlemanly than those more fortunate than themselves, or inflict pain on those less powerful, unless in the interests of discipline. Dr Thomas Arnold in his Headmaster's address to the Scholars of Rugby School summed up these priorities: 'What we must look for here is, first, religious and moral principles, secondly, gentlemanly conduct, thirdly, intellectual ability.' The reality of these 'religious educations' was often much more strenuous and malevolent, including

[210]

a strong strain of bullying, especially in the minor, less-well-off public schools. By the 1830s, the public schools were under attack for their dissolute ways, 'their immorality, exclusivity and restricted curriculum' (J. Richards 1988, p. 10).

The initial modernization of the public schools may be conveniently and perhaps too readily dated from Arnold's headmastership (*sic*) at Rugby School in 1828. He instituted a variety of educational and institutional reforms, founded on an emphasis on the principles of 'Christian morality, self-government in the form of the prefectorial or monitorial system, and an appeal for a liberal curriculum' (Reed 1964, p. 5). Arnold's method was one of almost Socratic example rather than rote learning, but it was disciplined not least by using older boys as *praepostores*.

This striving to disciplined conduct, the training of character, was emulated by some of the other public schools. However, despite these wider reforms, including a greater emphasis on authoritarian control, the mid-century remained a period of relative stagnation for these schools. Criticisms, not least from the growing middle classes, continued. They sought a more systematic education for their sons, socially, intellectually, and indeed morally. In partial answer to this, the Royal Commission was established in 1861, reporting in 1864 in favour of curricular and prefectorial reform, along with games and fagging. The Headmasters' Conference was formed in 1869, and this acted as a catalyst to further standardization (Wilkinson 1964, p. 22). Between 1841 and 1900 half the present-day public schools were established.

Late nineteenth-century public schooling was more utilitarian in orientation, but still 'a powerful device for insulating and socializing an élite and for protecting the values of the aristocracy, moral fervour and gentlemanliness' (Weinberg 1967, p. 52). At public school, boys were made incipient leaders and professional men, in the context of changes in economic class structure, internal industrial base, and international relations. The growth of the German and the United States economies jolted the mid-Victorian lack of interest in the Empire (Pelling 1960). Imperial British power could no longer be sustained without effort, and the public schools were looked to to provide a set of leaders, administrators, and organizers appropriate to a revived imperialism. The end of the century thus saw schooling caught in a number of difficult tensions and contradictions – most obviously between the preservation of traditional values and the demands of more bureaucratic governmental agencies, the expanding professions, and more competitive capitalist enterprise. Neither civil service bureaucracy nor modern professionalism and industrialism sat very easily with the taken-for-granted assurance of the public school product.

A more specific tension was around the pursuit of sport. On the one hand, the games ethic was clearly not enough for a training for 'successful' modern imperial, industrial, and state leadership; on the other, the power and pervasiveness of sports persisted in all sorts of ways, not least in association with the rise of muscular Christianity. The late nineteenth century saw a consolidation of organized games, and 'by the 1890s athletics became a mania which characterised the public schools until well after World War I' (J. Richards 1988, p. 11). The ideology of sports, and the character-building and sense of team spirit that were supposed to follow, easily mirrored the prevalent ideology of patriotism and imperialism of the end of the century. Thus colonial administrators may have been recruited and selected on the basis of public school character, gentlemanliness, and even prefectorial experience, but the applicability of the sport–patriotism complex to the realities of imperialist leadership is quite a different matter. Who exactly was assumed to be in or not in the 'macro-team' of patriotic imperialism is not difficult to guess. The point is made starkly in a testimonial letter for the selection of the Colonial Service: 'He would maintain the best traditions of English government over subject races. He is a gentleman, a man of character.'[1]

The nineteenth-century expansion of schooling throughout the economic classes brought other public selves for boys and young men – new moralities, and new practices of 'individuality' and 'collectivity'. In some cases these institutions were sites for the reproduction of *hierarchy* itself rather than hierarchy for a specific task. Such hierarchies, abstract or practical, have clear relevance for the formation of public selves, themselves hier-archical. Of more novel interest were the changing relations of culture and government in schooling, which constituted the indi-vidual public selves in quite distinct ways, particularly through the formation of literary education (Hunter 1988).[2] The expanding approaches of popular education had as their object not '"man" as the bearer of a divided ethical substance awaiting aesthetic reconciliation or "the subject" as the bearer of an unconscious being awaiting theoretical clarification' but rather 'the formation of a highly specific profile of cultural attributes, . . . the attributes of a citizenry'. The object of this cultural–governmental complex was 'the individual as the member of a population whose health, literacy, criminal tendencies, private sentiments and public conduct are the concern of government'. Yet the paradox was, and in some ways still is, that this reshaping of individual citizens was 'operationalised through forms of conscientiousness which permitted individuals to govern themselves' (ibid., p. ix). What is of course largely missing from Hunter's account is gender, specifically the reproduction of the public selves of men as members of this new 'citizenry'. This account of public selves may be seen in terms of 'men' in several ways: in the activities of particular *public men*, notably the new breed of cultural and intellectual administrators, like David Stow, James Kay-Shuttleworth, and much later Matthew Arnold (as an HM Education Inspector in the 1860s[3]); in the establishment of new forms of *schoolmasters*, with their own disciplinary, spatial, and pedagogical technologies; in the education of the '*schoolchildren*' themselves; and in the creation of *men citizens*.

In all these cases men's public selves were (re)produced. I shall briefly give some detail on the first two, although all four are closely interrelated. Both Stow and Kay-Shuttleworth were concerned with the relationship of the organization of space and the goals of education, on school premises with trained masters (*sic*). Stow made two major contributions: the introduction of the raised stepped platform in the classroom, and of the playground, the 'uncovered schoolroom': 'In seeking to attach the schoolmaster's "moral observation" to the free play in which each child revealed its "true character and dispositions", the playground served as an emblem for the new non-coercive system' (Hunter 1988, p. 60). Kay-Shuttleworth instituted teacher training from religious societies to the government, and also reformed that training through the production of the character-forming moralizing environment of the residential teaching training colleges, the so-called Normal School. The relationship between the principal and the trainees reproduced the future relationship of teacher and pupil, in habits of 'punctuality, industry, cleanliness, order and subordination' (ibid., p. 63). This was achieved through moral surveillance and the encouragement of moral *self*-direction: self-conscious subjectivities within a total environment.

[213]

Aspects of the modernization of the public schools have definite parallels with the deployment of 'education', and particularly literary education, 'as a discipline in an apparatus aimed at the cultural transformation of whole populations' (ibid., p. 5). Both were seats of authoritarian teaching, classroom discipline, and often rote learning. Yet, in both, progressives promoted quasi-democratizations – the teaching of that moral substance that can be applied anywhere – 'that men are superior'; that there is a neutral method. In both state and public schools, *rational, moral* methods were seen as the way to produce modern public selves of men.

A further link across educational class was in the growth of organized youth movements in the late nineteenth century. While middle-class and upper-class boys were sent away to be schooled and to learn their Christian gentlemanliness, lower-middle-class and working-class boys, especially the sons of the slightly-better-off urban workers, were sent to the Christian care of the Boys' Brigade, the Boy Scouts, the Church Lads' Brigade, the Army Cadet Force, and other similar ventures. A number of such youth movements, generally single gender, for boys and young men, and for girls and young women, were created, and then expanded around the turn of the century. These typically involved a mixture of patriotic, religious, military, educational, and sporting activities and ethics, and the advancement of muscular Christianity, and were typically organized and administered by the middle classes. Many, though not all, were uniformed, and most also brought a range of awards, badges, targets, rewards, and punishments as a definite structure to the youthful identity. The youth was (to be) disciplined, and through that a required 'manliness' was to be maintained, trained, or expressed. As Colonel Bennett of the Queen's Cadet Battalion, Stoke Newington, explained:

The habits of order, discipline and good conduct inculcated could not fail to beneficially affect [the cadets'] characters at an age when most susceptible to good or evil influences, training them to become loyal, manly and self-respecting members of society.[4]

[214]

It will be clear from these examples that public selves, particularly as general categories, may include moral aspects within moral discourses. This may be most apparent in middle-class public selves of men, be they the gentlemanly duty, honour, and self-sacrifice of military officers, schoolboys, or professionals – the 'sacrifice of a certain amount of individual liberty in order to ensure certain professional objects' (Dicey 1867, p. 177a).[5]

More bodily, yet more subtle, examples of men's moralities are to be found in the realm of sport, which, in its organized forms at least, became in the late nineteenth century an important arena for the reproduction and display of men's public selves. Although it is possible to play many sports in private, doing sport in private is something of a contradiction in terms. Sport entails the use of rules that are at least minimally public. From the 1860s onwards many organized team games were subject to definite codification. This process had class, ethnic, and gender bases. Upper- and middle-class white men were prominent not only in the administration of the British Empire but also in the codification of sport, processes that were themselves facilitated through the public school system. The Empire was not only administered by such men, but it was also a means of diffusion of these newly codified sports (Bott 1931; Mangan 1986). By 1890, fifteen sports had national codifying bodies in Britain.

Such codification and rationalization can thus be related back to the modernization of the public school system, even though they themselves often embodied forms of anti-modernism,[6] as in the modern resurrection of classical ideals. Team sports particularly embodied the ideals of schooling in which discipline, regularity, and stoicism were valued; thus schooling and sports were closely linked in the latter part of the nineteenth century to the development of men's public selves, especially for the middle and upper classes. These ideals were further institutionalized on the national and international scale by the revival of the Olympic movement. The first modern Games were held appropriately in Athens in 1896. These were simply a gathering of those who happened to be available, including diplomats from the British Embassy. National teams were not instituted until 1912. In this case modern public selves were paradoxically being formed in relation to pro- and anti-modernist imagery.

Meanwhile, and particularly from the 1880s, sport was also becoming an increasingly important set of institutions in the lives of working-class men. The case of football is instructive here. The Football Association was formed in 1863, initially under the domination of southern clubs of gentlemen amateur players, which proceeded to win the FA Cup for ten years from its inception in 1872.[7] In 1883 Blackburn Olympic (*sic*) defeated Old Etonians 2 – 1 after extra time, so becoming the first northern side to win the Cup, and beginning a period of northern domination for nearly twenty years. This also marked the end of the rule of the gentlemen clubs and the rise of clubs of working-class men. For example, the Blackburn Olympic side consisted of three weavers, a loomer, a gilder, two iron foundry workers, a clerk, a master plumber, a licensed victualler, and a dentist – largely respectable working-class men who were part-time sportsmen and for whom the emergent professional payment was important. Furthermore, professional sport brought new moral and bodily regimes – new ways of governing the self, soul, and body in public. For example, the week before the 1883 Final, the Blackburn team went to a Blackpool hotel for special training and 'build-up'. This consisted of rising at 6, a glass of port and two raw eggs, walk along the sand, return for breakfast of porridge and haddock, dinner of leg of mutton, tea of more porridge and a pint of milk, supper of half a dozen oysters. The public construction of this particular working-class self extended to diet, exercise, timekeeping – by mouth, muscle, and minute, as well as desire between men.[8]

In this century, sport has been transformed partly through the supersession of Olympianism by commerce and collective gaze. It has also been changed from a site of playing and watching to a resource for consumption, appreciation, speculation, and imagery. Sport has been vital to the reproduction of men's public selves in other kinds of ways, including mass, often working-class participation; mass, often working-class spectatorship; the creation of sporting heroes; the homoerotic contact with seen men; the glow of being with men watching men. Sport is now no longer just a modernist challenge, within the bounds of collectivism, individual achievement, and hierarchy; it is a plaything for idle reflection, both 'live' and in slow motion, beyond the bounds of postmodernism.

Public men as psyches: personalities and subjectivities

The representation of public men as psyches has long been the special concern of religious and spiritual institutions. The late nineteenth century saw the establishment of the modern 'disciplines' of psychology and psychoanalysis as men's new sciences of the psyche – the application of 'rational' public domain methods to the inner world. Accordingly, psychology and psychoanalysis bring with them the particular associations of men's power and rational institutionalization of the public domains. Experimental psychology is usually dated from the 1860s with Wilhelm Wundt's work in Germany. In 1867 he introduced the first course on the subject at the University of Heidelberg; in 1873–4 he wrote the first textbook on experimental psychology, *The Principles of Physiological Psychology*; and in 1879 he opened the first psychological laboratory at the University of Leipzig. Meanwhile at Harvard University William James was working on his 'functionalist' psychology, following the establishment of the first psychological laboratory in 1875.[9] Like most academic disciplines at the time, the prominent exponents were men. By the end of the nineteenth century the development of psychological sub-specialisms, including structuralism, gestaltism, behaviourism, hormic (purposive) psychology, and dynamic psychology, had begun – all special forms of men's knowledge of the psyche, soon to be accompanied by psychoanalysis itself.

Presumed divisions between the public and private domains inevitably had their psychological equivalents reproduced in the 'person', the 'personality', the public and private 'faces', or even *the face* itself as public and *other parts of the body* as private. Much mainstream psychology and psychoanalysis have done a great deal to reproduce the public–private dichotomy within the psyche of the person.[10] For example, we may find the public face of the person represented as 'persona', 'behind' which stands (some would say, lurks) a less conscious psyche: the conscious stands before the subconscious and unconscious; the ego before the id.

It is important to note that, in referring to psychoanalysis here, I am speaking most directly of the *historical discourse* of psychoanalysis and of the relevance of psychoanalysis for understanding modern (potentially postmodern) *experience*. I am not speaking

[217]

directly to the place of psychoanalysis as an explanation of men, important though that may well be within the contexts of social structures. Psychoanalytic explorations of men's public selves involve both elements of private selves ('private men') that comprise public selves, and elements of public selves that are internal and intra-psychic rather than external and behavioural. Psychoanalytic perspectives are also important in describing projections of the inner upon the outer, internal contradictions, sources of conflict and resistance to change in masculinities, and developmental and socio-sexual dynamics. Psychoanalysis necessarily addresses the significance of the body for men's sense of self, including the changing significance of the sexual in the experience of the body. Psychoanalysis has also raised contradictions between knowing that all we have is experience, even if it is abstract or 'secondhand', and being intensely sceptical of the meaningfulness of that experience: the phallus may be dominant yet symbolic.

While confession, absolution, dream analysis, and fantasy all have long histories in religious and other discourses, psychoanalysis as conscious praxis is modern. It is quite difficult to date the beginnings of psychoanalysis, not least because of the complexities of Freud's own biography, following Breuer's analytic work in the early 1880s. During his study visit to Charcot's neurological clinic in 1885–6, Freud was to learn of literature by Tardieu and others on child sexual abuse, and of the physiological effects of violence to children at the Paris morgue (Masson 1984). Freud opened his private practice in 1886, and in 1896 delivered the famous 'Aetiology of Hysteria' lecture to the Society for Psychiatry and Neurology in Vienna. This set out his theory that neurosis arose from early sexual traumas; in the face of major opposition, he was to publicly retract the 'seduction theory' in 1905. In many ways this debate between infantile experience and fantasy has set the terms for the subsequent elaboration of psychoanalysis. Additionally, much of the impetus for Freud's work appears to have come from the attempt to understand the 'problem' of 'female psychology'. The problem of 'male psychology'/ 'the psychology of men' is only recently being addressed more consciously and critically. Despite this, the diversification of psychoanalysis into the numerous schools and sub-schools has produced a wide variety of accounts of the psyche, which can often be re-read as both stories by men and stories partly about men. Not only do Freudian, Jungian, Adlerian, and other psycho-analyses provide explicit and implicit accounts of men and masculinities, and indeed of women and femininities, they can also be understood as statements on the predicament of men in public patriarchies. To put this another way, the movement to public patriarchies involves men's domination of the psycho-logical and psychodynamic arenas. This raises two interrelated issues: the historical significance of the development of psy-choanalysis in the development of public patriarchies; and the significance of psychoanalysis for the analysis of public patriarchies.

As already discussed, the period 1870–1920 was one of huge economic and social transformations, and it may be tempting to 'explain' the 'rise' of psychoanalysis as an (ideological?) effect of such causes from, say, factory to monopoly capitalism.[11] Barry Richards (1986), writing on the growth of modern 'psychological practice', also notes the use of 'institutionalized psychologism' (Berger 1965) for the 'repair of identities', for corporate, non-violent means of control, or more likely both. Commodification of personal relationships, whether for burgeoning consumerism or imminent expressivism, might be seen as following the satisfaction of basic, material needs for the bourgeoisie, the increasing contra-dictions of the bourgeois 'family', and the growth of the 'personal problem', 'welfare', and the 'welfare state'.

These movements were also part of major structural changes in gender, ethnic, and other relations. Accordingly psychoanalysis might be understood as part of men's attempt to restore or extend patriarchal authority in the light of 'disturbances' in the family, and part of men's prefigurative practice to create the collective father of the emerging modern state. Psychoanalysis thus becomes part of the shift from the power of the private father to the power of the public patriarchs, professionals, state managers, and workers, as well as sometimes part of the reaction and resistance to that process.

State powers, supporting yet overriding the power of the father, complicate the problem of the 'absent father'. With the phenomenon of the absent father, patriarchal power is para-doxically reproduced through an absence rather than a presence. Furthermore, sonhood, while presumably powerful in the re-production of fathering, absent or otherwise, is most directly experienced in relation to the mother, present. Sonhood is in this

[219]

situation a double absence, an experience of absence in relation to an absence. State power reinforced these absences to further abstraction: the father from whom the son is absent is himself absented by the state. The son is not relating to a non-entity. With such changes in the direct power of the father, public patriarchal power operated both in objective relations, as with state laws, and in the creation of the discourse of the subjective. Indeed, psychoanalysis practised by more powerful men on less powerful women can be an exemplar of public patriarchies, the placing of private patriarchal relations of subjectivity into the patriarchal public domains, albeit initially in the privacy of the consulting room, later to become a public, if 'anonymous', case.

Psychoanalysis both in its early Freudian development and its more recent development, partly with the influence of feminist praxis, has been important in placing child abuse and child sexual abuse into public speech, whereby child abuse and child sexual abuse are material/psychoanalytic. This connection has become of greatest significance with the 'rediscovery' of 'child abuse' in recent years. Psychoanalysis also offers a way of bringing men's subjectivity more fully into the public domains. This may be indirectly, in the sense of men's relationship to other men perpetrators of child abuse and other violences, itself 'known' psychoanalytically. We (men) know ourselves by virtue of our relation with others similar, men, who themselves are known through the subjectivity of children and women who have suffered abuse. This may represent a shift in our consciousness as men. Furthermore, just as infantile trauma and other traumas from violence, for example rape, have become part of public domain, particularly professional, debates, so men's adult traumas have become public – most obviously in the recognition of 'shellshock' in the First World War, 'battle fatigue' in the Second, and other forms of 'post-traumatic stress syndrome' in military and other disasters since.[12]

The relevance of psychoanalysis for masculinities is complex. Partly it offers various 'Achilles heels' for men, showing vulnerability, contradictions, and possible rationalizations; and it creates space for the public(iz)ation of the sufferings of others violated by men. Meanwhile, it has facilitated even more oppressive means of men dominating others and each other, most obviously in the infamous Freudian representations of women and women's sexuality. The subtlety of its emancipatory potential is paralleled by the subtlety of its potential control: masculinities are not just impacted upon in these processes, they are psycho-analytically reformulated.

The significance of psychoanalysis, however, lies not only in social subjectivity, but also in relation to the visual, to looking, to voyeurism, and their increasing importance at the turn of the century. There are definite affinities between psychoanalysis and the 'birth of the movies', mass popular pornography, the film star phenomenon, the public sex scandal, the emotional gold rush of Hollywood, *in making the construction of private subjectivities a matter of the public domains*. Transference, projection, and reflection may be constructed in both psychoanalysis and film, the silver screen. As Eric Rhode (1976, p. 24) points out: 'the crucial concept of transference, in which the patient "projects" his fantasies onto what he feels to be the impersonal screen-like mind of the analyst finds its analogy in the cinema and other . . . optical inventions.'

Men's public subjectivities were intensely complicated by reflective capacities of 'public figures', whom men could identify with or against, cheer or jeer, emulate or dismiss. These figures, most obviously film stars (both women and men) but also arguably sporting heroes, provided material for multiple and ambiguous meanings – sexual, violent, self-ish, self-less. Both film and sports offer delusional states for men's public selves: in mass entertainment, glamour, narcissism. This is thus partly, though not only, a sexual process for men.

There are also clear parallels between psychoanalysis, film, and the dream. Men's sexuality too may be dreamlike, and objects of desire, whether film stars or 'girlfriends', are ideally 'out of this world', with a luminosity of their own. Film is a dream world, the cinema a dream palace. Interestingly, Freud's recognition of the dream, in the near completion of *The Interpretation of Dreams* in 1896, occurred at the same time as the dreamlike innovations of Lumière and other film makers. Although the pioneers of film saw themselves as working very much within the realms of science, they also elaborated the themes of futurism and futurist art. One of Edwin Porter's major films, *The Life of an American Fireman* (1902), begins with a fireman asleep in his office, who dreams (as shown in an inset) of a mother putting her baby to bed – with the suggestion that this mother and child, already threatened by fire, could be in the fireman's own house. Identification, fear, anxiety, are all here, even if the story is disappointing to modern eyes

(Rhode 1976, p. 41). Jed Sekoff (1987) has speculated that the film that Freud went to on his visit to New York as part of the famous Clark lectures in 1909 may have been one that was showing in New York at the time that included a dream sequence. According to Ernest Jones, he saw one with a 'primitive chase' sequence. Freud watched it with amusement; Ferenczi was quite excited. Paradoxically, film and psychoanalysis both bring a 'sharper accent' to everyday life, and yet deal in the unconscious, including senses of aura, transcendence, shadow, and projection (Izod 1988, pp. 44–5).

Such structured fantasies have existed in relation to the extension of universal cultural censorship. The extension of the means of producing and circulating texts and images throughout the world was accompanied by the possibility of (and the imagination of) the worldwide prohibition of such texts and images, local censorship, and moral crusades, but the *social institution* of the contemplation of wider change and restriction in text and image. The film became part of the heightened sexual awareness of the period, with greater display and greater censorship – 'hygiene' and 'repression' going hand in hand, both consciously and unconsciously. Part of its conscious and unconscious appeal was its possible censure, real or imagined. Like pornography more generally, where transgression is the law (Kaite 1988), film is the unspeaking camera eye on the 'real drama' – a pornographic medium. Pornography is the specific institutionalization of the general features of film form.

This has had profound implications for the construction of masculinities. 'Men' and their significations are just as amenable to censorship as are films and novels. In one sense, what we are now includes, sparks off from, these cultural significations of film and other cultural productions. We, as masculinities, are partly, though no less profoundly, produced in/on film – the most *material* of media, its fleetingness surely transparent.

Public men as senses: signs and perceptions

The social and gendered construction of public men extends not just to persons, selves, and psyches, but to the very construction of the senses – to what counts as signs and perceptions, and to what necessarily defines persons, selves, and psyches in the first place. The significance of public patriarchies for men's senses lies partly in the historical process of publicization, the historical possibility that everything, all senses may be brought into and become part of the public domains – everything may become, perhaps is, public domains signs, perceptions, and material experiences (thereof).[13] The significance of public patriarchies also lies in processes of consolidation, of fragmentation, and of fracturing. In the first case, there is the possibility at least of the consolidation and extension of men's gender class power over the senses. Diversification and fragmentation refer to the social, multiple, and often inconsistent ways in which masculinities (and femininities) can be shown, labelled, signified, 'expressed'. The separations and divergences of sexuality, procreation, paternal authority, and so on into separable relatively specialized public domain institutions create further hierarchies and (often *dualist*) differentiations. These can in turn easily become associated with the fracturing of experience of masculinities and of being a man, while experience is also more generally subject to its own fracturings.

Signs
Sensory and sensual differentiations and significations are historically structured psychocultural experiences. The separations of procreation, sexuality, nurture, and violence elaborated in public patriarchies are both institutional and psycho-significatory phenomena. They may become institutionalized in the public domains, just as public domain fragmentations may become instilled in immediate material sensual experiences. These processes may be recognized in historical processes of infant development, upon which the very senses of the infant are built, in connections between infant and adult life, and in historical processes of cultural life in general. First, infant psychodynamic processes may be represented as having particular and special power. Separations from the mother may be represented as separations from fusion; acts of individuation; material losses and gains. Separations from the father may be constructed differently, as abstract losses, either in emulation or in searches for the Other. These kinds of possible separations, historically formed, may be seen as creating stresses and strains for the infants, and thus fields for the accumulation of signs and significations. Accordingly, sexuality and sexual desire, as systems of signs in themselves, develop differentially for the

infant boy and infant girl. Such infant psychodynamic processes are fundamentally still *representations*.

A second kind of representation of signs is the supposed connection of infant processes and the subsequent adult construction of significations. An example of this is the reference to the psychological concept of splitting into adult life. In the terms of the present analysis, what is called 'splitting' – the distinct separation of 'love'/'hate', 'good'/'bad', onto different parts of the body of the mother (or other) – may co-relate with the historical separations of material activities (procreation, sexuality, nurture, and so on). Splitting as a psychological process of tension-management may be represented as recurring or being restimulated in subsequent institutional and organizational practices. The gap between the 'good'/'bad' may be institutionally re-formed (or so represented) within the sexual, in the gap between the 'maternal'/'erotic' or some other contrast; alternatively the 'erotic' may be assumed to arise in gaps, overlaps, contrasts, ambiguities between other elements that are split, as signs. Indeed the erotic may be intensified in the to-ing and fro-ing of movement from a particular meaning/sign. In such ways the non-sexual can (for men) become sexual, by paradoxical virtue of being non-sexual – even by a fragment more or less (of a surface or skin) than expected. More grossly, the appeal of stripping comes from *not* displaying the body, just as the desirability of 'flashing' derives from the putting *it* away and the taking *it* out again. Here signification becomes assault.[14] Even organizations may be *macro-flashings*, gross displays of men, just by being there, men in power together, like grandiose homoerotic self-advertisements. Institutions may be held to reproduce, perhaps restimulate, the sexualities of previously experienced gaps, and public domain institutions offer all manner of powerful signs and associations of gaps and separations – computers, trade figures, filing cabinets, guns. Certain institutions, notably total institutions and bureaucratic institutions, create the contradiction that they are their own social world and that they are separated off from the wider social world: the contradiction of *a* social world and *the* social world. In such separations, sexualities and sexual desire are signified. Such institutions, the building blocks of the public domains, are for men typically full of gaps/signs, and filled with diffuse sexuality.

Thirdly, significations may not of course necessarily be linked to infant psychodynamics but may be seen as part of the structuring of cultural life in general. In this sense, men do many strange things in public as part of exerting power over women, and as examples of the peculiarities of men's cultural meanings. For example, men may appear to act on, rather than be, or even embody, life there – through work, money, power, status violence, strength, an almost 'magical' means to achieve that being there, that embodiment (or rather fail to achieve that being or embodiment). This can be looked at in many different ways. Such processes, such alienations from our 'human species-being', can be *represented* as projections – projections of what Jungians would call our 'anima' *onto the outside world*. In this latter view, men's actions in the public domains produce and are produced by men's projection of 'anima' externally rather than accepting its residence internally, with consequences of domination, violence, and suffering for others. Such references to projections are themselves representations.

Interestingly, significatory interpretations of 'projection' are themselves understandable in terms of materialist approaches to trafficking in women in kinship systems (Rubin 1975),[15] and conversations of gender/economic class solidarity between men (Cockburn 1983).[16] An alternative framework is provided by Luce Irigaray (1985, p. 172) when she says:

> Reigning everywhere, although prohibited in practice, hom(m)osexuality is played out through the bodies of women, matter, or sign, and heterosexuality has been up to now just an alibi for the smooth workings of man's relations with himself, of relations among men.[17]

Similarly, in discussing Karl Theleweit's (1987) work on the German Freikorps in the 1920s, Cynthia Cockburn (1988, p. 311) comments:

> The dread of women emerges as a terror men feel regarding the precise location and integrity of their self-boundaries, and their identification of women with what lies outside those boundaries and threatens to overwhelm them.[18]

In men's 'projections', women are material signs between men, externalized signs of that which we are/are not, and that which appears or is felt to threaten that which is not what we are/are not. Sexual violence and hierarchic heterosexuality may be structured, yet passing, fleeting engagements with these 'projections' onto Others. What is called 'men's sexuality' or 'male desire' itself derives from sets of signs in different situations and structures. Particular men at particular moments may, consciously or unconsciously, 'see' signs of desire, however supposedly 'trivial': by *appearance* (e.g. hair, dress), *situation* (e.g. place, space), *qualities* (e.g. present, lacking), and so on. In this, we (men) also become signs ourselves; like sandwich men with placards, or wearers of sloganizing T-shirts, we bear signs, become, are them.

Perception

Finally, the movements towards public patriarchies also entail changes in what perception is assumed to be. This is most obviously so in the expansion of visual powers, in direct surveillance, through the sight of the written word, and through the impact of public domain institutions in which sight, surveillance, and writing became more extensive. Visual powers also became increasingly dominant over other senses and types of sensory powers, such as hearing. At the same time, all the senses underwent social transformation. For example, modernization and postmodernization involved deodorization (Corbin 1986; Duroche 1990) and reodorization (cf. desexualization and resexualization, Hearn & Parkin 1987). The turn of the century brought new valuations of voyeurism (looking), glottophilia (talking) and frottophilia (touching), as both forms of perception in general and constructions of men's sexualities (Bailey 1990). A sensory perspective on public patriarchies links closely with both the critique of perception as a 'male construct' (Duroche 1990) and the claim for female perception as located in touch and the body (Irigaray 1985). For men this may suggest that the appropriate pro-feminist stance is 'talking the body'.[19]

Distinctions and changes in perception and sensory significances have been and remain gendered, though in highly variable, by no means dichotomized, ways. It may be possible to make connections between public domains, men's perceptions, and the visual, and private domains, women's perceptions, and non-visual senses, but this is only a very broad set of equations. From a different perspective, public patriarchies might be considered as moving towards a totality of oppression founded on a totality of the senses rather than a totality of social divisions.

Afterword
Beyond public men?

So those are some of the ways we have got here.

In saying all this, one of the assumptions of this text has been that some of the major features of modern contemporary masculinities can be located in the events of the late nineteenth and early twentieth centuries. That movement towards public patriarchies has provided the specific historical problem of 'public men', and in doing so made it contestable in both interpersonal and structural politics, struggles, and reflections. The movement to public patriarchies opened up both the incorporation of subjectivity into the public domains and the possibilities for radical challenges of subjectivity, for example in the new politics of sexuality at the turn of the century.

The move to public patriarchies is thus clearly a multi-faceted process. It involves rearrangements of legal and other practices around procreation, fatherhood, the family, marriage, nurture, sexuality, violence; it involves the growth of law, the state, the nation, the professions, the polity, suffrage, and public political participation; it involves the transformation of not just paid work, economic relations, organizations and organizational size, structure and form, but also culture more generally; it involves changing and new interrelations of culture, imaging, media – sexuality and organization; it involves movements from modernism to postmodernism; and it involves social, temporal, and spatial changes, of urbanization and electronicization, and much more. It is a series of, not always easily paralleled or neatly compatible, changes in the locating of 'men' and 'masculinities'. Through this array of changes, and indeed others, men as public men are *located* and *created*.

In these and other ways, public men have come to be seen and have come to see ourselves as reset at the *centre* of discourse: as the One to the Other(s). This is not cause to suggest being at the centre is new: in many societies 'God' has been male for a long time. No, it is merely to remark on the changed and changing

[227]

way men have come to sit at the centre (and on the left and right hands as well). This (re)centring – historical, spatial, social – is of intense interest and concern; it speaks to the knowledge that our (men's) cover is being blown. The movements to public patriarchies and the *bringing into* the public domains that ensues carry the seeds of their own destruction, the decentring of this transitory and temporary recentring. The creation of the public paradoxically leads in time to its dissolution.

Contemporary feminisms, particularly since the 1960s, have raised the possibility that public men could be problematic *to breaking point*. Contemporary society may have some of its bases in the turn of the century, but has now moved on in a mass of ways – in the state(s), international relations, global organization, technologies, greater militarism, and wilder extravagancies of postmodernism. These movements, perhaps beyond public patriarchies, to what may provisionally be called post-public patriarchies may bring the deconstruction (and sometimes new possibilities of destruction) of public/modern men and masculinities – a second fall after the first fall (Sennett 1977) and rise of 'public man'/'public men'.

What shape might such post-public patriarchies take? There are many alternatives; some of them probably incipient. They include the increasing incorporation of the private in the public, and the public in the private; the further consolidation and fragmentation of the public domains; and the destruction, some might say imploding, of the public domains (the culmination of their own logic).

Within (post-)public patriarchies, public men exist within many contradictions, of which two are probably the most important. First, there is the contradiction between *publicization* – the dominance of the public, the possibility of all things being made public – and the *fracturing of experience* in the public domains. Second, there is the contradiction between the *consolidation of men as a gender class* and the *fragmentation of men and masculinities* as the monolith of 'white heterosexual able-bodied men' is increasingly shown to be a myth. Post-public patriarchies offer even greater possibilities for oppression in and of the public domains, and even greater immersion in subjectivity as a means, even an end, of radical critique.

These contradictions are of course closely interrelated, in the sense that publicization provides the means for the consolidation

[228]

of the gender class of men through the currencies of the public domains. Similarly, the fracturing of public domain experience feeds into the fragmentation of men and masculinities, although paradoxically this latter process also arises from the collective organization of men and the assertion of forms of identity of men. Such organizations of types of men and assertion of identities of men may indeed in some circumstances provide bases for the renewed consolidation of the gender class of men. In other words, these apparent contradictions may also be mutually reinforcing in some senses.

Men, individually and collectively, now exist in definite, recognizable relations both to the increasingly international capabilities of men (both possible and actual) in economic exploitation, in militarism, in methods of domination and destruction ('mass' and 'precision'), in ecological, nuclear, biological, and chemical capabilities and disasters, and also to peaceful organization and resistance; and the momentary, fragmentary, fleeting, and seemingly arbitrary and random associations of signs and sets of signs, of all and anything – in images, adverts, films, looks, gazes, cuts, slips, splits, bits, and so on, even the casting of famine as video sign. Men are increasingly able to control city spaces and the earth's surface through satellites, electronic surveillance, control of movement and entrances to buildings, and even electronic tagging of people. Such interventions are of course supplemented by video phones, pocket communicators, and the range of computer technologies. Again publicization/consolidation and fracturing/fragmentation may go hand in hand. It is possible for *anything*, however fragmented, to be in the public domains – a taperecording of men eating breakfast played over a tableau of foam, kangaroos, and music hall memorabilia, sprinkled with nail clippings. More bizarre examples are constructed in contemporary pornography built on bits of bodies, and yet international in its scope and organization. 'Men' are increasingly a universal world gender class and increasingly fragmented, beyond even identity.

There is, however, a more precise contrast to be drawn between public patriarchies and such emerging post-public patriarchies in terms of the representation of the private domains. While in public patriarchies the activities of the private domains are increasingly managed or represented as amenable to management in the public domains, in post-public patriarchies the technologies of the public domains re-create the artefacts and experiences of the private domains in new public forms and varieties. The (public) means of construction of public patriarchies by which private patriarchies are organized themselves begin to construct those privatenesses. This is perhaps most seen in the public re-invention of fathers and the 'rights' of fathers, despite and because of the supersession of fathers with increasing divorce and other rearrangements of families; governmental attempts to make fathers 'more responsible', especially in their payment of maintenance; media glorification of fathers in text and image; the mythologizing of the father and the supposed need for men to (re)find 'our fathers'; the fetishism of the family tree; the scientization of fatherhood in DNA testing and the placing of reproductive technology at the service of heterosexual families and fathers; the ambiguity of fathers' 'fame' in child abuse and child sexual abuse; the portrayal of father–infant intimacy in popular glossy photography and child pornography; state licensing of AID (or ID) clinics in keeping with their reinforcement of 'the need for a father'.[1]

Similarly, and paradoxically, the public domains are the last havens of men's secret selves and sexualities. Consumption, including sexual consumption, can be increasingly made apparently individualized; as in 'personics' – the making of CD discs of personalized selected music. Sexuality 'itself' may become open to further technologization through video dating, telephone sex; the creation of sexual virtual realities,[2] more material/idealized succubi and simulacra, and the harmonization of person/sexual qualities/preferences in pre-programmed personal bleepers so that 'compatibles' register when they are within the vicinity of each other. In the face of all this, appeals to 'reflexive modernization' are touchingly humanist, rationalist, and of course ungendered.

So why should men attempt to act against patriarchy at this particular point in (post-)public patriarchies? There are of course responses to demands from women, action from principles of justice and equality, and from sheer anger and outrage, as well as self-interested material reasons, such as increased possibilities for love and the avoidance of nuclear annihilation. But such *motivations* do not fully capture the structural complexity of men's possible opposition to (post-)public patriarchies. This is partly because being 'against patriarchy' cannot be simply reduced to public or private responses, just as it cannot be reduced to a matter of either just theory or just practice. Men's actions against patriarchies are always problematic, always contradictory, always partial – the prospect of a 'total strategy' is illusory. Thus it involves a recognition of, and acceptance of, responsibility in the social power of men, and a deconstruction of 'men', a disintegrated self. It involves an association with the mass of men, and a separation from them. It also involves a problematic relationship with feminism, in the sense that the questions feminism asks can never be fully answered (Hearn 1992). It may draw on anti-organizational practice and an awareness of the limitations of such practice; it is within and against patriarchies.[3]

We can 'return' to the private domains, but, as noted, if all is, potentially, public, this may be an illusory privacy. As action against patriarchy, it also depends on how we might return there – to be? to reassert fatherhood? to gain 'access' to children? to care? not to care? do work? not do work? be violent? be non-violent? We can certainly challenge and organize against dominant modes of public men – attempt to challenge and change them – by pro-feminist politics against violence, torture, brutality, war, heterosexism, and for an anti-sexist culture.

We can also reformulate the public/private divides/differences, show their arbitrariness, even folly, not just through acknowledging the private in the public and vice versa, but by acting and speaking in ways that seek to transcend them, so deconstructing them in practice and politics.

The notion of 'public men' needs to be deconstructed: the authority of men in public has to be undermined as much as the authority of men in private. Saying that brings me to the uneasy conclusion that, while we need to critique men, we need also to look with doubt upon reorganizations of men, new solidarities of men, and new identities of men; all of these may have to go if men are to be de-centred. We need to fully recognize and change men's powers, and to support women's liberation, and yet at the same time to undermine 'our' identities as men.[4] Thus all new identities of men, including those that are anti-sexist, gay, bisexual, even pro-feminist, should be treated with wariness. Everything we do remains in the Public Eye, or potentially so. Deconstructing and de-centring men is, as always, a theoretical analysis, a political direction,[5] and a personal experience; and all of these remain open questions.

[231]

Notes

Foreword: Pluralizing perspectives

1 I have explored these issues before in a number of different ways, for example experientially, politically, theoretically. See, for example, Hearn 1983, 1986, 1987a, 1987b.

2 This is a very important issue in recent feminist debates on knowledge and epistemology, including the critique of logocentrism and phallocentrism. See, for example, Irigaray 1985, Grosz 1987, Weedon 1987.

3 Although the association of men, men's domination, and the public domains is well established in societies following Western political and economic traditions, and indeed in the majority of societies throughout the world, this is not a universal rule. This association is not recognized in all societies: in a few, women dominate public life; and in some, the meanings of the public and the private are quite different from those of Western society (Moore 1987).

4 I shall generally use the terms 'public domain' and 'patriarchy' when referring to other writers who themselves use the singular, and the terms 'public domains' and 'patriarchies' in developing my own analysis.

5 In the early stages of writing this book, I was forced to look self-critically at the use and conceptualization of the term *'public man'*. I started writing: 'When I use the term "public man", I am using it in a particular and consciously critical way. I am not following the use of Richard Sennett 1977, although I find his analysis provocative and stimulating. Moreover, although he devotes most of his discussion to men in the public domain, including such gender-specific activities as heterosexual affairs and prostitution, he does not explore his notion of "public man" in terms of the issues of men, masculinities, or gender relations. Because of this I struggled long to see whether the term "public man" is the one I wish to use, or whether the concept is inadequate, fundamentally flawed. The main reason I decided to retain it is that "public man" is shorter and neater than "men in the public domains".'

Then I realized my mistake – I had been using the term 'public man' both *because* of and *despite* Sennett's use of it. Yet why this glorification of men into *'man'*, the Absolute of 'Man' – just like 'Man and his Environment', 'Man in the World Today', 'The Ascent of

[232]

Man', and so on? I had been trying to use 'public man' as a shorthand for *'men* in the public domains'. Now, the term 'public men' seems the obvious one to use, meaning as it does men in the public domains.

6 I am indebted to work with Wendy Parkin on the construction of the public and the private domains through (dis)able-bodiedness (Hearn & Parkin 1991).

7 In the private domains, *man singular* ('private man') is presumed dominant – it is the prescription of singularity and individuality that is ideological, not the dominance of men. Here *patriarchy*, relatively unsullied, is presumed. Private man appears individual, yet, as O'Brien 1981 points out, supposedly private fatherhood is actually an arrange-ment *between men* in the public domain rather than a specific relation between an individual man and an individual woman. While the ideology of private (domain) hierarchy has been replaced to some extent by the *ideology* of equality in the private domains, that of 'individuals' remains (see Ch. 9).

8 There is an extensive literature and debate on these questions of dominance, difference, social divisions, and otherness. See, for ex-ample, Harding 1986, esp. Ch. 7, du Cille 1990, Collins 1990.

9 As this book is about men and/in the public domains, it appears to be a form of self-affirmation – at first sight at least, an instance of that which it describes. It is 'situationally eponymous'. This contrasts with those attempts to *write publicly* about *speech in private* – what it is 'really' like in private. The act of writing the public version of the private transforms or destroys the former private-ness; a secret becomes of interest only by virtue of its breaking or breakability.

Chapter 1: Introduction: the problem of public men

1 For fuller discussion of Marx on gender and praxis see O'Brien 1979, and Hearn 1987a, 1991a.

2 This is explored by G. Lloyd 1984 and Brittan 1989.

3 A continuing problem in any work of this sort is the nature of historical sources, and specifically the *usually* patriarchal nature of literature, produced by men, in both the present and the past (Allen 1986). In saying this I am not suggesting a blanket dismissal of either past literature or literature written by most men as worthless. Despite the difficulty of dealing with patriarchal sources of literature, it is necessary to neither caricature nor dismiss them. The past is not there for pillage or abuse. While men were and are patriarchal, not all were; nor were all all the time. Rather I see most such literature as written within specific historical sets of assumptions, emphasizing particular issues, avoiding others. Such information tends to be produced in relation to malestream traditions, rather than in relation to repro-duction; even less so as a positive response to feminism. This applies

as much to 'primary' sources as it does to 'secondary' sources produced since. Indeed, the distribution between primary and secondary,
and the hierarchical relation expressed between them, is itself an
instance of a hierarchical way of thinking. 'Primary' sources were
written at different, earlier times, and in their own social context.

A further complication in historical research and writing on men is
whether we can really talk of 'men' in times past. Or, to be more
precise, when I write of 'men' in the past how do I deal with the fact
that I am writing with(in) my own consciousness of 'men' now. One
answer to this, and a relatively conventional one, is to immerse myself
within the material of the period and subsequent accounts of it. A
probably related approach is to be sensitive to the different ways in
which 'men' have not necessarily been seen as 'men' in the past. For
example, this may involve referring to a medicalized notion of 'the
homosexual', rather than to 'the gay' or 'the gay man'. Another, and
in some respects contradictory, approach is to seek connections
between contemporary senses of 'men' or 'masculinities' and past
senses; not necessarily to seek 'origins', but to engage with a history
of the present. Additionally, there are the critical insights to be gained
by the application of contemporary theorizing on men to past
material, even though this may at first appear to entail the imposition
of concepts derived from different historical experiences. The
interplay of approaches, sometimes in their difficult disjunction, has
been the most consistent guide to an appreciation of the past – and
thus the present (Hearn 1991b).

4 For an extended critique of the 'separate spheres' perspective, see
Bose 1987.

5 Citing Katz 1983.

6 A fuller discussion of different positions amongst men's responses to
feminism is included in Hearn 1987a.

7 See several chapters in Hearn & Morgan 1990, Hearn 1989a.

8 This appears a very promising approach to gender, patriarchies, and
men. Relevant discussions of the relation of gender and value are
included in Hearn 1983, 1987a, and Holter 1984.

Chapter 2: Public men in the malestream

1 Different conventions are used in different social sciences and other
disciplines (Spender 1981). A particularly interesting case is
anthropology, which ranges from its imperialist legacy to critical
relativism onto feminist analysis (Moore 1987).

2 I am grateful to John Barker for research on this question. The 1850
Act also contains a strange inconsistency in contrasting the 'masculine
gender' (a social construct) with 'females' (a biological construct). For
further discussion on the terminology of gender in relation to issues
of 'men' and 'masculinities', see Hearn 1989b, Hearn & Collinson
1990.

3 Cited in Keane 1984.
4 The bringing of women into the productive labour force and the commodification of household tasks are, of course, historical concepts rather than historical factual givens. For example, women are also part of the productive labour force, and in agricultural societies usually do the majority of the manual work. The very definition of production and reproduction is itself problematic.
5 See Bologh 1990 for an extended discussion of Weber's relation to masculine thinking.
6 Different historical transformations provide rich material for giving substance to what may appear trans-historical experiences of being a man. Historical changes of this type occur over and over again, and indeed any historical change may feed these senses of potential in being a man (cf. O'Brien 1981).
7 I am grateful to John Remy for alerting me to this aspect of national socialism. For example, Ernst Kriek's 1932 *Nationalpolitische Erziehung*, a training manual used by German army officers and soldiers from 1933 to 1934, argues that capitalism as a mode of production and a form of culture was effete and effeminizing for men.
8 The negative consequences of the onset of the public domains have been particularly important in the analysis of the consequent *psychological* dimensions of rationalization. For example, David Riesman 1969 in *The Lonely Crowd* and William H. Whyte 1956 in *Organization Man* turned their attention to the dubious social benefits of 'other-directedness' and corporate 'togetherness' respectively.
9 A persistent aspect of liberal romanticism is the attempt to re-create a community within association. It has been especially important in the development of organization theory and management thinking, following the human relations movement of the inter-war and early post-war years.
10 For critiques of Lasch see Tucker & Treno 1980, and Barrett & McIntosh 1982.
11 The presence of discourse also includes silence, absence, and difference. Jacques Derrida 1976 has been prominent in theorizing difference as simultaneous presence and absence.
12 We are here dealing with the problem of the operationalizing of Foucault's ideas in terms of possible 'truths'. As Nancy Fraser 1981 has discussed, this seems to be a possible area of political weakness in his theorizing.
13 See Hearn & Parkin 1987, p. 169. The usefulness or otherwise of Foucault's work for feminism is strongly debated.
14 Although Elias is addressing the transition from the medieval to the modern here, the final phrase of the extract – 'in dreams, in books and pictures' – does seem particularly evocative of the turn of the century, with the growth of mass media, mass circulation newspapers and magazines, and perhaps above all films (see Ch. 8).

Chapter 3: Patriarchy, public patriarchy, and related critiques

1 This conclusion stems from feminist work on the public/private from the perspectives of discourse theory and critical theory. In particular Nancy Fraser 1989 has detailed some of the ways in which the public and the private may overlap and be distinct from production and reproduction.

2 See, for example, Rowbotham 1979, Alexander & Taylor 1980, Beechey 1979, Walby 1989.

3 These different social bases of patriarchy, other than those that arise from capitalism, include biology (Firestone 1970), sexuality (MacKinnon 1982), the domestic mode of production (Delphy 1977, 1984), kinship pattern (Weinbaum 1978), biological reproduction and the care of dependent children (O'Brien 1981), reproduction more generally (Vogel 1983, Hearn 1987a), sex-affective production (the production of sexuality, bonding, and affection as the core processes of society) (Ferguson & Folbre 1981; A. Ferguson 1989).

4 Forms of labour other than narrowly defined productive labour include reproductive labour (O'Brien 1981), sexual labour (Hearn & Parkin 1987), people work (Goffman 1961; Stacey 1981, 1982), emotion labour (Hochschild 1983), childwork (Hearn 1983), and solitary labour (Lynch 1989).

5 I have found Dorothy Smith's writing, and particularly her critique of political economy (Smith 1989), very useful on these issues.

6 Another reason for speaking of *patriarchies* rather than patriarchy lies in the danger of reifying society and nation with the use of the singular. Patriarchy singular is usually used to refer to a particular society, nation, or type of society or nation, and in so doing patriarchal definitions of societies and/or nations are reproduced. Political units, like nations, and social units, like societies, are themselves usually the result of patriarchal definition, sometimes arbitrarily so, as in the drawing of imperialist straight lines to determine national boundaries.

7 For a discussion of some of the confusions in the term 'capitalist patriarchy' see Hearn 1987a, pp. 53–4.

8 This dual view of the state, as both patriarchal and mediator of capitalistic and patriarchal relations, echoes analysis of economic class relations as both technical and social relations of production (Cardechi 1977).

9 A very useful review of the Scandinavian theorists, along with the related work of Mary Ruggie 1984, is provided by Yvonne Summers 1989.

10 This formulation parallels Habermas's (1984, 1987) distinction between the 'system', which consists of the public administrative system and the private sector market, and the 'life world', which consists of the public sphere of opinion formation and the private world of intimacy and the family.

11 Whereas in 1986 Walby writes of 'sexuality in patriarchal relations', in 1989 she reframes this as 'patriarchal relations in sexuality', perhaps in greater recognition of the relative autonomy and significance of sexuality.

12 An interesting question is the relationship of Walby's six structures of patriarchy to other composite approaches, such as Foord & Gregson's 1986 four forms of relations, namely, biological reproduction, hetero-sexuality, marriage, and the nuclear family. In *The Gender of Oppression* (Hearn 1987a) I distinguished four forms of reproduction (sexual, biological, generative, physical/violent) which are organized through four dominant institutions of patriarchy (hierarchic hetero-sexuality, fatherhood, the professions, and the state, respectively), and two forms (paid work and ideology) which are not organized through specifically patriarchal institutions.

Walby's analysis of the elements of patriarchy has much in common with my own; interestingly they were formulated quite separately and published within a year. Her analysis is more historical; mine more theoretical. She includes a category of culture while I include a category of ideology; she sees capitalist work relations as a separable site, while I prefer to see them largely as developments of other patriarchal relations, such as those of sexuality and violence, even though the reproduction of labour power is certainly an identifiable category. I include an open-ended category of practices around the social organization of nurture and generative reproduction, which she incorporates largely within her analysis of the family and the state. However, the main difference is the nature of the theoretical tasks in hand: she is concerned with analysing *sites* and *arenas* where patri-archal relations are to be found; I am more concerned with types of *social relations* and *social processes* that are specifically patriarchal. This affects the categories developed and their detailed description. For example, I do not see sexuality as specifically patriarchal, though I do see 'hierarchic heterosexuality' as such.

The two sets of concepts used by Walby and myself are compared in Table 3.2. Each of the sites, arenas, social relations, and social

Table 3.2 Comparison of Walby's (1986, 1989) and Hearn's (1987a) approaches to patriarchy

Walby (sites and arenas)	*Hearn* (social relations and social processes)
Capitalist work	Reproduction of labour power
The family	Procreation
The state	Regeneration/degeneration
Violence	Violence
Sexuality	Sexuality
Culture	Ideology

processes exists in relation to private domains and public domains: they effectively contribute to the social creation and reproduction of multiple, pluralized domains – and hence plural public men and public masculinities.

13 I am grateful to discussions with Øystein Gullvåg Holter on historical change in Norway.

Chapter 4: Public patriarchy: some initial implications for men and masculinities

1 This is one of the major themes amongst the 'pessimistic progressives' (pp. 35–8).

2 This has been promoted most clearly by some Scandinavian feminists, notably Hernes 1984, 1987a, b.

Chapter 5: Public patriarchies, public men, public domains, and public masculinities

1 The following points are developed from Hearn & Collinson 1990.

2 Difference-iation and de-differentiation are apparently contrasting social processes emphasized in different postmodernist accounts. In keeping with the concept of *différence*, both would seem to be reciprocally relevant to postmodernist theorizing and supposedly postmodernist societies.

3 See, for example, Grosz 1987. On pro-feminism and postmodernism see Hearn 1989a, 1989b. Such critiques of the public/private division draw on broader feminist debates on the meaning and significance of the notion that 'the personal is political'. On the interrelation of 'work' and 'sexuality', see Hearn & Parkin 1987.

4 These four different foci have some equivalences to the differentiation between the four subsequent chapters (Chs 6–9).

5 See, for example, Hindess 1987.

6 The question of disjunctions in space and movement is a major theme in the intersection of geography and postmodernism (Soja 1989).

7 I am grateful to Kirsten Hearn for pointing this out in her address to the Anti-Clause 28 Rally in Manchester, April 1988.

8 These four different meanings of the private and the public have some equivalences to the meanings emphasized in the four subsequent chapters (Chs 6–9). See n4 above.

9 This theme is explored further in Hearn & Collinson 1990.

10 Not only do the private and the public have various meanings in terms of the spatial, the temporal, the social, and the psychological, but these different frames of meaning may themselves in turn be com-

bined together to construct particular meanings of the private and the public. For example, the public and the private domains might be seen as particular and different forms of interrelation of the spatial and the social. Accordingly, public domains might be seen as the social contained *within* the spatial; while private domains might be seen as the spatial contained within the social.

11 This echoes Bob Connell's (1987, p. 85) comment: 'The social definition of men as holders of power is translated not only into mental body-images and fantasies, but into muscle tensions, postures, the feel and texture of the body.'

12 This is a brief statement on a very complex theoretical and practice area. The interrelation of reproductive materialism and cultural materialism in some form of cultural reproductive materialism is a question deserving close attention in the future.

Chapter 6: Public men as social relations

1 There are many different methodological ways of understanding broad changes in the social structuring of public patriarchies. They are described here as changes in the social forms of social elements of public patriarchies, and as such may refer to changes in *social structural relations*, in the extent of the *public domains*, in the nature and structure of public *discourses*, as well as in a number of types of more specific social arrangements, such as in *inter-organizational relations*. Whichever of these formulations is seen as the most useful, they all refer to social phenomena of great generality that are represented in the development of individual institutions and organizations. As such, this chapter is concerned with *relational* social phenomena. Furthermore, although these altered formulations are methodologically distinct, it is of course possible to conceptualize social change as occurring simultaneously in more than one, and in interrelated ways, for example as simultaneously social structural and discursive.

2 The extent to which Britain experienced economic decline relative to its competitors is subject to considerable debate and variation in interpretation. See, for example, Kindleberger 1964, Saul 1976, Pollard 1989, Feinstein & Prest 1972. The novelty of this late nineteenth-century situation may be compared with British imperial decline after the Second World War, and the consequent problematizations of masculinity (Tolson 1977).

3 Citing Brown 1981.

4 For relevant discussions of men's domination of the medical profession see Parry & Parry 1976, Donnison 1977, Ehrenreich & English 1979, Hearn 1982, Showalter 1987.

5 Jeffrey Weeks (1989, p. 45) notes: 'Many British and American doctors were influenced by the work of French medical men on the dangers of contraception, particularly that of L. F. E. Bergeret 1868, translated as *Conjugal Onanism* . . .'

6 Citing Routh 1879, pp. 9–17, and noting that many of these diseases were also supposedly attendant upon higher education of women. Also see L. Hall 1991, Ch. 1.

7 Citing D'Emilio & Freedman 1988.

8 The gulf between the principles and practices of men sexual radicals, New Thinkers, and Fabians in the late nineteenth and early twentieth centuries has been explored by Brandon 1990. Also see Seers 1977, Leach 1981, Bland 1986, Copelman 1986, D. Morgan 1992.

9 The term 'new man' was even coined as a response to these changes (Showalter 1991).

10 For an extended discussion of the relationship of patriarchalism, bureaucracy, and clientelism, see K. Ferguson 1984.

11 See Lewis 1980, 1986, Rowan 1985, Brookes 1986, Dwork 1986.

12 Comparisons can be made here with the 'paternalistic' and 'tutelary' nature of the state explored by Hernes and Borchorst & Siim (see pp. 63–4).

13 Analyses of the relationship of the state and sexuality have been developed, or not developed, largely within the frameworks of political theory, with its own distinct ideologies. Accordingly, state theory has been dominated by two major malestream traditions – liberal and Marxist (Burstyn 1983; MacKinnon 1983). In the first, the state is a social accumulation of powers, rights, duties, and obligations from the previously unfettered individual of civil society – the personal freedom of the individual is lost to the contract of collective benefit. In the second, the state is a social structural form which contributes, sometimes determinedly, to the social construction of economic classes, including individuals within them – collective freedom is gained or lost according to the particular domination of class relations within and indeed outside the state. In neither tradition does sexuality usually figure as a central element for either individual or collective. Having said that, there is no obvious reason why the liberal tradition could not be elaborated in relation to sexuality; there are clear reasons around the pre-eminence of economic class why Marxist theory of the state has difficulties with both gender and sexuality as central elements in theorizing.

In contrast, feminist scholarship on the state often makes questions of sexuality, and indeed violence, central, and this has been seen in specific disciplinary areas like feminist criminology and feminist juris-prudence and more generally in feminist political theory. Hartmann's 1979 work, though not exclusively on the state, has, by theorizing patriarchy in terms of men's restrictions of women's access to economically productive resources and on women's sexuality, been important in agenda-setting. Burstyn 1983, in one of the few Marxist feminist direct critiques on the state as a system of 'male dominance', argues that '[w]omen's labour and sexuality are the two most important things to control for any society of male dominance' (p. 64). For her, men's control of women's sexuality is a pervasive feature of the state, and 'capitalist states, like all other states, have functioned, in the final analysis, to preserve and in new ways extend masculine control' (p. 65), so that as much emphasis needs to be given in analysis to gender as to economic class.

MacKinnon 1982, 1983, 1989 has set out a radical feminist analysis of sexuality, the state, and society. For her, sexuality is fundamental, comparable to the status of work in Marxist analysis. Thus sexuality is not just something to be controlled, as in Burstyn's theorizing, but is 'that social process which creates, organizes, and directs desire, creating social beings we know as women and men, as their relations create society' (1982, p. 516). From this, what is called the state and state law follows, as structured areas of male dominance. She proposes that 'the state is male in the feminist sense'; 'the way the male point of view frames an experience is the way it is framed by state policy'; 'formally, the state is male in that objectivity is its norm' (1983, p. 644; cf. Connell 1990). And yet elements of that state may be used politically on occasions to challenge dominant sexual practices, such as sexual harassment and pornography, through the pursuit of feminist jurisprudence. If MacKinnon is correct in her approach, and I think she substantially is, we would expect to find a series of significant changes in the relationship of sexuality and the state in the move to public patriarchies.

14 Quoted in Bland 1986, p. 138.
15 The Social Purity and Hygiene Movement had an important and shifting influence throughout this period. Drawn from the ranks of the church, teaching, medicine, the political parties, and some feminist organizations, the movement promoted sexual restraint and campaigned against pornography, prostitution, venereal disease, and even masturbation. See Humphries 1988, Mort 1987.
16 See Ch. 7, n17, pp. 246–7.
17 Quoted in Harrison 1982, p. 284.
18 This section draws heavily on Radford 1988.
19 The Married Women's Property Act, 1870, had given wives the right to keep their own earnings. A useful analysis of economic class variations in women's strategies for resistance to marriage is provided by Joan Perkin 1988.
20 See R. v. Jackson (1891) in the Courts of Appeal. It was only in 1991 that rape in marriage was recognized in English courts.
21 The 1895 Act provided the basic grounds for separation and maintenance orders until 1960.
22 Quoted in Harrison 1982, p. 399.
23 Cited by Temkin 1987, p. 82.
24 On law reform on the 'feeble-minded' see Simmons 1978.
25 For further discussion on the relation of law, family, and patriarchy, see Laurin-Frenette 1982, Polan 1982, Boris & Bardaglio 1983, Law 1983, O'Donovan 1985, 1986, Grossberg 1985a, 1985b, McLean & Burrow 1988, Duxbury 1989.
26 This view of political development *as a consequence* of men's domination of the inheritance and indeed accumulation of property raises a number of major philosophical and practical problems and issues – most notably, is gender the basis of property, as Marx 1975

suggests in 'The Economic and Philosophical Manuscripts' (see Hearn 1991a)?

27 In 1902, William Thomas Pike edited what was presumably seen at the time as a useful reference work, *West Yorkshire at the Opening of the Twentieth Century: Contemporary Biographies*; 818 biographies were included of politicians, nobility and gentry, clergy, professionals, business people, artists, writers, scientists – and all 818 were men.

28 There are innumerable examples of this pervasive and *both explicit and implicit* domination by and of men. A convenient and immediately transparent illustration is T. H. S. Escott's discussion of the state of the 'nation' and its 'people' in the 1870s – *England: Her People, Polity and Pursuits*, first published in 1879. The book discusses the changing nature of class society, and does so strictly in terms of the changing nature of men – be they aristocratic, democratic, or plutocratic. Thus, for Escott, England's people includes 'sons of newly-enriched farmers', 'typical country gentlemen', 'men of extensive culture', 'gentlemen of a finished type', 'men of the people', 'professional men', 'merchant-peers and merchant-statesmen', 'young men of birth and fashion', but no women and few working-class men. For him, while the 'race' and 'stock' of England was changing, it was doing so with a good deal of economic intermingling of types of (gentle)men – and was thus in fairly safe hands. 'The people' was a male concept, and a cultural and economic one at that.

29 Reprinted in Hanham 1968, p. 205.

30 A particularly complex issue was feminist and purity campaigning on the temperance question, in which women and men worked against alcohol abuse, often in association with campaigns against prostitution and other perceived immoralities. While the increasing involvement of large numbers of women can be seen as part of 'a maternal struggle', an extension of the home, it can also be understood as a major factor in moving women towards active public domain politics (Epstein 1981, Bordin 1990). Also see pp. 116–17 on the 'population problem' and n15 above on the Social Purity and Hygiene Movement.

31 Citing Radzinowitz 1956.

32 Citing Western 1956, and Teichman 1940.

33 Interestingly, since the Crown Private Estates Act of 1873 a separation has been made between the public (now Civil List) income and the private wealth of the monarch. According to this statute, the latter can not only be invested but also be taxed. This could be said to date the state's formal separation of the public and private faces of the monarchy.

Chapter 7: Organizations of men (1): size, structures, and hierarchies

1 Wendy Parkin (1989, pp. 118–19) has brought together many of the overlapping contemporary forms of men's domination of organizations and bureaucracies – the public over the private; production over reproduction; the labour market for men over that for women; the 'work role' of men over the dual or triple roles of women.

She goes on to describe how male domination is perpetuated within organizations:

> – men, predominantly in positions of power, authority and leadership and holding high-status, highly-paid posts, over women in low-status, low-paid positions with little authority, power and influence;
> – men as intellectual workers over women as manual workers . . . ;
> – men as professionals over women as semi-professionals . . . ;
> – men as manual workers in non-domestic trades over women as manual workers in domestic trades . . . ;
> – men as full-time permanent workers over women as part-time and temporary workers;
> – men in 'central', non-boundary roles over women in 'boundary roles', whom they interview and select;
> – men as registered unemployed over women not registered as unemployed;
> – men's heterosexuality over women's sexuality, lesbianism, and men's gayness: this domination being both a basis and a reinforcement of the oppressions within all the above.

In view of all the associations of organizations and domination, and organizations and men, it is not surprising that organizations and organization theory might be subject to feminist critiques. A major feminist critique of bureaucracy has been completed by Kathy Ferguson 1984 under the title *The Feminist Case Against Bureaucracy*, while others, such as Cynthia Cockburn 1989, 1990, 1991 and Beverly Burris 1989, have focused on more particular organizational features. Also see K. Ferguson 1987, Hearn & Parkin 1983, 1986–7, 1987, 1992, Hearn *et al.* 1989.

2 Useful distinctions may be made between mixed-gender organizations and single-gender organizations. In most mixed-gender organizations, it is men who have dominated, and indeed continue to dominate. Thus the societal intensification of public patriarchies is reproduced in 'mini public patriarchies' within the limits of particular organizations. Accordingly, a number of broad types of organization may be distinguished (see Figure 7.1). Type 4 might be the most common; types 1, 3, and 5 much less so. In the case of type 2, men

	Dominated by:		
	Women	Men	Women and men
Women only	1	–	–
Men only	–	2	–
Women and men	3	4	5

Membered by:

Figure 7.1 Types of organization by gender divisions

dominated certain sectors of the public domains through the exclusion of women.

3 The concept of 'people work' was first used by Erving Goffman 1961 in *Asylums*; more recently it has been elaborated by Margaret Stacey 1981, 1982. Also see Ch. 3, n4, p. 236.

4 The exclusion of women from banking and related sectors was near complete until the 1870s. The first woman clerk was appointed by the Bank of England in 1893 (Dohrn 1988). An extensive discussion of men clerks in banks, counting houses, insurance, and similar establishments is contained in Gregory Anderson's 1976 *Victorian Clerks*.

5 See Holcombe 1973, Anderson 1976, 1988, Lowe 1987, Zimmeck 1986. A recent collection on contemporary continuations and continuities in this trend is Jane Jenson *et al.*'s 1988 collection, *Feminization of the Labour Force*.

6 While the Liberal reforms of the 1900s are usually portrayed as the beginnings of the modern welfare state, following a period of relative economic stagnation, the 1890s were in fact a period of even more rapid growth in government, despite relative stagnation in the wider economy. In contrast, the 1900s were a period of relatively slow growth in government and rapid growth in the wider economy. Relatively large public sector deficits, due to relatively high central government current expenditure on goods and services in the period 1900–2, were first suddenly reduced in 1903, and then gradually resolved to near balance by 1913. Indeed, if local authorities are included as public authorities, current balance operated from 1904 to 1913, with the exception of 1909 (Feinstein & Prest 1972). A detailed study of the growth of state employment 1890–1950 is Abramovitz & Eliasberg 1957. A useful collection on the historical approach to public administration has been edited by Lee 1974.

7 The penny post was begun in 1840, book post in 1848, postal cards in 1870, postal orders in 1881, and parcel post in 1883. The Savings Bank was established in 1861. Telegraphs were taken over nationally in 1870 and the gradual takeover of the telephone system was completed in 1911 (Holcombe 1973, p. 164).

8 See Holcombe 1973, Anderson 1976, Cohn 1985, Grint 1988, Lowe 1987, and Lewis 1988. Gendered analyses of the state are provided by Aron 1987 (on the United States) and Deacon 1989 (on Australia).

9 Cited in Holcombe 1973, p. 165. Also see Lowe 1987, p. 17.

10 Cohn's 1985 study emphasizes the relative importance of managerial intervention and power in facilitating women's participation in the Post Office. He specifically rejects the 'cheap labour' hypothesis, as on that basis women, working on lower pay levels, would be the 'rational' managerial choice in all sectors – and instead draws attention to additional economic incentives to employ women in sectors where labour costs are particularly high. In such situations the economic incentive may override sexist beliefs, social norms limiting interaction between women and men in organizations, and men's resistance to change. In addition, the Post Office case appears to have been affected by the personal influence of a number of Postmaster-Generals relatively sympathetic to the employment of women (Lowe 1987, pp. 17–18).

11 Cited in Anderson 1976, p. 113.

12 Special mention should also be made of Keith Grint's 1988 recent study of pay and gender relations in the Post Office 1870–1961, with particular emphasis on the inter-war period. He is especially helpful in pointing to the multiple nature of social causes and the contradictions facing particular actors and groups, such as men managers. In general terms he concludes that it has been men who have inhibited equal pay, and it has been market forces that have stimulated state-induced equal pay. Having said that, it is important to acknowledge that the demand for state employment is itself the product of gender and other political relations.

13 This section draws extensively on Joyce 1980.

14 On a similar theme, David Collinson & Margaret Collinson 1989 address some of the contemporary contradictions for men and the formation of 'masculine identity' in the workplace – between lack of power there and power over women. Accordingly the workplace and their own culture were perceived as symbols of freedom and autonomy (inhibited by middle-class politeness), despite their lower pay and less comfortable working conditions, and pension, sickness and holiday provisions. Masculine identity and specifically 'the preoccupation with masculine sexuality . . . reflected the men's concern to deny their [own] subordinate position within the organization' (p. 98). Also see Collinson 1992.

15 Links between economic class cultures and masculinities are, however, problematic on several counts. Most importantly, class culture is sometimes used to refer to class cultures of men, rather than of women. Secondly, class culture may place a prime emphasis upon the construction of masculinity through activities *in the public domains*. Thirdly, there are various contradictions between masculinities and class cultures. Working-class masculinities may be characterized by collective values, but may also be characterized by contradictory independence – in terms of either the supposedly independent status

of the waged worker or an individual, or, perhaps more interestingly, the supposedly independent status of the man in the private domain, as father, husband. Middle-class masculinities may be characterized by not only individualism but also collective values, whether in terms of the collectivity of individual middle-class waged (or 'salaried') workers or the collectivity of men, as fathers, husbands, men. Public domain toughness may be combined with private domain kindness, just as public domain generosity may be combined with private domain tyranny. The emphasis on the public domain and economic class dimension of men's lives as the prime basis of masculinities neglects these contradictory interrelations of the private and the public. It also reinforces the association of selected elements of the public domains and economic class bases of masculinities with the character of economic class culture that is supposed to exist in agendered, thus 'masculine', terms.

16 Kathy Ferguson 1984 sees both women in bureaucracies and the clients of bureaucracies as equivalent to the 'second sex', the Other, to the One of the male-dominated bureaucracy.

17 In this respect it is important to note that some of the managerial pioneers, most obviously Frederick Taylor, but also Henry Ford and many others, were centrally concerned, even obsessed, with control and hence anxiety about that control. Gareth Morgan (1986, pp. 204–8), drawing on Sudhir Kakar 1970 and others, shows how such anal-compulsive approach to organization and managements can be connected to anal sexuality at various degrees or levels of repression or sublimation. A comparable analysis of John Harvey Kellogg, the Massachusetts industrialist and author of *Man, the Masterpiece, or Plain Truths Plainly Told, About Boyhood, Youth and Manhood* 1886, has been provided by Jackson Lears (1981, pp. 13–14). Kellogg was adamant about the dangers for boys and men of 'sensual self-indulgence: in food, in sleep, and above all, in sex', especially masturbation, and even erotic dreams and nocturnal emissions. Against these he urged 'the will', and the practising of a strict personal regime, including:

1. Kneading and pounding on the abdomen each day to promote evacuation before sleep and thus avoid 'irritating' congestion.
2. Drinking hot water, six to eight glasses a day (same end in view).
3. Urinating several times each night (same end in view).
4. Avoiding alcohol, tobacco, and tea because they stimulated lecherous thoughts.
5. Taking cold enemas and hot sitz baths each day.
6. Wearing a wet girdle to bed each night.

Norman Dixon 1976 has explored similar dynamics in British army officers in the nineteenth and early twentieth centuries. Men's experiences of 'hidden anxieties' in the context of the 'natural urges'/'self-control' discourse are documented by Lesley Hall 1991. Such psychological dynamics developed alongside and within (not antithetically to) structural relations and structural change.

18 This parallels Cardechi's 1977 analysis of the dual productive function of management under capitalism.

19 The term 'macho management' became popular in the 1980s, in association with a new liberal individualism. The use of 'macho' in this and other contexts is a form of implicit racism in its Hispanic referencing.

20 Bureaucracies and bureaucratization have long been presented as gender-neutral or agendered. The Weberian thesis of rationalization raises this theme of agendered technical rationality to the level of a major and macro societal process. In this view, agendered bureaucratization is the most visible manifestation of agendered societal rationalization.

21 The wider connections between 'rationality' and 'masculinity' have been taken up by feminist and other scholars – some through psychology and the domination of the analytic part of the personality over the expressive; some through science and epistemology; others have related 'masculine' rationality, or the complex of masculinity/ rationality, to the domination of production over reproduction (Hartsock 1983, Holter 1984). Although these diverse approaches are not equivalents, they all attempt to deconstruct taken-for-granted connections of masculinity and rationality, often through emphasizing relations and relationality, as against linear cause and linearity, in conventional malestream definitions (of both masculinity and rationality). Even within more abstract forms of rationality, like logic, there are issues of *incompleteness* rather than completeness; parallel computations rather than one overriding computation; as well as a lack of logic about any closed system of logic.

Chapter 8: Organizations of men (2): processes, sexualities, and images

1 This section draws on Hearn 1990b.

2 This raises a major political, and indeed methodological, question – namely, the nature of the connection between the public domain control of the *sexual* power and oppression of the father, and the possibly compensatory increase in *sexual* power and oppression in the public domains, not least in mass market pornography at the turn of the century and other times.

3 Cited in Walby 1986, p. 116.

4 Citing Wood 1842, p. 33.

5 Cited in Mackie & Pattullo 1977, p. 163.

6 Recent studies have found high levels of sexual harassment in

workgroups and organizations where women are entering what were formerly men's territories (Hearn & Parkin 1987, pp. 81 ff).

7 See Gordon 1976 and Edwards 1986 for more general discussions of the construction of women's sexuality in the nineteenth century.

8 Cf. MacKinnon 1983 on men's eroticization of the non-erotic.

9 Comparisons may be made between fears of women's sexuality in the First World War (Lewis 1984, p. 185) and in Second World War factories (T. Harrison 1943, Hearn & Parkin 1987, pp. 26–9).

10 Also see Lambertz 1985 for an analysis of other similar incidents, including the prosecution and discharge of a head carder for his sexual pressurizing and even assault on young women under his authority in Oldham in 1887.

11 There are difficulties of constructing exact figures on this development until the 1911 Census, as prior to that shop keepers (mainly men) were included together with shop assistants (increasingly women). Even so, it may be noted that the proportion of the total of 'dealers' (both keepers and assistants) who were women increased from 18.6 per cent in 1861 to 30.5 per cent in 1911 (see Holcombe 1973, App. 3). The very notion of 'assistants' is of course ideological.

12 Partly as a critique of both determinism and Marxism, the major objects of Foucault's work have been sites, arenas, positionings, and discourses other than narrowly economic and capitalist ones. They have included technologies of the state, the professions, and other people-processors. There is no reason why his sceptical discursive approach should not be applied to the arenas of production and consumption.

13 These examples are taken from de Vries 1968.

14 For other materials on the changing norms around sexuality and dress at the end of the century, compare Bott & Clephane 1932 and Wilson 1976.

15 On French music hall programmes, see Zucker 1964. For more general discussion of the meaning of Frenchness in British culture, see Kimmel 1987.

16 There are of course many facets to the growth of mass media and mass culture. Important media not examined here are music hall (Bailey 1986), popular press (A. Lee 1976), and radio. The last gave new possibilities for the extension of men's (emotional) power, not least in the rise of fascism. For a more general discussion of the relationship of popular culture to politics, and specifically socialism at the turn of the century, see C. Waters 1990.

17 Before looking at photography and film, it is worth noting that images are not usually taken, formed, to *specifically portray* 'masculinity'. Much more importantly, masculinities *do not pre-exist* image-making (just as agents always act in pre-existing social structures and histories). Rather than conceiving of images being *of* masculinity it is accurate to see masculinities *as* images. The photographic metaphor, 'pictures of men', does seem inappropriate here (Hearn & Melechi 1992).

18 Some of these photographs have recently been 'brought to life' in the

television series *The Civil War* written by Ken Burns, Ric Burns, and Geoffrey C. Ward. Also see Batty & Parish 1987, Frassanito 1978.

19 This section draws on Hearn 1988b.

20 This occurred in 1878 according to Keith Reader 1979, p. 4, and in 1884 according to D. J. Wenden 1975, p. 12.

21 This is not to be confused with the film *The Kiss* (1929) directed by Belgian Jacques Feyder, and starring Greta Garbo in her last silent film.

22 Cited in Low 1948, p. 58.

23 A detailed analysis of the relationship of sexuality and censorship in early film, 1909–25, is provided by Annette Kuhn 1988.

24 The contemporary Page 3 phenomenon has its parallel in the 'Regimental Pets' portrayed in the illustrations of *Ally Sloper's Half Holiday* – a weekly entertainment magazine brought out at the turn of the century with the beginnings of the Saturday half-day holiday. The magazine, a mixture of the *Sun* and *Tit Bits*, included drawings of large-chested women in military uniform alongside humorous and satirical articles.

25 See Dubbert 1979, Filene 1986, Kimmel 1987, Mangan & Walvin 1987.

26 For a fuller discussion of the significance of the western, including its relation to the frontier and racial subtext, see Hearn & Melechi 1992. A comparable fictional genre is the 'male romance' or 'eastern', developed from the 1880s by Rider Haggard (e.g. *She*), Rudyard Kipling (e.g. *He Who Would Be King*), and other men novelists. In these, men forsake the company of women, and instead go off to Asia or perhaps Africa in bands/bonds on adventures into the unknown. Such unknown places constitute the racialized imperialist male imaginary of the time (see Bristow 1991, Showalter 1991). These themes have continued into contemporary genres, such as science fiction and space movies.

27 I am grateful to Gary Wickham 1990a and Antonio Melechi for drawing my attention to the specificity of the global.

28 In discussing this interrelation of fragmentation and monolithic culture, it is important that we guard against any underlying sense or explanation through balance or equilibrium. The interrelation of fragmentation and 'unity' is an illustration of difference not of homoeostasis.

29 A discussion of the shortcomings of culturalist explanations of masculinity is provided by Carrigan, Connell & Lee 1985.

30 For analyses of the specific establishment of brotherhoods and fraternities in the Victorian era see Carnes 1989, Clawson 1989; a more general text on the creation of 'tradition' in this period is provided by Hobsbawm & Ranger 1983.

31 Among many useful surveys of modernist art and literature in this period see Ford 1961, Cox & Dyson 1972, Berman 1983, Karl 1985, Lunn 1985, Symons 1987, and Woolf & Seed 1988. While these overwhelmingly emphasize men, women's activity is being increasingly documented (e.g. Garb 1986).

32 The supersession of the Angelic Invalid by the Sensual Woman in Victorian imagery is described by Drinka 1985.

33 Coincidentally this theme is also noted in a recent conference paper by David Morgan 1990.

34 There is clearly no determined pattern here – slightly later and contrasting examples are the association of dadaism (c.1916–22) and anarchism, and of surrealism (c.1917–?) with Marxism, in the eyes of Andre Breton at least. On Marinetti and facism, see J. Davies 1988.

35 The artist most obviously spanning these movements is the painter and illustrator, Aubrey Beardsley.

36 These notions carry within them contradictions between the notion of doom and the notion of rebirth, which have particular resonance in contemporary Britain.

37 The specific homosexual desire for soldiers had been recognized since at least the early nineteenth century. This is evidenced in the reputation of the 'other ranks' of H.M. Brigade of Guards, and in the appendix on 'The love of soldiers and related matters' to the first German edition of Symond's *Sexual Inversion* (Fussell 1975, p. 279). Fussell goes on to explore the more general British homoerotic tradition, especially in literature and poetry (pp. 279 ff).

38 For a discussion of the way in which the gender class of men is partly and *paradoxically* maintained through the construction of a falsely monolithic notion of 'man' and 'masculinity', and the obscuring of the fragmentation of 'men' and 'masculinities', see Hearn & Collinson 1990.

39 I am thinking here of MacKinnon's 1982 theorization of sexuality as the basis of gender. This might therefore suggest that 'sexuality' between men is as important as 'sexuality' between men and women as the bases of the gender class of men.

40 One of the particular features of the pub for men is that it is for most there a place of *consumption*. Several recent commentators have suggested that consumption may be of increasing importance as against production in the construction of contemporary Western masculinities (Chapman & Rutherford 1988, Morgan 1992).

41 See Ann Game 1989 for a relevant psychoanalytic linguistic account of this relation, and Irigaray 1985, especially the essays 'Women on the market' and 'Commodities among themselves', for a more general analysis of women as exchanges between men. Also see p. 225, p. 252.

42 Shortly after using the term 'phallusy', I came across *Exposing Nuclear Phallacies* (Russell 1989).

43 There are, however, difficulties around the very notion of 'homoeroticism', especially within a heterosexist culture, particularly the invoking of 'homosexual desire' that is most unambiguously shown in private domains. Similarly, the very notions of 'heterosexuality' and 'homosexuality' as separable and isolatable forms of men's public sexualities are open to deconstruction and critique. For a more general critique of the notion of 'sexual orientation', see Hearn 1991b, 1992.

Chapter 9: Public men as persons: selves, psyches, and senses

1 Cited in Heussler 1963, p. 20. A twentieth-century account of the public school construction of masculinity is provided by Heward 1988.

2 The following section provides only the mere indications of the arguments of Hunter's *Culture and Government*. To place his work in context it is necessary, first, to compare the difference between the structuring of the emergence of modern forms of education and the structuring of dominant practice of such education; and, second, to locate literary education within and in relation to other educational practices.

3 It is tempting to speculate on parallels between the impact of Thomas Arnold on the modernization of the public scholar and the impact of his son, Matthew Arnold, on the modernization of state schools, in his capacity as Her Majesty's School Inspector. Not only is there the intriguing question of the relations between father–son and private–public education, but there is also the irony of Matthew Arnold's dual role as the champion of non-elite liberal education and the founder of modern cultural criticism.

4 Cited in Springhall 1977, p. 15.

5 Cited in Reader 1966, p. 159.

6 An extensive discussion of anti-modernism and American culture at the turn of the century is provided by Lears 1981.

7 This information is taken mainly from John Golby's Radio 4 programme, on 'The history of organised sport', last broadcast 1990.

8 See n17 below.

9 The idea of the nervous system paralleled the innovation of telegraph lines in the 1850s and 1860s, followed by the telephone proper in 1875 (Drinka 1985, pp. 68–9).

10 The distinction between the external social world, with its personal and other social relationships, and the internal world of the person and the personality is widespread in a number of fields, notably social psychology and psychoanalysis. Such distinctions can, of course, be further applied to both 'parts' of the person.

11 The next five paragraphs draw on Hearn 1987b.

12 The recognition of the extent of trauma in some cases is such that it is now possible to gain compensation for emotional trauma for relatives of those involved in disasters.

13 Stephen Kern (1983, pp. 316–17) observes: 'Already in 1913 the camera was tagged "a democratic art", as the camera eye penetrated everywhere and as its cheap admission prices and mixed seating arrangements brought the highbrow culture of the theater to the working classes.' This illustrates the way in which emphases upon signs and upon material experience are in no way inconsistent.

14 Comparison may be made with cutting in/of discourse: 'Is not the

most erotic portion of a body where *the garment gapes?* . . . it is intermittence . . . which is erotic' (Barthes 1976, pp. 9–10).

15 Lilian Rubin's work on the traffic in women, the social system of women as commodities for exchange between men, represents a development of Claude Lévi-Strauss's 1949 analysis of women as signs. Comparison may also be made with Jacques Lacan's assessment of the signification of 'women' as signs between men within phallocentric culture, even to the point of the body of the women 'becoming' the phallus, as in the pin-up. For a discussion of Lacanian analysis of popular culture see Easthope 1986, especially on masculinity and joking.

16 On men's use of women as means of exchange in power and conversation between men in workplaces, Cockburn (1983, pp. 134–5) observes that:

> The solidarity forged between men as a group of males is part of the organised craft's defence against the employer. Many women . . . will confirm . . . that they (the men) make a big show of apologising for 'bad language' . . . . The social currency of the composing room is women and woman-objectifying talk, from sexual expletives and innuendo through to narration of exploits and fantasies. . . . Women are the subject of a traffic among men that serves the purpose of forging solidarity within the workshop . . .

17 Luce Irigaray argues that '[t]he production of women, signs, and commodities is always referred back to men' (1985, p. 171), and that 'exchanges upon which patriarchal societies are based take place exclusively among men' (p. 192). In this sense 'the *very possibility of a sociocultural order requires homosexuality* as its organizing principle' (p. 192; emphasis in original).

18 The link between social structural and psychoanalytic explanations of child abuse by men is discussed by Hearn 1990a.

19 See Brittan 1989, Hearn 1991b, on 'talking the body', following Jardine 1987.

Afterword: Beyond public men?

1 This refers to the announcement by the UK government in the person of Virginia Bottomley, the Minister of State for Health, of the creation of the Human Fertilisation and Embryology Authority. This organization is to have statutory authority to license clinics and other establishments for 'assisted conception'. In issuing such licences, she said that the new authority would have two prime concerns: the welfare of the child and the need of the child for a father (Mihill 1991).

2 The technologically imaginable possibilities of 'teledildonics'

(simulated sex at a distance) now include the combination of tele-presence virtual reality technology with the telephone network. In such a way realistic senses of the sight, sound, and touch of the self and others could be received, transmitted, and interchanged, not just between two people but large numbers many miles apart. The moral, legal, and emotional implications of such sexualities are multiple and difficult to predict. See Rheingold 1991.

3 Comparisons can be drawn with being 'in and against the state' (London Edinburgh Weekend Return Group 1980). This issue takes on a special urgency as one arena for anti-sexist work by men is the state and its various agencies. Having faith in the possibility of men doing such work as teachers, youth workers, social workers, and so on, necessitates attention to theories of the state that make the relationship of gender power and historical change explicit. 'Being in and against gender' is more problematic.

4 For a critique of the identity of men 'as men', see Stoltenberg 1990, p. 182.

5 I am thinking here of the dangers of men organizing public domain political events, such as conferences, meetings, organizations, for men only. The exclusion of women from them is a fundamental political act/error. Such political practice may often be paradoxical, in the sense that it may mean the use of our em(power)ment to de-power ourselves.

Bibliography

Abramovitz, M. & Eliasberg, V. F. 1957. *The Growth of Public Employment in Great Britain*. Princeton, NJ: Princeton University Press.

Adburgham, A. 1964. *Shops and Shopping 1800–1914. Where, and in what Manner the Well-dressed Englishwoman Bought her Clothes*. London: Allen & Unwin.

Addelson, K. P. 1982. Words and lives. In *Feminist Theory. A Critique of Ideology*, N. O. Keohane, M. Z. Rozaldo & B. C. Gelpi (eds), 176–88. Brighton: Harvester.

Alexander, S. 1976. Women's work in nineteenth century London; a study of the years 1820–1850. In *The Rights and Wrongs of Women*, J. Mitchell & A. Oakley (eds), 59–111. Harmondsworth: Penguin.

Alexander, S. & Taylor, B. 1980. In defence of 'patriarchy'. *New Statesman* **99**, 2250, 1 February, 161.

Allen, A. & Morton, A. 1961. *This is Your Child: The Story of the National Society for the Prevention of Cruelty to Children*. London: Routledge & Kegan Paul.

Allen, J. 1986. Evidence and silence: feminism and the limits of history. In *Feminist Challenges: Social and Political Theory*, C. Pateman & E. Gross (eds), 173–89. Sydney: Allen & Unwin.

Allen, J. 1989. Men, crime and criminology: recasting the questions. *International Journal of the Sociology of Law* **17**, 19–39.

Anderson, G. L. 1976. *Victorian Clerks*. Manchester: Manchester University Press.

Anderson, G. (ed.) 1988. *The White-Blouse Revolution. Female Office Workers Since 1870*. Manchester and New York: Manchester University Press.

Aristotle. 1962. *The Politics*. Harmondsworth: Penguin; trans. T. A. Sinclair. Rev. trans. T. J. Saunders, 1981.

Aron, C.S. 1987. *Ladies and Gentlemen of the Civil Service. Middle-Class Workers in Victorian America*. New York and Oxford: Oxford University Press.

Atkins, S. & Hoggett, B. 1984. *Women and the Law*. Oxford and New York: Basil Blackwell.

Atkinson, P. 1979. The problem with patriarchy. *Achilles Heel* **2**, 18–22.

Baden-Powell, R. 1908. *Scouting for Boys*. London: Horace Cox.

Bagehot, W. 1928. *The English Constitution*. Oxford: Oxford University Press.

Bailey, P. (ed.) 1986. *Music Hall. The Business of Pleasure.* Milton Keynes: Open University Press.

Bailey, P. 1990. Parasexuality and glamour: the Victorian barmaid as cultural prototype. *Gender and History* 2(2), 148–72.

Bailey, V. & Blackburn, S. 1979. The Punishment of Incest Act 1908: A case study in law creation. *Criminal Law Review* November, 709–18.

Banks, J. A. & Banks, O. 1964. *Feminism and Family Planning in Victorian England.* Liverpool: University of Liverpool.

Barker, D. 1983. How to curb the fertility of the unfit: the feeble-minded in Edwardian England. *Oxford Review of Education* 9(3), 197–211.

Barrett, M. 1987. The concept of difference. *Feminist Review* 26, 29–41.

Barrett, M. & McIntosh, M. 1982. *The Anti-social Family.* London: Verso.

Barthes, R. 1976. *The Pleasure of the Text.* London: Cape.

Batty, P. & Parish, P. 1987. *The Divided Union. The Story of the Great American War 1861–65.* Topsfield, Mass.: Rainbird; London: Salem House.

Beales, D. 1969. *From Castlereagh to Gladstone 1815–1885.* London: Nelson.

Beckett, J. R. (ed.) 1892. *Bradford Portraits (Pictorial and Biographical) of Influential Citizens of Bradford.* Bradford: M. Field & Sons.

Beechey, V. 1979. On patriarchy. *Feminist Review* 3, 66–82.

Benfield, R. 1976. *Bijou Kinema. A History of Early Cinema in Yorkshire.* Sheffield: Sheffield City Polytechnic.

Benson, S. P. 1986. *Counter Cultures: Saleswomen, Managers and Customers in American Department Stores, 1890–1940.* Urbana, Ill.: University of Illinois Press.

Berger, P. 1965. Towards a sociological understanding of psychoanalysis. *Social Research* 32, 26–41.

Berman, M. 1983. *All That Is Solid Melts Into Air. The Experience of Modernity.* London: Verso.

Bland, L. 1982. 'Guardians of the Race' or 'Vampires upon the nation's health'? Female sexuality and its regulation in early twentieth century Britain. In *The Changing Experience of Women*, E. Whitelegg *et al.* (eds), 377–88. Milton Keynes: Open University Press.

Bland, L. 1986. Marriage laid bare: feminists take issue with marital sex 1880–1914. In *Labour and Love, Women's Experience of Home and Family 1850–1940*, J. Lewis (ed.), 123–46. Oxford: Basil Blackwell.

Bland, L., McCabe, T. & Mort, P. 1978. Sexuality and reproduction: three official instances. In *Ideology and Cultural Production*, M. Barrett, P. Corrigan, A. Kuhn & J. Wolff (eds), 78–111. London: Croom Helm.

Bologh, R. W. 1990. *Love or Greatness? Max Weber and Masculine Thinking – a Feminist Inquiry.* London and Boston: Unwin Hyman.

Borchorst, A. & Siim, B. 1987. Women and the advanced welfare state – a new kind of patriarchal power? In *Women and the State. The Shifting Boundaries of Public and Private*, A. S. Sassoon (ed.), 128–57. London: Hutchinson.

Bordin, R. 1990. *Woman and Temperance. The Quest for Power and Liberty*

1873–1900. New Brunswick, NJ and London: Rutgers University Press; Philadelphia, Pa: Temple University Press, 1981.

Boris, E. & Bardaglio, P. 1983. The transformation of patriarchy. The historic role of the state. In *Families, Politics and Public Policy*, I. Diamond (ed.), 70–93. New York: Longman.

Bose, C. E. 1987. Dual spheres. In *Analyzing Gender. A Handbook of Social Science Research*, B. B. Hess & M. M. Ferree (eds), 267–85. Newbury Park, Ca: Sage.

Bott, A. 1931. *Our Fathers (1870–1900)*. London: Heinemann.

Bott, A. & Clephane, I. 1932. *Our Mothers. A Cavalcade in Pictures, Quotation and Description of Late Victorian Women 1870–1900*. London: Gollancz.

Brand, E. A. 1965. *Modern Supermarket Operation*. New York: Fairchild Publications.

Brandon, R. 1990. *The New Women and the Old Men. Love, Sex and the Woman Question*. New York and London: W. W. Norton.

Braverman, H. 1974. *Labor and Monopoly Capital*. New York: Monthly Review Press.

Brehony, K. 1985. Popular control or control by experts? Schooling between 1880 and 1902. In *Crises in the British State 1880–1930*, M. Langhan & B. Schwartz (eds), 256–73. London: Hutchinson.

Briggs, A. 1964. The political scene. In *Edwardian England 1901–1914*, S. Nowell-Smith (ed.), 43–101. London and New York: Oxford University Press.

Bristow, J. 1991. *Empire Boys*. London and New York: Routledge.

Brittan, A. 1989. *Masculinity and Power*. Oxford: Blackwell.

Brod, H. 1983–4. Work clothes and leisure suits: the class bias of the men's movement. *M* **11** (Winter), 10–12, 38–40; reprinted in M. Kimmel & M. Messner (eds), *Men's Lives*. New York: Macmillan, 1990.

Brod, H. 1987. Introduction: themes and theses of men's studies. In *The Making of Masculinities. The New Men's Studies*, H. Brod (ed.), 1–18. Boston and London: Allen & Unwin.

Bromley, P. M. & Lowe, N. V. 1987. *Family Law*, 7th edn. London: Butterworths.

Brookes, B. 1986. Women and reproduction c. 1880–1919. In *Labour and Love. Women's Experience of Home and Family 1850–1940*, J. Lewis (ed.), 149–71. Oxford: Basil Blackwell.

Brophy, J. & Smart, C. 1982. From disregard to disrepute: the position of women in family law. In *The Changing Experience of Women*, E. Whitelegg *et al.* (eds), 207–25. Milton Keynes: Open University Press.

Brown, C. 1981. Mothers, fathers, and children: from private to public patriarchy. In *Women and Revolution. The Unhappy Marriage of Marxism and Feminism*, L. Sargent (ed.), 239–67. New York: Maple; London: Pluto.

Brownlow, K. 1973. *The Parade's Gone By . . . .* London: Sphere. 1st pub. 1968.

Brownlow, K. 1991. *Behind the Mask of Innocence – Sex, Violence, Prejudice,*

Crime. Films of Social Conscience in the Silent Era. London: Jonathan Cape.

Bunyan, T. 1977. *The History and Practice of the Political Police in Britain.* London: Quartet.

Burawoy, M. 1979. *Manufacturing Consent: Changes in the Labor Process under Monopoly Capitalism.* Chicago: University of Chicago Press.

Burnham, J. 1941. *The Managerial Revolution.* New York: Peter Smith.

Burrell, G. & Hearn, J. 1989. The sexuality of organization. In *The Sexuality of Organization,* J. Hearn, D. Sheppard, P. Tancred-Sheriff & G. Burrell (eds), 1–28. London and Newbury Park, Ca: Sage.

Burris, B. H. 1989. Technocratic organization and gender. *Women's Studies International Forum* 12(4), 447–62.

Burstyn, V. 1983. Masculine dominance and the state. In *The Socialist Register 1983,* R. Miliband & J. Savile (eds), 45–89. London: Merlin.

Canaan, J. E. & Griffin, C. 1990. The new men's studies: Part of the problem or part of the solution? In *Men, Masculinities and Social Theory,* J. Hearn & D. H. J. Morgan (eds), 206–14. London and Cambridge, Mass.: Unwin Hyman.

Cardechi, G. 1977. *On the Economic Identification of Social Classes.* London: Routledge & Kegan Paul.

Carnes, M. C. 1989. *Secret Ritual and Manhood in Victorian America.* New Haven, Conn. and London: Yale University Press.

Carrigan, T., Connell, R. W. & Lee, J. 1985. Toward a new sociology of masculinity. *Theory and Society* 14(5), 551–604.

Chapman, R. & Rutherford, J. (eds) 1988. *Male Order. Unwrapping Masculinity.* London: Lawrence & Wishart.

Child, J. 1969. *British Management Thought.* London: Allen & Unwin.

Clark, M. G. & Lange, L. (eds) 1979. *The Sexism of Social and Political Theory.* Toronto: University of Toronto Press.

Clawson, D. 1980. Class struggle and the rise of bureaucracy. In *The International Yearbook of Organization Studies,* D. Dunkerley & G. Salaman (eds), 1–15. London: Routledge & Kegan Paul.

Clawson, M. A. 1989. *Constructing Brotherhood. Class, Gender and Fraternalism.* Princeton, NJ: Princeton University Press.

Cockburn, C. 1983. *Brothers. Male Dominance and Technological Change.* London: Pluto.

Cockburn, C. 1988. Masculinity, the Left and feminism. In *Male Order. Unwrapping Masculinity,* R. Chapman & J. Rutherford (eds), 303–29. London: Lawrence & Wishart.

Cockburn, C. 1989. Equal opportunities: the short and the long agendas. *Industrial Relations Journal* 20(3), 213–25.

Cockburn, C. 1990. Men's power in organizations: 'equal opportunities' intervenes. In *Men, Masculinities and Social Theory,* J. Hearn & D. H. J. Morgan (eds), 72–89. London and Boston: Unwin Hyman.

Cockburn, C. 1991. *In the Way of Women: Men's Resistance to Sex Equality in Organizations.* Basingstoke: Macmillan.

Cohen, E. W. 1965. *The Growth of the British Civil Service, 1780–1939.* London: Cass.

Cohn, S. 1985. *The Process of Occupational Sex-Typing*. Philadelphia, Pa: Temple University Press.

Collins, P. H. 1990. *Black Feminist Thought*. Boston and London: Unwin Hyman.

Collinson, D. L. 1992. *Managing the Shopfloor: Subjectivity, Masculinity and Workplace Culture*. Berlin: de Gruyter.

Collinson, D. L. & Collinson, M. 1989. Sexuality in the workplace: the domination of men's sexuality. In *The Sexuality of Organization*, J. Hearn, D. Sheppard, P. Tancred-Sheriff & G. Burrell (eds), 91–109. London and Newbury Park, Ca: Sage.

Collinson, D. L. & Hearn, J. 1990. Unities and differences between men and masculinities. (2) The fragmentation of management and the management of fragmentation. Paper at British Sociological Association Annual Conference, 'Social Divisions and Social Change', University of Surrey, April. University of St Andrews: mimeo.

Collinson, D. L. & Hearn, J. 1992. Men, masculinities and managements: unities, differences and their interrelationships. *Academy of Management Review* 17.

Connell, R. W. 1987. *Gender and Power*. Cambridge: Polity.

Connell, R. W. 1990. Gender, the state and sexual politics. Theory and appraisal. *Theory and Society* 19, 507–44.

Copelman, D. M. 1986. 'A new comradeship between men and women': family, marriage and London's women teachers, 1870–1914. In *Labour and Love. Women's Experience of Home and Family 1850–1940*, J. Lewis (ed.), 175–93. Oxford: Basil Blackwell.

Corber, R. J. 1990. Representing the 'unspeakable'. William Godwin and the politics of homophobia. *Journal of the History of Sexuality* 1(1, July), 85–101.

Corbin, A. 1986. *The Foul and the Fragrant: Odor and the French Imagination*. Cambridge, Mass.: Harvard University Press. 1st pub. in French 1982.

Cox, C. B. & Dyson, A. E. (eds) 1972. *The Twentieth Century Mind. History, Ideas, and Literature in Britain. I. 1900–1915*. London: Oxford University Press.

Davidoff, L. 1979. The separation of home and work? Landladies and lodgers in nineteenth and twentieth century England. In *Fit Work for Women*, S. Burman (ed.), 64–97. London: Croom Helm.

Davidoff, L. 1990. 'Adam spoke first and named the orders of the world': Masculine and feminine domains in history and sociology. In *The Politics of Everyday Life: Continuity and Change in Work, Labour and the Family*, H. Corr & L. Jamieson (eds), 229–55. London: Macmillan.

Davidoff, L. & Hall, C. 1986. *Family Fortunes*. London: Hutchinson.

Davidson, A. I. 1986. Archaeology, genealogy, ethics. In *Foucault: A Critical Reader*, D. C. Hoy (ed.), 221–33. Oxford: Basil Blackwell.

Davies, J. 1988. The futures market: Marinetti and the facists of Milan. In *Visions and Blueprints. Avant-garde Culture and Radical Politics in Early Twentieth-Century Europe*, E. Timms & P. Collier (eds), Manchester, Manchester University Press.

Davies, M. W. 1982. *Woman's Place is at the Typewriter: Office Work and Office Workers, 1870–1930*. Philadelphia, Pa: Temple University Press.

Deacon, D. 1989. *Managing Gender. The State, the New Middle Class and Women Workers 1830–1930*. Melbourne: Oxford University Press.

Delgado, A. 1979. *The Enormous File. A Social History of the Office.* London: John Murray.

Delphy, C. 1977. *The Main Enemy. A Materialist Analysis of Women's Oppression.* London: WRRC. 1st pub. in French 1970.

Delphy, C. 1984. *Close to Home. A Materialist Analysis of Women's Oppression.* London: Hutchinson. 1st pub. in French 1970 onwards.

D'Emilio, J. 1983. Capitalism and gay identity. In *Desire. The Politics of Sexuality*, A. Snitow, C. Stansell & S. Thompson (eds), 140–52. London: Virago; New York: Monthly Review.

D'Emilio, J. & Freedman, E. 1988. *Intimate Matters: A History of Sexuality in America.* New York: Harper & Row.

Derrida, J. 1973. *Speech and Phenomena.* Evanston, Ill.: Northwestern University Press.

Derrida, J. 1976. *Of Grammatology.* Baltimore, Md: Johns Hopkins University Press.

Derrida, J. 1978. *Writing and Difference.* London: Routledge & Kegan Paul.

De Vries, L. 1968. Text by James Lower. *Victorian Advertisements.* London: John Murray.

Dewey, L. & O'Dell, P. 1971. D. W. Griffiths. In *A Concise History of the Cinema. Volume One. Before 1940*, P. Cowie (ed.), 10–16. London: Zwemmer; New York: Barnes.

Dicey, A. V. 1867. Legal etiquette. *Fortnightly Review* (New Series) 2 (August), 169–79.

Dicey, A. V. 1914. *Law and Public Opinion in England during the Nineteenth Century*, 2nd edn. London: Macmillan, 1962.

Dixon, N. 1976. *On the Psychology of Military Incompetence.* London: Jonathan Cape.

Dohrn, S. 1988. Pioneers in a dead-end profession: the first women clerks in banks and insurance companies. In *The White-Blouse Revolution. Female Office Workers since 1870*, G. Anderson (ed.), 48–66. Manchester: Manchester University Press.

Donnison, J. 1977. *Midwives and Medical Men.* London: Heinemann.

Drinka, G. F. 1985. *The Birth of Neurosis. Myth, Malady, and the Victorians.* New York: Touchstone.

Dubbert, J. L. 1979. *A Man's Place. Masculinity in Transition.* Englewood Cliffs, NJ: Prentice-Hall.

Du Cille, A. 1990. 'Othered' matters: reconceptualising dominance and difference in the history of sexuality in America. *Journal of the History of Sexuality* 1(1, July), 102–27.

Durham, M. 1985. Suffrage and after: feminism in the early twentieth century. In *Crises in the British State 1880–1930*, M. Langan & B. Schwartz (eds), 179–91. London: Hutchinson.

Duroche, L. 1990. Male perception as social construct. In *Men,*

Masculinities and Social Theory, J. Hearn & D. H. J. Morgan (eds), 170–85. London and Boston: Unwin Hyman.

Duxbury, N. 1989. Exploring legal tradition: psychoanalytical theory and Roman Law in modern continental jurisprudence. *Legal Studies* **9**, 84–98.

Dwork, D. 1986. *War is Good for Babies and Other Young Children*. London: Routledge & Kegan Paul.

Dworkin, A. 1983. *Right Wing Women. The Politics of Domesticated Females*. London: Women's Press.

Dyer, R. 1985. Male sexuality in the media. In *The Sexuality of Men*, A. Metcalf & M. Humphries (eds), 28–43. London: Pluto.

Easthope, A. 1986. *What a Man's Gotta Do. The Masculine Myth in Popular Culture*. London: Paladin.

Edwards, R. 1979. *Contested Terrain*. New York: Basic.

Edwards, S. S. M. 1986. *Female Sexuality and the Law*. Oxford: Martin Robertson.

Eekelaar, J. 1978. *Family Law and Social Policy*. London: Weidenfeld & Nicolson.

Ehrenreich, B. & English, D. 1979. *For Her Own Good. 150 Years of the Experts' Advice to Women*. London: Pluto.

Eisenstein, Z. 1981. *The Radical Future of Liberal Feminism*. New York: Longman.

Elias, N. 1982. *State Formation and Civilization. The Civilizing Process, Volume 2*. Oxford: Basil Blackwell.

Ellis, J. B. 1869. *The Sights and Secrets of the National Capital: A Work Descriptive of Washington City in all its Various Phases*. Chicago: Jones, Junkin & Co.

Elshtain, J. B. 1981. *Public Man, Private Woman*. Oxford: Martin Robertson.

Englishwoman's Review 1889. 15 May, 205 ff.

Epstein, B. L. 1981. *The Politics of Domesticity: Women, Evangelism, and Temperance in Nineteenth-Century America*. Middletown, Conn.: Wesleyan University Press.

Escott, T. H. S. 1879. *England: Her People, Polity and Pursuits*. Extracts from 1881 edn in *Culture and Society in Britain 1850–1890*, J. M. Golby (ed.), 27–31. Oxford: Oxford University Press, 1986.

Feinstein, C. H. & Prest, A. R. 1972. *National Income, Expenditure and Output of the U.K. 1855–1965*. Cambridge: Cambridge University Press.

Felski, R. 1989. Feminist theory and social change. *Theory, Culture and Society* **6**(2), 219–40.

Ferguson, A. 1982. Patriarchy, sexual identity, and the sexual revolution. In *Feminist Theory. A Critique of Ideology*, N. O. Keohane, M. Z. Rosaldo & B. C. Gelpi (eds), 147–61. Brighton: Harvester; Chicago: University of Chicago Press.

Ferguson, A. 1989. *Blood at the Root*. London: Pandora.

Ferguson, A. & Folbre, N. 1981. The unhappy marriage of patriarchy and capitalism. In *Women and Revolution*, L. Sargent (ed.), 313–18. Boston: South End Press.

Ferguson, H. 1989. Rethinking child protection practices: a case for history. In *Taking Child Abuse Seriously*, Violence Against Children Study Group, 121–42. London: Unwin Hyman.

Ferguson, K. E. 1984. *The Feminist Case against Bureaucracy*. Philadelphia, Pa: Temple University Press.

Ferguson, K. E. 1987. Work, text, and act in discourses of organization. *Women and Politics* 7(2), 1–21.

Field, J. 1980. 'When the Riot Act was read': a pub mural of the Battle of Southsea, 1874. *History Workshop* 10 (Autumn), 152–63.

Filene, P. G. 1986. *Him/Her/Self. Sex Roles in Modern America*, 2nd edn. Baltimore, Md: Johns Hopkins University Press.

Firestone, S. 1970. *The Dialectic of Sex*. New York: Morrow; London: Jonathan Cape.

Foord, J. & Gregson, N. 1986. Patriarchy: towards reconceptualisation. *Antipode* 18, 181–211.

Ford, B. (ed.) 1961. *The Modern Age, Volume 7 of the Pelican Guide to English Literature*. Harmondsworth: Penguin.

Ford, C. & Harrison, B. 1983. *A Hundred Years Ago. Britain in the 1880s in Words and Photographs*. Harmondsworth: Penguin Allen Lane.

Foster, J. 1974. *Class Struggle and the Industrial Revolution. Early Industrial Capitalism in Three English Towns*. London: Weidenfeld & Nicolson.

Foucault, M. 1981. *The History of Sexuality. Volume One: An Introduction*. Harmondsworth: Penguin. 1st pub. in French 1976.

Fowler, L. 1985. Women and work – sexual harassment, patriarchy and the labour process. Unpub. ms. MSc Industrial Sociology, Bradford: University of Bradford.

Fraser, N. 1981. Foucault on modern power: empirical insights and normative confusions. *Praxis International* 1(3, October), 272–87.

Fraser, N. 1989. *Unruly Practices. Power, Discourse and Gender in Contemporary Social Theory*. Cambridge: Polity.

Fraser, W. H. 1981. *The Coming of the Mass Market 1850–1914*. London: Macmillan.

Frassanito, W. A. 1978. *Antietam. The Photographic Legacy of America's Bloodiest Day*. New York: Scribners.

Friedan, B. 1963. *The Feminine Mystique*. New York: W. W. Norton.

Fussell, P. 1975. *The Great War and Modern Memory*. New York and London: Oxford University Press.

Game, A. 1989. Research and writing: 'secretaries and bosses'. *Journal of Pragmatics* 13, 343–61.

Garb, T. 1986. *Women Impressionists*. New York: Rizzoli; Oxford: Phaidon.

Giddens, A. 1981. *The Class Structure of the Advanced Societies*. London: Hutchinson. 1st pub. 1973.

Gilligan, C. 1982. *In a Different Voice: Essays on Psychological Theory and Women's Development*. Cambridge, Mass.: Harvard University Press.

Gillis, J. R. 1985. *For Better, For Worse. British Marriage, 1600 to the Present.* New York and Oxford: Oxford University Press.

Goffman, E. 1961. *Asylums.* New York: Anchor.

Golby, J. M. & Purdue, A. M. 1984. *The Civilisation of the Crowd.* London: Batsford.

Gooch, J. 1974. *The Plans of War. The General Staff and British Military Strategy c.1900–1916.* London: Routledge & Kegan Paul.

Gordon, L. 1976. *Woman's Body, Woman's Rights: A Social History of Birth Control in America.* New York: Grossman.

Griffin, S. 1982. The way of all ideology. In *Feminist Theory. A Critique of Ideology,* N. O. Keohane, M. Z. Rosaldo & B. C. Gelpi (eds), 273–92. Brighton: Harvester; Chicago: University of Chicago Press.

Grint, K. 1988. Women and equality. The acquisition of equal pay in the Post Office 1870/1961. *Sociology* 22(1, February), 87–108.

Grossberg, M. 1985a. Crossing boundaries: nineteenth century domestic relations law and the merger of family and legal history. *American Bar Foundation Research Journal* 4, 799–847.

Grossberg, M. 1985b. *Governing the Hearth: Law and the Family in Nineteenth Century America.* Chapel Hill, NC: University of North Carolina Press.

Grosz, E. A. 1987. Feminist theory and the challenge to knowledges. *Women's Studies International Forum* 10(5), 475–80.

Guillaumin, C. 1980. The practice and power of belief in nature, Part I: the appropriation of women. *Feminist Issues* 1(2), 3–28.

Gummett, P. 1980. *Scientists in Whitehall.* Manchester: Manchester University Press.

Habermas, J. 1975. *Strukturwandel der Offentlichkeit: Untersuchungen zu einer Kategorie der burgerlichen Gesellschaft.* Luchterhand: Neuwied.

Habermas, J. 1984. *The Theory of Communicative Action, Vol. 1, Reason and the Rationalization of Society,* trans. T. McCarthy. Boston: Beacon.

Habermas, J. 1987. *The Theory of Communicative Action, Vol. 2, Lifeworld and System: A Critique of Functionalist Reason,* trans. T. McCarthy. Boston: Beacon.

Hakim, C. 1979. *Occupational Segregation.* London: Department of Employment Research Paper No. 9.

Halbert, M. 1989. Feminist epistemology: an impossible project? *Radical Philosophy* 53, 3–7.

Hall, L. A. 1991. *Hidden Anxieties. Male Sexuality, 1900–1950.* Cambridge: Polity.

Hall, M. 1989. Private experiences in the public domain: Lesbians in organizations. In *The Sexuality of Organization,* J. Hearn, D. Sheppard, P. Tancred-Sheriff & G. Burrell (eds), 125–38. London and Newbury Park, Ca: Sage.

Hamilton, R. 1883. Popular education in England and Wales before and after the Elementary Education Act of 1870. *Journal of the Royal Statistical Society* 46 (June), 283–340.

Hamilton, R. 1890. Popular education in England and Wales since 1882. *Journal of the Royal Statistical Society* 53 (March), 50–105.

Hamilton, R. 1967. *Affluence and the French Worker in the Fourth Republic.* Princeton, NJ: Princeton University Press.

Hanham, W. 1968. *The Reformed Electoral System in Great Britain 1832–1914*, London: Historical Association.

Hanmer, J. 1990. Men, power and the exploitation of women. In *Men, Masculinities and Social Theory*, J. Hearn & D. H. J. Morgan (eds), 21–42. London and Boston: Unwin Hyman.

Harding, S. 1986. *The Science Question in Feminism.* Milton Keynes: Open University Press.

Harrison, B. 1978. *Separate Spheres. The Opposition to Women's Suffrage in Britain.* London: Croom Helm.

Harrison, B. 1982. *Peaceable Kingdom. Stability and Change in Modern Britain.* Oxford: Clarendon Press.

Harrison, R. & Mort, F. 1980. Patriarchal aspects of nineteenth century state formation: property relations, marriage and divorce, and sexuality. In *Capitalism, State Formation and Marxist Theory*, P. Corrigan (ed.), 79–109. London: Quartet.

Harrison, T. (ed.) (Mass Observation) 1943. *War Factory: A Report.* London: Gollancz.

Hart, J. 1978. Police. In *Crime and Law in Nineteenth Century Britain*, W. R. Cornish, J. Hart, A. H. Manchester & J. Stevenson, 177–211. Dublin: Irish University Press.

Hartmann, H. 1979. The unhappy marriage of Marxism and Feminism: towards a more progressive union. *Capital and Class* 8(2), 1–33.

Hartsock, N. 1983. *Money, Sex and Power. Toward a Feminist Historical Materialism.* New York and London: Longman.

Harvey, A. D. 1978. *Clarissa* and the Puritan tradition. *Essays in Criticism* **xxvii**, 38–51.

Harvey, A. D. 1989. Female sexuality. *History Workshop* **27** (Spring), 242–3.

Haug, F. 1987. *Female Sexualization.* London: Verso. 1st pub. 1983.

Hearn, J. 1982. Notes on patriarchy, professionalisation and the semi-professions. *Sociology* **16**(2), 184–202.

Hearn, J. 1983. *Birth and Afterbirth: A Materialist Account.* London: Achilles Heel.

Hearn, J. 1986. Patriarchy, masculinity and psychoanalysis. Unpub. ms., Bradford: University of Bradford.

Hearn, J. 1987a. *The Gender of Oppression. Men, Masculinity and the Critique of Marxism.* Brighton: Wheatsheaf; New York: St Martin's.

Hearn, J. 1987b. Patriarchy, masculinity and psychoanalysis. Paper at 'Psychoanalysis and the Public Sphere' Conference, North East London Polytechnic/Free Associations, October. University of Bradford: mimeo.

Hearn, J. 1988a. Child abuse: violences and sexualities to young people. *Sociology* **22**(4, November), 531–44.

Hearn, J. 1988b. Speaking the unspeakable: The historical development of organisations and men's sexuality in the public domain. British Sociological Association Conference, 'Sociology and History', University of Edinburgh, March. University of Bradford: mimeo.

Hearn, J. 1989a. Reviewing men and masculinities – or mostly boys' own papers. *Theory, Culture and Society* 6(4), 665–89.

Hearn, J. 1989b. *Some Sociological Issues in Researching Men and Masculinities*, Hallsworth Research Fellowship Working Paper No. 2. Manchester: Department of Social Policy and Social Work, University of Manchester.

Hearn, J. 1990a. 'Child abuse' and men's violence. In *Taking Child Abuse Seriously*, The Violence Against Children Study Group, 63–85. London: Unwin Hyman.

Hearn, J. 1990b. State organisations and men's sexuality in the public domain 1870–1920. In *The State, Private Life and Political Change*, L. Jamieson & H. Corr (eds), 50–72. London: Macmillan.

Hearn, J. 1991a. Gender: biology, nature and capitalism. In *Marx: Cambridge Companions to Philosophy*, T. Carver (ed.), 222–45. New York: Cambridge University Press.

Hearn, J. 1991b. Recent developments in the critical study of men and men's bodies – or trying to talk men's bodies. In *Kropp og Kjonn*, O. G. Holter (ed.). Oslo: Norges Rad for Anvelt Samfunnsforskning (NORAS).

Hearn, J. 1992. The personal, the political and the theoretical: the case of men's sexualities and sexual violences. In *Men and Feminism* (provisional title), D. Porter (ed.). London: Routledge.

Hearn, J. & Collinson, D. 1990. Unities and differences between men and masculinities. (1) The categories of men and the case of sociology. Paper at British Sociological Association Annual Conference, 'Social Divisions and Social Change', University of Surrey, April. University of Bradford: mimeo.

Hearn, J. & Melechi, A. 1992. The Transatlantic gaze: youth, masculinities and the American Imaginary. In *Mediated Men. Images of American Males in the Mass Media*, S. Craig (ed.). Newbury Park, Ca: Sage.

Hearn, J. & Morgan, D. H. J. (eds) 1990. *Men, Masculinities and Social Theory*. London and Boston: Unwin Hyman.

Hearn, J. & Parkin, P. W. 1983. Gender and organizations: a selective review and a critique of a neglected area. *Organization Studies* 4(3), 219–42.

Hearn, J. & Parkin, P. W. 1986–7. Women, men and leadership: a critical review of assumption, practices and change in the industrialized nations. *International Studies on Management and Organization* 16(3–4), 3–32.

Hearn, J. & Parkin, P. W. 1987. *'Sex' at 'Work'. The Power and Paradox of Organisation Sexuality*. Brighton: Wheatsheaf; New York: St Martin's.

Hearn, J. & Parkin, P. W. 1991. The narratives of oppressions: from paradigms and metaphors to gender and sexuality to the interrelations of multiple oppressions. Paper presented at 'Towards a new theory of organisations' Conference, Keele University, April. University of Bradford: mimeo.

Hearn, J. & Parkin, P. W. 1992. Women, men, management and

[264]

leadership. In *Women in Management Worldwide*, 2nd edn, N. Adler & D. Izraeli (eds). New York: M. E. Sharpe.

Hearn, J., Sheppard, D., Tancred-Sheriff, P. & Burrell, G. (eds) 1989. *The Sexuality of Organization*. London and Newbury Park, Ca: Sage.

Henderson, I. T. 1974. *Pictorial Souvenirs of Britain*. Newton Abbot: David & Charles.

Hendrick, H. 1990. *Images of Youth: Age, Class and the Male Youth Problem, 1880–1920*. Oxford: Clarendon.

Hernes, H. M. 1984. Women and the welfare state. The transition from private to public dependence. In *Patriarchy in a Welfare Society*, H. Holter (ed.), 26–45. Oslo: Universitetsforlaget.

Hernes, H. M. 1987a. *Welfare State and Woman Power*. Oslo: Norwegian University Press.

Hernes, H. M. 1987b. Women and the welfare state: the transition from private to public dependence. In *Women and the State. The Shifting Boundaries of Public and Private*, A. S. Sassoon (ed.), 72–92. London: Hutchinson.

Hernes, H. M. 1988a. Scandinavian citizenship. *Acta Sociologica* **31**(3), 199–215.

Hernes, H. M. 1988b. The welfare state citizenship of Scandinavian women. In *The Political Interests of Gender. Developing Theory and Research with a Feminist Face*, K. B. Jones & A. G. Jonasdottir (eds), 187–213. London and Newbury Park, Ca: Sage.

Heussler, R. 1963. *Yesterday's Rulers*. Syracuse, NY and Oxford: Syracuse University Press; London: London University Press.

Heward, C. 1988. *Making a Man of Him. Parents and their Son's Education at an English Public School 1929–50*. London: Routledge.

Hey, V. 1986. *Patriarchy and Pub Culture*. London: Tavistock.

Higgs, R. J. 1987. Yale and the heroic ideal, *Götterdämmerung* and palingenesis, 1865–1914. In *Manliness and Morality. Middle-class Masculinity in Britain and America 1800–1940*, J. A. Mangan & J. Walvin (eds), 160–75. Manchester: Manchester University Press.

Hindess, B. 1987. *Politics and Class Analysis*. Oxford: Blackwell.

Hirst, P. & Woolley, P. 1982. *Social Relations and Human Attributes*. London: Tavistock.

Historical Abstract of British Labour Statistics, 1886–1968 1971. London: HMSO.

Hobsbawm, E. & Ranger, T. (eds) 1983. *The Invention of Tradition*. Cambridge: Cambridge University Press.

Hochschild, A. R. 1983. *The Managed Heart. The Commercialization of Human Feeling*. Berkeley, Ca: University of California Press.

Holcombe, L. 1973. *Victorian Ladies at Work. Middle-Class Working Women in England and Wales 1850–1914*. Newton Abbot: David & Charles.

Hollway, W. 1984. Gender difference and the production of subjectivity. In *Changing the Subject*, J. Henriques, W. Hollway, C. Urwin, C. Venn & V. Walkerdine, 227–63. London: Methuen.

Holter, H. (ed.) 1984. *Patriarchy in a Welfare Society*. Oslo: Universitetsforlaget.

Hower, R. M. 1949. *The History of an Advertising Agency*. Cambridge, Mass.: Harvard University Press.

Humm, M. 1989. *The Dictionary of Feminist Theory*. New York and London: Harvester Wheatsheaf.

Humphries, S. 1988. *A Secret World of Sex. Forbidden Fruit: The British Experience 1900-1950*. London: Sidgwick & Jackson.

Hunter, I. 1988. *Culture and Government*. London: Macmillan.

Hurst, G. B. 1942. *Closed Chapters*. Manchester: Manchester University Press.

Hutchins, B. L. 1915. *Women in Modern Industry*. London: G. Bell & Sons.

Irigaray, L. 1985. *This Sex Which Is Not One*. New York: Cornell University Press. 1st pub. in French 1977.

Izod, J. 1988. *Hollywood and the Box Office 1895-1986*. London: Macmillan.

Jackson, D. 1990. *Unmasking Masculinity. A Critical Autobiography*. London and Boston: Unwin Hyman.

Jackson, H. 1976. *The Eighteen Nineties*. Hassocks: Harvester. 1st pub. 1913.

Jacoby, R. 1977. *Social Amnesia. A Critique of Conformist Psychology from Adler to Laing*. Boston: Beacon, 1975; Hassocks: Harvester.

James, J. S. 1986. *Stroud's Judicial Dictionary of Words and Phrases*, 5th edn, vol. 1. London: Sweet & Maxwell.

Jardine, A. 1987. Men in feminism: odor di homo or compagnons de route. In *Men in Feminism*, A. Jardine & P. Smith (eds), 54–61. London: Methuen.

Jefferson, T. 1987. Beyond paramilitarism. *British Journal of Criminology* **27**(1, Winter), 47–53.

Jenson, J., Hagen, E. & Reddy, C. (eds) 1988. *Feminization of the Labour Force*. Cambridge: Polity.

Joyce, P. 1980. *Work, Society and Politics. The Culture of the Factory in Later Victorian England*. London: Methuen.

Kaite, B. 1988. The pornographer's body double: transgression is the law. In *Body Invaders. Sexuality and the Postmodern Condition*, A. and M. Kroker (eds), 150–68. London: Macmillan.

Kakar, S. 1970. *Frederick Taylor: A Study in Personality and Innovation*. Cambridge, Mass.: MIT Press.

Karl, F. R. 1985. *Modern and Modernism. The Sovereignty of the Artist 1885-1925*. New York: Atheneum.

Katz, J. 1983. The invention of heterosexuality. Paper presented at the New York Institute for the Humanities seminar on Sexuality and the Consumer Culture.

Keane, J. 1984. *Public Life and Late Capitalism: Towards a Socialist Theory of Democracy*. Cambridge: Cambridge University Press.

Kellogg, J. H. 1886. *Man, the Masterpiece, or Plain Truths Plainly Told, About Boyhood, Youth and Manhood*. Battle Creek, Mich. Chicago, Ill.: Modern Medicine Pub., 1894; London: Pacific Press, 1890.

Kelly, J. 1979. The doubled vision of feminist theory: a postscript to the 'Women and Power' Conference. *Feminist Studies* **5**(1, Spring), 216–27.
Kennedy, P. 1980. *The War Plans of the Great Powers 1880–1914*. London: Allen & Unwin.
Kent, S. K. 1987. *Sex and Suffrage in Britain 1860–1914*. Princeton, NJ and Oxford: Princeton University Press.
Kern, S. 1983. *The Culture of Time and Space*. London: Weidenfeld & Nicolson.
Kimmel, M. S. 1986. Teaching about men: retrieving women's studies' long lost brother. *Journal of the National Association for Women Deans, Administrators & Counselors* **49**(4, Summer), 13–21.
Kimmel, M. S. 1987. The contemporary 'crisis' of masculinity in historical perspective. In *The Making of Masculinities. The New Men's Studies*, H. Brod (ed.), 121–53. Boston and London: Allen & Unwin.
Kindleberger, C. P. 1964. *Economic Growth in France and Britain 1851–1950*. Oxford: Oxford University Press; Cambridge, Mass.: Harvard University Press.
Klein, V. 1965. *Britain's Married Women Workers*. London: Routledge & Kegan Paul.
Kocka, J. 1980. *White Collar Workers in America 1890–1940. A Social–Political History in International Perspective*. London and Beverly Hills, Ca: Sage. Trans. M. Kealey.
Kriek, E. 1932. *Nationalpolitische Erziehung*. Leipzig: Armanen-Verlag.
Kuhn, A. 1988. *Cinema, Censorship and Sexuality, 1909–1925*. London and New York: Routledge.

Labour Law Commissioners on Working of Master and Servant Act, 1875. Second and Final Report, *Parliamentary Papers*, **xxx** (1157–1).
Lambertz, J. 1985. Sexual harassment in the nineteenth century English cotton industry. *History Workshop* **19** (Spring), 29–61.
Lasch, C. 1977. *Haven in a Heartless World: The Family Besieged*. New York: Basic Books.
Lasch, C. 1979. *The Culture of Narcissism*. New York: W. W. Norton.
Lasch, C. 1984. *The Minimal Self. Psychic Survival in the Troubled Times*. London: Pan; New York: W. W. Norton.
Laurin-Frenette, N. 1982. The women's movement, anarchism and the state. *Our Generation* **15**(2, Summer), 27–39.
Law, S. A. 1983. Women, work, welfare and the preservation of patriarchy. *University of Pennsylvania Law Review* **131**(6, May), 1250–61.
Leach, W. 1981. *True Love and Perfect Union: The Feminist Reform of Sex and Society*. London: Routledge & Kegan Paul.
Lears, T. J. J. 1981. *No Place of Grace. Antimodernism and the Transformation of American Culture 1880–1920*. New York: Pantheon.
Lee, A. J. 1976. *The Origins of the Popular Press 1855–1914*. London: Croom Helm; Totowa, NJ: Rowman & Littlefield.
Lee, J. M. (ed.) 1974. *Approaches to the Study of Public Administration. Part 4: The Historical Approach*. Milton Keynes: Open University Press.

Leed, E. 1979. *No Man's Land. Combat and Identity in World War I.* London and New York: Cambridge University Press.

Legge, K. 1987. Women in personnel management: uphill climb or downhill slide? In *In a Man's World: Essays on Women in Male-Dominated Professions,* A. Spencer & D. Podmore (eds), 33–60. London: Routledge.

Lévi-Strauss, C. 1949. *The Elementary Structure of Kinship.* Boston, Mass.: Beacon.

Lewis, J. 1980. *The Politics of Motherhood: Child and Maternal Welfare in England 1900–1939.* London: Croom Helm.

Lewis, J. 1984. *Women in England 1870–1950: Sexual Divisions and Social Change.* Brighton: Wheatsheaf; Bloomington, Ind.: Indiana University Press.

Lewis, J. 1986. The working-class wife and mother and state intervention, 1870–1918. In *Labour and Love. Women's Experience of Home and Family 1850–1940,* J. Lewis (ed.), 99–120. Oxford: Basil Blackwell.

Lewis, J. E. 1988. Women clerical workers in the late nineteenth and early twentieth centuries. In *The White-Blouse Revolution. Female Office Workers since 1870,* G. Anderson (ed.), 27–47. Manchester: Manchester University Press.

Lloyd, A. (ed.) 1984. *Movies in the Silent Years.* London: Orbis.

Lloyd, G. 1984. *The Man of Reason. 'Male' and 'Female' in Western Philosophy.* London: Methuen.

London Edinburgh Weekend Return Group 1980. *In and Against the State.* London: Pluto.

Low, R. 1948. *The History of British Film 1896–1929, Volume 1.* London: Allen & Unwin.

Low, R. 1971. *The History of British Film 1896–1929, Volume 4.* London: Allen & Unwin.

Lowe, G. S. 1987. *Women in the Administrative Revolution.* Cambridge: Polity.

Lucie-Smith, E. 1972. The other arts. In *The Twentieth Century Mind. History, Ideas, and Literature in Britain 1900–1918,* C. B. Cox & A. E. Dyson (eds), 485–511. London: Oxford University Press.

Lunn, E. 1985. *Marxism and Modernism.* London: Verso.

Lynch, K. 1989. Solidary labour: its nature and marginalisation. *Sociological Review* 37(1, February), 1–14.

McClelland, K. 1989. Some thoughts on masculinity and the 'Representative Artisan' in Britain, 1850–1880. *Gender and History* 1(2), 164–77.

McKechnie, S. n.d. *Popular Entertainment through the Ages.* London: Sampson Low, Marston & Co.

McKendrick, N., Brewer, J. & Plumb, J. H. 1983. *The Birth of a Consumer Society: The Commercialization of Eighteenth Century England.* London: Hutchinson.

Mackie, L. & Pattullo, P. 1977. *Women at Work.* London: Tavistock.

MacKinnon, C. A. 1979. *The Sexual Harassment of Working Women.* New Haven, Conn.: Yale University Press.

BIBLIOGRAPHY

MacKinnon, C. A. 1982. Feminism, marxism, method and the state: an agenda for theory. *Signs* 7(3), 515–44.

MacKinnon, C. A. 1983. Feminism, marxism, method and the state: toward feminist jurisprudence. *Signs* 8(4), 635–58.

MacKinnon, C. A. 1989. *Toward a Feminist Theory of the State*. Cambridge, Mass. and London: Harvard University Press.

McLean, S. A. & Burrow, N. 1988. *The Legal Relevance of Gender. Some Aspects of Sex-Based Discrimination*. London: Macmillan.

Mandell, M. J. 1968. *Advertising*. Englewood Cliffs, NJ: Prentice-Hall.

Mangan, J. 1986. *The Games Ethic and Imperialism: Aspects of the Diffusion of an Ideal*. Harmondsworth: Viking Penguin; Manchester: Manchester University Press.

Mangan, J. A. & Walvin, J. (eds) 1987. *Manliness and Morality. Middle-class Masculinity in Britain and America, 1800–1940*. Manchester: Manchester University Press.

Marinetti, F. T. 1971. *Marinetti: Selected Writings*, ed. C. W. Flint. New York: Farrar, Straus & Giroux.

Markin, R. J. 1963. *The Supermarket: An Analysis of Growth, Development and Change*. Washington: Washington State University Press.

Marx, K. 1975. Economic and philosophical manuscripts. In *Early Writings*. Harmondsworth: Penguin.

Masson, J. M. 1984. *The Assault on Truth. Freud's Suppression of the Seduction Theory*. New York: Farrar, Straus & Giroux.

Matthews, G. 1987. *'Just a Housewife'. The Rise and Fall of Domesticity in America*. New York and London: Oxford University Press.

Meyrowitz, J. 1986. *No Sense of Place. The Impact of Electronic Media on Social Behaviour*. Oxford: Oxford University Press.

Midwinter, E. C. 1968. *Victorian Social Reform*. London: Longman. 14th impression 1988.

Mies, M. 1986. *Patriarchy and Accumulation on the World Scale*. London: Zed.

Mihill, C. 1991. Virgin birth law 'adequate'. *Guardian*, 12 March, 1.

Miles, R. 1988. *The Women's History of the World*. London: Michael Joseph.

Minor, I. 1979. Working-class women and Matrimonial Law Reform, 1890–1914. In *Ideology and the Labour Movement*, D. E. Martin & D. Rubenstein (eds), 102–24. London: Croom Helm; Totowa, NJ: Rowman & Littlefield.

Mitchell, B. R. & Deane, P. 1962. *Abstract of British Historical Statistics*. Cambridge: Cambridge University Press.

Moore, H. 1987. *Feminism and Anthropology*. Cambridge: Cambridge University Press.

Morgan, D. H. J. 1990. In search of post-modern man. Paper at British Sociological Association Annual Conference, 'Social Divisions and Social Change', University of Surrey, April. University of Manchester: mimeo.

Morgan, D. H. J. 1992. *Discovering Men*. London and New York: Routledge.

Morgan, G. 1986. *Images of Organization*. Newbury Park, Ca: Sage.

Mort, F. 1985. Purity, feminism and the state: sexuality and moral politics, 1880–1914. In *Crises in the British State 1880–1930*, M. Langan & B. Schwartz (eds), 209–25. London: Hutchinson.
Mort, F. 1987. *Dangerous Sexualities. Medico-Moral Politics in England since 1830*. London: Routledge & Kegan Paul.
Motherson, K. 1979. Wider we. Towards an anarchist politics. In *Women are the Real Left*, M. J. Sjoo & K. Motherson. Manchester: Matri/anarchy.

O'Brien, M. 1979. Reproducing Marxist man. In *The Sexism of Social Political Theory, Women and Reproduction from Plato to Nietzsche*, M. G. Clark & L. Lange (eds), 99–116. Toronto: University of Toronto Press.
O'Brien, M. 1981. *The Politics of Reproduction*. London: Routledge & Kegan Paul.
O'Brien, M. 1990. *Reproducing the World*. Boulder, Col.: Westview.
O'Donovan, K. 1985. *Sexual Divisions in Law*. London: Weidenfeld & Nicolson.
O'Donovan, M. 1986. Family law and legal theory. In *Legal Theory and Common Law*, W. Twining (ed.), 184–94. Oxford and New York: Blackwell.
O'Leary, C. C. 1962. *The Elimination of Corrupt Practices at British Elections, 1868–1911*. Oxford: Clarendon.
Ortner, S. 1974. Is female to male as nature is to culture? In *Woman, Culture and Society*, M. Z. Rosaldo & L. Lamphere (eds), 67–87. Stanford, Ca: Stanford University Press.
Otter, L. 1986. Domestic violence: a feminist perspective: implications for practice. In *Gender Reclaimed, Women in Social Work*, H. Marchant & B. Waring (eds), 104–19. Sydney: Hale & Iremonger.

Pankhurst, C. 1913. *The Hidden Scourge and How to End it*. London: E. Pankhurst.
Parkin, W. 1989. Private experiences in the public domain: sexuality and residential care organizations.In *The Sexuality of Organization*, J. Hearn, D. Sheppard, P. Tancred-Sheriff & G. Burrell (eds), 110–24. London and Newbury Park, Ca: Sage.
Parry, N. & Parry, J. 1976. *The Rise of the Medical Profession*. London: Croom Helm.
Pelling, H. 1960. *Modern Britain, 1885–1955*. Edinburgh: Thomas Nelson.
Perkin, J. 1988. *Women and Marriage in Nineteenth Century England*. London: Routledge.
Pike, W. T. (ed.) 1902. *West Yorkshire at the Opening of the Twentieth Century: Contemporary Biographies*, Pike's New Century Series No. 6. Reprinted Edinburgh: Peter Bell, 1986.
Pinchbeck, I. 1981. *Women Workers and the Industrial Revolution, 1750–1850*. London: Virago.
Pleck, J. & Pleck, E. (eds) 1980. *The American Man*. Englewood Cliffs, NJ: Prentice-Hall.

Poffenberger, A. T. 1925. *Psychology in Advertising*. New York: McGraw-Hill.

Polan, D. 1982. Toward a theory of law and patriarchy. In *The Politics of Law. A Progressive Critique*, D. Kairys (ed.), 294–303. New York: Pantheon.

Pollard, S. 1989. *Britain's Prime and Britain's Decline. The British Economy, 1870–1914*. London: Edward Arnold.

Radford, L. M. T. 1988. The law and domestic violence against women. Doctoral thesis, Bradford: University of Bradford.

Radzinowitz, L. 1956. *A History of English Criminal Law and its Administration from 1750. Vol. II. The Clash between Private Initiative and Public Interest in the Enforcement of the Law*. London: Stevens.

Ramazanoglu, C. 1988. *Feminism and the Contradictions of Oppression*. London: Routledge.

Rawlence, C. 1990. *The Missing Reel*. London: Collins.

Reader, K. 1979. *The Cinema. A History*. London: Hodder & Stoughton; New York: David McKay.

Reader, W. J. 1966. *The Rise of the Professional Classes in Nineteenth Century England*. London: Weidenfeld & Nicolson.

Reed, J. R. 1964. *Old School Ties. The Public Schools in British Literature*. Syracuse, NY: Syracuse University Press.

Remy, J. 1988. Patriarchy and fratriarchy as forms of androcracy spawned in the men's hut 'womb'. Paper at British Sociological Association Conference, 'Men, Masculinity and Social Theory', University of Bradford, July.

Remy, J. 1990. Patriarchy and fratriarchy as forms of androcracy. In *Men, Masculinities and Social Theory*, J. Hearn & D. H. J. Morgan (eds), 43–54. London and Cambridge, Mass.: Unwin Hyman.

Rheingold, H. 1991. *Virtual Reality*. London: Secker & Warburg.

Rhode, E. 1976. *A History of the Cinema from its Origins to 1970*. London: Allen Lane.

Richards, B. 1986. Psychological practice and social democracy. *Free Associations* 5, 105–36.

Richards, J. 1984. *Age of the Dream Palace*. London: Routledge & Kegan Paul.

Richards, J. 1988. *Happiest Days: The Public Schools in English Fiction*. Manchester: Manchester University Press.

Riesman, D. in collaboration with R. Denney and N. Glazer 1969. *The Lonely Crowd: A Study of the Changing American Character*. New Haven, Conn. and London: Yale University Press. 1st pub. 1950.

Rosaldo, M. Z. 1974. Women, culture and society: a theoretical overview. In *Women, Culture and Society*, M. Rosaldo & L. Lamphere (eds), 17–42. Stanford, Ca: Stanford University Press.

Rose, L. 1986. *Massacre of the Innocents. Infanticide in Great Britain 1800–1939*. London and Boston: Routledge & Kegan Paul.

Routh, C. H. F. 1879. *The Moral and Physical Evils Likely to follow practices intended as Checks to Population be not Strongly Discouraged or Condemned*. Reprinted from the Medical Press and Circular, October 1878.

Routh, G. 1980. *Occupation and Pay in Great Britain 1906–79*, 2nd edn. London: Macmillan.

Rowan, C. 1985. Child welfare and the working-class family. In *Crises in the British State 1880–1930*, M. Langan & B. Schwartz (eds), 226–39. London: Hutchinson.

Rowbotham, S. 1979. The trouble with patriarchy. *New Statesman* **98**, 2544/5, 21/28 December, 970–1.

Rubin, G. 1975. The traffic in women: notes on the 'political economy' of sex. In *Toward an Anthropology of Women*, R. R. Reiter (ed.), 157–210. New York: Monthly Review Press.

Ruggie, M. 1984. *The State and Working Women*. Princeton, NJ: Princeton University Press.

Russell, D. E. H. (ed.) 1989. *Exposing Nuclear Phallacies*. New York and Oxford: Pergamon.

Saul, S. B. 1976. *The Myth of the Great Depression 1873–1896*, 2nd edn. London: Macmillan.

Savile, J. 1988. Review. Leonore Davidoff and Catherine Hall, *Family Fortunes*. *History Workshop* **26**, 188–90.

Scott, W. D. 1913. *The Psychology of Advertising*. Boston: Small Maynard.

Second Report of the Royal Commission Appointed to Inquire into the Civil Establishments of the Different Offices of State. 1888. *Parliamentary Papers*.

Seers, H. D. 1977. *The Sex Radicals. Free Love in High America*. Lawrence: The Regents Press of Kansas.

Sekoff, J. 1987. Freud and film. Paper at 'Psychoanalysis and the Public Sphere' Conference, London: North East London Polytechnic/Free Association, October.

Sennett, R. 1977. *The Fall of Public Man*. New York: Knopf.

Shipman, D. (ed.) 1982. *The Story of Cinema. An Illustrated History, Volume One*. London: Hodder & Stoughton.

Showalter, E. 1987. *The Female Malady: Women, Madness and English Culture 1830–1980*. London: Virago.

Showalter, E. 1991. *Sexual Anarchy*. London: Bloomsbury.

Siim, B. 1987. The Scandinavian welfare state – towards sexual equality or a new kind of male domination. *Acta Sociologica* **30** (3/4), 255–70.

Siim, B. 1988. Towards a feminist rethinking of the welfare state. In *The Political Interests of Gender. Developing Theory and Research with a Feminist Face*, K. B. Jones & A. G. Jónasdóttir (eds), 160–86. London and Newbury Park, Ca: Sage.

Silverstone, R. 1976. Office work for women: an historical review. *Business History* **18**, 98–110.

Simmons, H. G. 1978. Explaining social policy: the English Mental Deficiency Act of 1913. *Journal of Social History* 11: 385–403.

Smiles, S. 1871. *Character*. London: John Murray.

Smith, D. E. 1987. Feminist reflections on political economy. *Studies in Political Economy* **30**, 37–59.

Soja, E. W. 1989. *Postmodern Geographies. The Reassertion of Space in Critical Social Theory*. London: Verso.

Soloway, R. A. 1982. *Birth Control and the Population Question in England, 1877–1930.* Chapel Hill, NC and London: University of North Carolina Press.

Sontag, S. 1978. *On Photography.* Harmondsworth: Penguin.

Spender, D. (ed.) 1981. *Men's Studies Modified.* Oxford: Pergamon.

Springhall, J. O. 1977. *Youth, Empire and Society: British Youth Movements 1883–1940.* London: Croom Helm.

Stacey, M. 1981. The division of labour revisited or overcoming the two Adams. In *Practice and Progress. British Sociology 1950–1980,* P. Abrams, R. Deern, J. Finch & P. Rocks (eds), 172–90. London: Allen & Unwin.

Stacey, M. 1982. Masculine or feminine powers? Action in the public domain. Paper at International Sociological Association Annual Conference, Mexico, August. University of Warwick: mimeo.

Stacey, M. 1986. Gender and stratification: one central issue or two. In *Gender and Stratification,* R. Crompton & M. Mann (eds), 214–23. Cambridge: Polity.

Stacey, M. 1988. *The Sociology of Health and Illness.* London and Cambridge, Mass.: Unwin Hyman.

Stacey, M. & Davies, C. 1983. *Division of Labour in Child Health Care: Final Report to the S.S.R.C.* Coventry: University of Warwick.

Stacey, M. & Price, M. 1981. *Women, Power and Politics.* London: Tavistock.

Starch, D. 1923. *Principles of Advertising.* New York: McGraw-Hill.

Stevenson, J. 1978. Civil disorder. In *Crime and Law in Nineteenth Century Britain,* W. R. Cornish, J. Hart, A. H. Manchester & J. Stevenson, 153–76. Dublin: Irish University Press.

Stoltenberg, J. 1990. *Refusing to be a Man. Essays on Sex and Justice.* New York: Meridian; London: Collins.

Stone, E. & Johnson, H. 1987. *Forensic Medicine.* London: Waterlow.

Strauss, S. 1983. *'Traitors to the Masculine Cause': The Men's Campaigns for Women's Rights.* Westport, Conn.: Greenwood.

Summers, Y. 1989. Women and citizenship: the insane, the insolvent and the inanimate? Paper at British Sociological Conference 'Sociology in Action', Plymouth, April. Revised version, 1991, in *Women, Sexuality and Power,* P. Abbott & C. Wallace (eds), 19–40. London: Macmillan.

Symons, J. 1987. *Makers of the New. The Revolution in Literature, 1912–1939.* London: Andre Deutsch.

Teichman, O. 1940. The yeomanry as an aid to the civil power 1795–1867. Part II. 1831–1867. *Journal of the Society for Army Historical Research* **19**, 127–43.

Temkin, J. 1987. *Rape and Legal Process.* London: Sweet & Maxwell.

Theleweit, K. 1987. *Male Fantasies. Volume One.* Cambridge: Polity.

The Times 1886. 29 June.

Thomis, M. I. & Grimmett, J. 1982. *Women in Protest 1800–1850.* London: Croom Helm.

Tolson, A. 1977. *The Limits of Masculinity.* London: Tavistock.

Tosh, J. 1991. Domesticity and manliness in the Victorian middle class: the family of Edward White Benson. In *Manful Assertions. Masculinities* in *Britain since 1800*, M. Roper & J. Tosh (eds), 44–73. London: Routledge.

Tucker, K. & Treno, A. 1980. The culture of narcissism and the critical tradition. An interpretive essay. *Berkeley Journal of Sociology* 25, 341–55.

Unger, R. 1975. *Knowledge and Politics*. New York: Free Press.

Unofficial Reform Committee 1912. *The Miner's Next Step*. Tonypandy: Davies printer.

Ursel, J. 1986. The state and the maintenance of patriarchy: a case study of family, labour and welfare legislation in Canada. In *Family, Economy and the State*, J. Dickinson & B. Russell (eds), 150–91. London and Sydney: Croom Helm.

Vicinus, M. 1985. *Independent Women: Work and Community for Single Women 1850–1820*. London: Virago.

Vogel, L. 1983. *Marxism and the Oppression of Women. Toward a Unitary Theory*. London: Pluto.

Walby, S. 1986. *Patriarchy at Work*. Cambridge: Polity.

Walby, S. 1989. Theorizing patriarchy. *Sociology* 23(2, May), 213–34.

Walby, S. 1990a. *Theorizing Patriarchy*. Oxford: Blackwell.

Walby, S. 1990b. Women's employment and the periodisation of patriarchy. In *Politics of Everyday Life. Continuity and Change in Work and the Family*, H. Corr & L. Jamieson (eds), 141–61. London: Macmillan.

Walkowitz, J. R. 1980. *Prostitution in Victorian Society: Women, Class and the State*. Cambridge: Cambridge University Press.

Waters, C. 1990. *British Socialists and the Politics of Popular Culture 1884–1914*. Manchester: Manchester University Press.

Waters, M. 1989. Patriarchy and viriarchy. *Sociology* 23(2, May), 193–211.

Webb, B. 1971. *My Apprenticeship*. Harmondsworth: Penguin.

Weber, M. 1930. *The Protestant Ethic and the Spirit of Capitalism*. London: Allen & Unwin, 1976.

Weedon, C. 1987. *Feminist Practice and Poststructuralist Theory*. Oxford and New York: Blackwell.

Weeks, J. 1977. *Coming Out: Homosexual Politics in Britain from the Nineteenth Century to the Present*. London: Quartet.

Weeks, J. 1989. *Sex, Politics and Society*, 2nd edn. London: Routledge & Kegan Paul. 1st edn 1981.

Weinbaum, B. 1978. *The Curious Courtship of Women's Liberation and Socialism*. Boston: South End Press.

Weinberg, I. 1967. *The English Public Schools. The Sociology of Elite Education*. New York: Atherton.

Wenden, D. J. 1975. *The Birth of the Movies*. London: MacDonald.

Western, J. R. 1956. The volunteer as an anti-revolutionary force. *English Historical Review* 71(281), 603–14.

Westwood, S. 1990. Racism, black masculinity and the politics of space. In *Men, Masculinities and Social Theory*, J. Hearn & D. H. J. Morgan (eds), 55–71. London and Boston: Unwin Hyman.

Whyte, W. H. 1956. *The Organization Man*. New York: Simon & Schuster.

Wickham, G. (ed.) 1987. *Social Theory and Legal Politics*. Sydney: Local Consumption Publications.

Wickham, G. 1990a. The political possibilities of post-modernism. *Economy and Society* 19(1, February), 121–49.

Wickham, G. 1990b. Sport and the formation of manners. Murdoch University, Australia: mimeo.

Wilkinson, R. 1964. *Gentlemanly Power: British Leadership and the Public School Tradition*. New York: Oxford University Press. Title in England *The Prefects*.

Williams, F. 1989. Swiss men give women the vote. *The Independent on Sunday*, 30 April.

Williams, R. 1976. *Keywords*. London: Fontana.

Willson, F. M. G. 1955. Ministries and boards: some aspects of administrative development since 1832. *Public Administration* 33 (Spring), 43–58.

Wilson, A. 1976. *The Naughty Nineties*. London: Book Club Associates/ Eyre Methuen.

Wilson, J. n.d. *Joseph Wilson, His Life and Work*. London: Lund Humphries (1923?).

Winter, M. F. & Robert, E. R. 1980. Male dominance, late capitalism and the growth of instrumental reason. *Berkeley Journal of Sociology* 24/25, 249–80.

Wolfram, S. 1983. Eugenics and the Punishment of Incest Act 1908. *Criminal Law Review* 508–18.

Wood, C. 1983. *Olympian Dreamers. Victorian Classical Painters 1860– 1914*. London: Constable.

Wood, R. 1987. Raging Bull: the homosexual subtext in film. In *Beyond Patriarchy. Essays by Men on Power, Pleasure and Change*, M. Kaufman (ed.), 266–76. Toronto: Oxford University Press.

Wood, W. R. (Sub-Commissioner for Bradford and Leeds) 1842. *Report of the Royal Commission on Children's Employment (Mines)*, Cmnd 380.

Woolf, J. & Seed, J. (eds) 1988. *The Culture of Capital: Art, Power and the Nineteenth-Century Middle Class*. Manchester: Manchester University Press; New York: St Martin's Press.

Woolf, J. D. 1925. *Writing Advertising*. New York: Ronald Press.

Zimmeck, M. 1984. Strategies and stratagems for the employment of women in the British Civil Service, 1919–1939. *The Historical Journal* 27(4), 901–24.

Zimmeck, M. 1986. Jobs for the girls: the expansion of clerical work for women, 1850–1914. In *Unequal Opportunities, Women's Employment in England 1800–1918*, A. John (ed.), 153–78. Oxford: Blackwell.

Zimmeck, M. 1988. Get out and get under: the impact of demobilisation on the Civil Service, 1918–32. In *The White-Blouse Revolution. Female Office Workers Since 1870*, G. Anderson (ed.), 88–120. Manchester: Manchester University Press.

Zucker, I. 1964. *A Sourcebook of French Advertising Art*. London: Faber & Faber.

Name index

Abramovitz, M. 244
Acton, Lord 177
Adburgham, A. 182
Addelson, K.P. 145
Alexander, S. 99, 236
Allbutt, H.A. 106
Allen, A. 122
Allen, J. 133, 233
Alma-Tadema, Sir Lawrence 201
Anderson, Gregory 244, 245
Anderson, G.L. 150, 152, 154, 157, 177, 245
Aristotle 30
Armat, Thomas 189
Arnold, Matthew 213, 251
Arnold, Sir Thomas 210–11, 251
Aron, Cindy Sondik 175, 176, 177–8, 245
Atkins, Susan 174, 181

Baden-Powell, Robert 109
Bagehot, Walter 128
Bailey, P. 180, 206, 226, 248
Bailey, V. 125
Banks, J.A. & Banks, O. 106
Bara, Theda 192
Bardaglio, P. 241
Barker, D. 116
Barker, John 234
Barrett, Michele 45, 74, 235
Barthes, R. 252
Batty, P. 248
Beales, D. 128
Beardsley, Aubrey 250
Beckett, J.R. 162
Beechey, V. 236
Benfield, R. 191
Benkert, Karoly Maria 15
Bennett, Colonel 214

Benson, Susan Porter 183
Bentham, J. 14
Berger, P. 219
Bergeret, L.F.E. 239
Berman, M. 196, 249
Blackburn, S. 125
Blackstone, W. 119
Bland, L. 115, 116, 125, 240, 241
Bologh, R.W. 235
Borchorst, Anette 54, 63–4, 141, 240
Bordin, R. 242
Boris, E. 241
Bose, C.E. 234
Bott, A. 136, 156, 215, 248
Bottomley, Virginia 252
Brand, E.A. 182
Brandon, R. 240
Braverman, Harry 36, 150
Brehony, K. 113
Breton, Andre 250
Breuer, J.F. 218
Briggs, A. 131
Bristow, J. 249
Brittan, A. 16, 233, 252
Brod, Harry 101–2
Bromley, P.M. 119
Brookes, B. 240
Brophy, Julia 120
Brown, Carol 16, 54, 55–7, 58, 65, 141, 239
Brownlow, K. 189, 192
Bunyan, T. 134
Burawoy, M. 163
Burnham, J. 165
Burns, Ken 248
Burns, Ric 248
Burrell, G. 170
Burris, Beverly 243

Burrow, N. 241
Burstyn, V. 71, 240, 241
Butler, Josephine 123

Canaan, J.E. 5
Cardechi, G. 236, 247
Carnes, M.C. 249
Carrigan, T. 107, 249
Chaplin, Charlie 194
Chapman, R. 250
Charcot, J. 218
Child, J. 165
Clark, M.G. 29
Clawson, M.A. 249
Clawson, Dan 163
Clephane, I. 248
Cockburn, Cynthia 50, 225, 243,
    252
Cohen, E.W. 154, 155, 158, 159
Cohn, S. 245
Collins, P.H. 233
Collinson, D. 234, 238, 250
Collinson, D.L. 167
Collinson, David & Collinson,
    Margaret 245
Connell, R.W. 107, 239, 241, 249
Cooper, Fenimore 194
Copelman, D.M. 240
Corber, R.J. 14
Corbin, A. 226
Cox, C.B. 249

Davidoff, Leonore 14–15, 77
Davidson, A.I. 209
Davies, J. 250
Davies, M.W. 150, 160
Davis, Celia 54, 62, 86
de Vries, L. 248
Deacon, D. 245
Deane, P. 154
Delgado, A. 177
Delphy, C. 236
D'Emilio, John 107, 240
Derrida, Jacques 74, 235
Dewey, L. 194
Dicey, A.V. 127, 215
Disraeli, B. 130
Dixon, Norman 246

Dohrn, S. 244
Donnison, J. 143, 239
Drinka, G.F. 249, 251
du Cille, 233
Dubbert, Joe L. 16, 100–1, 249
Durham, M. 116
Durkheim, E. 28
Duroche, L. 226
Duxbury, N. 241
Dwork, D. 240
Dworkin, Andrea 53
Dyer, R. 193
Dyson, A.E. 249

Easthope, A. 252
Edison, Thomas 188–9
Edwards, S.S.M. 248
Edwards, Richard 152
Eekelaar, J. 121
Ehrenreich, B. 239
Eisenstein, Zillah 54, 57, 58
Elias, Norbert 39–40, 235
Eliasberg, V.F. 244
Ellis, John B. 176
Elshtain, Jean Bethke 48
Emerson, Ralph Waldo 33
English, D. 239
Epstein, B.L. 242
Escott, T.H.S. 242

Fairbanks, Douglas 194
Farr, Dr Samuel 124
Fawcett, Henry 156–7, 159
Feinstein, C.H. 239, 244
Felski, R. 32
Ferenczi, S. 222
Ferguson, A. 39, 90, 236
Ferguson, H. 115
Ferguson, Kathy E. 153, 240,
    243, 246
Feyder, Jacques 249
Filene, Peter G. 166, 249
Firestone, Shulamith 89, 236
Folbre, N. 90, 236
Foord, J. 78, 237
Ford, C. 187, 249
Foster, J. 161
Foucault, Michel 38–9, 107, 152,

235, 248
Fowler, Lesley 178
Fraser, Nancy 56–7, 235, 236
Fraser, W.H. 182
Frassanito, W.A. 248
Freedman, E. 240
Freud, S. 39, 72, 218, 222
Friedman, Betty 18
Friese-Greene, William 188
Fussell, Paul 204, 250

Game, Ann 250
Garb, T. 249
Garbo, Greta 192, 249
Giddens, A. 162
Gilligan, C. 76
Gillis, J.R. 109
Gish, Lillian 192
Gladstone, W.E. 130–1
Goffman, Erving 236, 244
Golby, John 251
Goldfish, Samuel/Goldwyn Sam
   192
Gooch, J. 135
Gordon, L. 125, 248
Gregson, N. 78, 237
Griffin, C. 5
Griffin, S. 75
Griffiths, D.W. 191, 194
Grimmett, J. 127
Grint, Keith 156, 158, 245
Grossberg, M. 241
Grosz, E.A. 170, 232, 238
Guillaumin, C. 54
Gummett, P. 136

Habermas, J. 32, 236
Haggard, Rider 249
Hakim, C. 152
Halbert, M. 75
Hale, Sir Matthew 123
Hall, Catherine 14–15
Hall, Lesley A. 117, 240, 246
Hall, Marny 107
Hamilton, R. 149, 162
Hanham, W. 129, 130, 242
Hanmer, J. 17
Harding, S. 233

Harrison, B. 132, 187, 241
Harrison, Brian 118
Harrison, R. 120
Harrison, T. 248
Hart, Jennifer 134–5
Hartmann, Heidi 54, 240
Hartsock, N. 247
Harvey, A.D. 15
Haug, F. 171
Hearn, J. 5, 7, 11, 42, 49, 80–1,
   89–90, 104, 142, 167, 170,
   226, 232–9, 241–3, 247–8,
   250–2
Henderson, I.T. 187
Hendrick, H. 109
Hernes, Helga Maria 63, 65, 73,
   141, 238
Heussler, R. 251
Heward, C. 251
Hey, V. 205
Higgs, R.J. 203
Hindess, B. 238
Hirst, P. 208
Hobbes, Thomas 30
Hobsbawm, E. 249
Hochschild, A.R. 236
Hoggett, Brenda 174, 181
Holcombe, L. 156, 158, 159,
   181, 244, 245, 248
Hollway, W. 117
Holter, Harriet 62–3, 65, 234,
   247
Holter, Øystein Gullvåg 238
Hower, R. 183
Hume, David 30
Humm, M. 45
Humphries, S. 241
Hunter, I. 212–14, 251
Hurst, Sir Gerald B. 163
Hutchins, B.L. 66

Irigaray, Luce 105, 225, 226,
   232, 250, 252
Izod, John 193, 222

Jackson, David 89
Jackson, H. 203
Jackson, R.R. 161

Jacobs, Aletta 106
Jacoby, Russell 36–8, 72
James, J.S. 119
James, William 217
Jardine, A. 252
Jefferson, T. 138
Jenson, Jane 244
Johnson, H. 12
Jones, Ernest 222
Joyce, Patrick 161, 162, 245

Kaite, B. 222
Kakar, Sudhir 246
Karl, Frederick R. 203, 204
Katz, J. 234
Kay-Shuttleworth, James 213
Keane, J. 235
Keaton, Buster 194
Kellogg, John Harvey 246
Kelly, Joan 45
Kennedy, P. 135
Kent, Susan Kingsley 132
Kern, Stephen 197, 251
Kimmel, Michael S. 13–14, 16,
    101, 102, 248, 249
Kindleberger, C.P. 239
Kipling, Rudyard 249
Kircher, T. 188
Kocka, Jurgen 183
Krafft-Ebing, R. von 16
Kriek, Ernst 235
Kuhn, Annette 184, 249

Lacan, Jacques 252
Lambertz, J. 248
Lange, L. 29
Lasch, Christopher 36–7, 72, 235
Laurin-Frenette, Nicole 54, 61,
    62, 73, 241
Law, S.A. 241, 249
Lawrence, Florence 192
Leach, W. 240
Lears, T. Jackson J. 246, 251
Lee, A. 248
Lee, J. 107, 244, 249
Leed, E. 204
Legge, Karen 167
Leibniz, G. 14

Leighton, Lord 201
Le Prince, (Louis) Augustin 188
Lévi-Strauss, Claude 252
Lewis, Jane 113, 117, 151, 159,
    240, 248
Lewis, J.E. 245
Lloyd, A. 190
Lloyd, G. 233
Lloyd, Hal 194
Locke, John 30–1
Low, R. 192
Lowe, G.S. 152, 244, 245
Lowe, N.V. 119
Lucie-Smith, E. 203
Lumière family 189
Lunn, Eugene 185, 203, 249
Lynch, K. 236

McCabe, T. 115, 125
McClelland, K. 99
Machiavelli, Niccollo 33
McIntosh, Mary 45, 235
McKechnie, S. 188, 189
McKendrick, N. 173
Mackie, L. 247
MacKinnon, Catharine A. 68, 89,
    90, 116, 171, 236, 240, 241,
    248, 250
MacLean, S.A. 241
McLuhan, Marshall 36
Mandell, M.J. 183
Mangan, J. 215
Mangan, J.A. 16, 249
Marey, Etienne 188
Marinetti, Filippo T. 203
Markin, R.J. 182
Marx, K. 6, 13, 28, 33–4, 233,
    241
Masson, J.M. 218
Matthews, G. 109
Melechi, Antonio 248, 249
Méliès, George 190
Meyrowitz, Joshua 87, 197
Midwinter, Eric C. 127
Mies, M. 78
Mihill, C. 252
Miles, Rosalind 48, 104, 105
Mill, John Stuart 33

Minor, I. 119
Mitchell, B.R. 154
Moore, Henrietta 47, 232, 234
Moore, Owen 194
Morgan, D. 240
Morgan, D.H.J. 132, 153, 234,
    250
Morgan, David 249
Morgan, Gareth 246
Morley, Samuel 162
Mort, Frank 16, 100, 115, 116,
    119, 120, 122, 125, 241
Morton, A. 122
Motherson, K. 200
Muybridge, Eadweard 188
Myers, C.S. 165

Nordau, Max 203

O'Brien, Mary 6, 7, 8, 29, 46,
    79, 80, 141, 232, 235, 236
O'Dell, P. 194
O'Donovan, M. 241
O'Donovan, Katherine 31, 32,
    46, 241
O'Leary, C.C. 129
Ortner, S. 47
Otter, L. 121

Pankhurst, Christabel 116
Parish, P. 248
Parkin, Wendy 86, 142, 170,
    226, 233, 236, 243, 247, 248
Parry, N. & Parry, J. 239
Parsons, T. 31
Pattullo, P. 247
Paul, Robert W. 189
Pearson, Karl 117
Pelling, H. 211
Perkin, John 241
Pickford, Mary 192, 194
Pike, William Thomas 242
Pinchbeck, I. 144
Plato 30
Pleck, Joseph & Pleck, Elizabeth
    15, 16, 100
Poffenberger, A.T. 184
Polan, Diane 46, 241

Pollard, S. 239
Porter, Edwin 221
Poynter, Sir Edward 201
Prest, A.R. 239, 244
Price, M. 44

Radford, L.M.T. 241
Radzinowitz, L. 242
Ramazanoglu, C. 49
Ranger, T. 249
Rawlence, Christopher 189
Reader, W.J. 251
Reader, Keith 188, 190, 249
Reed, J.R. 211
Remy, John 67, 138, 153, 200,
    235
Rheingold, H. 253
Rhode, Eric 186, 187, 190, 221–2
Richards, Barry 219
Richards, J. 191, 211, 212
Richardson, Samuel 15
Riesman, David 235
Robert, E.R. 71, 72
Rosaldo, Michelle Z. 47
Rose, L. 111, 112
Routh, Dr C.H.F. 105, 239
Rowan, C. 240
Rowbotham, S. 236
Rubin, G. 225, 252
Ruggie, Mary 236
Russell, D.E.H. 250
Russell, George 123
Rutherford, J. 250
Rye, Maria Susan 155

Saul, S.B. 239
Savile, John 15
Scott, Walter Dill 184
Seed, J. 249
Seers, H.D. 240
Sekoff, Jed 222
Sennett, Richard 3, 35, 36, 37,
    228, 232
Shipman, D. 190
Showalter, E. 239, 240, 249
Siim, Birte 54, 63–4, 141, 240
Silverstone, R. 152
Simmons, H.G. 116, 241

Skladanowsky, Max and Emil 189
Smart, Carol 120
Smiles, Samuel 109
Smith, Dorothy E. 236
Smith, G.A. 190
Soja, E.W. 238
Soloway, R.A. 116
Sontag, S. 187
Spender, D. 234
Springhall, J.O. 251
Stacey, Margaret 28–9, 44, 45, 54,
    62, 86, 117, 141, 236, 244
Starch, D. 184
Stevenson, John 127, 133
Stoltenberg, J. 253
Stone, E. 112
Stow, David 213
Strauss, S. 132
Summers, Yvonne 48, 236
Symons, J. 249

Tardieu, A.A. 218
Taylor, B. 236
Taylor, F. 246
Teichman, O. 242
Temkin, Jennifer 123, 124, 241
Theleweit, Karl 225
Thomis, M.I. 127
Tolson, A. 239
Tosh, J. 109
Treno, A. 235
Trewey, E. 189
Tucker, K. 235
Turpin, Ben 194

Unger, R. 32
Ursel, Jane 54, 57–61, 65, 141

Valentino, Rudolf 194
Vicinus, M. 144
Victoria, Queen 136
Vogel, L. 236

Walby, Sylvia 49, 54, 65–6, 159,
    173–4, 177, 236, 237, 247

Walkowitz, Judith R. 132
Walvin, J. 16, 249
Ward, Geoffrey C. 248
Waterhouse, John William 201–2
Waters, C. 248
Waters, Malcolm 45, 48, 51–2
Watts, George Frederick 201
Webb, Beatrice 162
Weber, Max 28, 33–4, 163, 168,
    235
Webley, Sir R.E. 159
Wedgwood, Josiah 173
Weedon, C. 232
Weeks, Jeffrey 15, 105, 106, 107,
    117, 239
Weinbaum, B. 236
Weinberg, I. 211
Wenden, D.J. 189; 190, 192,
    194, 249
West, Sir Algernon 158, 159
West, Mae 192
Western, J.R. 242
Westwood, S. 138
White, Pearl 193
Whyte, William H. 235
Wickham, Gary 126, 208, 249
Wilkinson, R. 211
Williams, F. 321
Williams, R. 31
Wilson, A. 248
Willson, F.M.G. 127
Wilson, Joseph 163
Windsor, Elizabeth 136–7
Winter, M.F. 71, 72
Wolfram, S. 125
Wood, C. 202
Wood, R. 179
Wood, W.R. 247
Woolf, J. 249
Woolf, J.D. 184
Woolley, P. 208
Wundt, Wilhelm 217

Zimmeck, M. 160
Zucker, I. 248

Subject index

able-bodiedness 3, 78, 233
academia 11–12, 165, 171, 184, 217
Acts of Parliament:
  Abbreviation Act 1830 32
  Ballot Act 1872 129
  Childrens Act 1908 121
  Coercion Act 1871 134
  Contagious Diseases Acts 122–3, 126, 132
  Corrupt and Illegal Practices Act 1883 129
  Criminal Law Amendment Act 1853 119
  Criminal Law Amendment Act 1885 15–16, 117, 123
  Crown Private Estates Act 1873 242
  Cruelty to Animals Act 1849 119
  Cruelty to Animals Act 1876 119
  Custody of Children Act 1891 113
  Dangerous Drugs Acts 1920 112
  Education (Forster) Act 1870 112
  Education (Balfour) Act 1902 112–13
  Employer and Workmen Act 1875 131
  Employers Liability Act 1880 98
  Explosive Substances Act 1883 134
  Factory Act 1833 111, 173
  Factory and Workshop Act 1878 98

First Irish Land Act 1870 134
First Reform Act 1832 128
Food and Drugs Act 1875 112
Hardwicke Act 1753 111
Incest Act 1908 125
Interpretation Act 1889 32
Interpretation Act 1978 32
Local Government Act 1888 133
Maintenance of Wives Act 1886 120
Married Women's Property Act 1870 241
Married Women's Property Act 1882 120
Maternity and Child Welfare Act 1918 113
Matrimonial Causes Act 1857 119
Matrimonial Causes Act 1878 119
Matrimonial Causes Act 1923 119
Middlesex Justices Act 1772 133
Mines and Collieries Act 1842 144
Municipal Franchise Act 1869 132
Notification of Births Act 1907 113
Obscenity Acts 126
Offences Against the Person Act 1861 112
Offices, Shops and Railway Premises Act 1963 181
Poor Law Amendment Act 1868 112, 121
Poor Law Amendment Act 1889 121

Poisons and Pharmacy Act
   1868 112
Prevention of Cruelty to and
   Protectior of Children Act
   1889 121
Qualification of Women Act
   1907 132–3
Representation of the People
   Act 1867 128–9
Representation of the People
   Act 1918 132
Russell Gurney Act 1876 110
Shops Act 1886 181
Summary Jurisdiction (Married
   Women) Act 1895 120
adultery 119–21, 176, 178–80,
   183–4
advertising 171, 180–1, 183–4,
   229
age 3–4, 78, 83, 99, 109, 112,
   149, 163
agency 8, 13, 70, 93–4, 102, 123,
   125, 208
aggregation 64–6
agriculture 44, 97–8, 235
alienation 17, 19, 172
andrarchy 48
androcracy 48, 67
anthropology 47
anti-feminism 2, 101
anti-modernism 200, 251
anti-patriarchalism see
   pro-feminism
anti-sexism 18–19, 123, 253
army see military
asexuality 176, 200
association 28, 33, 36, 85, 147,
   235
authority 59, 62, 71, 109, 145,
   152–3, 160, 162, 165, 181,
   183, 219, 243

'barmaid' 205–6
betrothal 111
biography 78, 208, 218, 242
biological reproduction 78, 80–1,
   84, 89–90, 96, 103–6, 108,
   223–4, 227, 237

biology 13, 21, 46, 234, 236
birth 78, 105
bisexuality 231
black people 166; see men, black;
   women, black
body, the 83, 89, 91, 116–17,
   125, 146, 198, 206, 208,
   218, 224–5, 239, 252
Boer War 116, 135
boys 83, 109, 112, 148, 157, 210,
   214, 223–4
boy scouts 100, 109, 214
bureaucracy 28, 33, 36, 98, 101,
   136–7, 144–7, 150–60, 177,
   211–12, 224, 240, 243,
   246–7
business 18, 72, 151

Canada 57–61
capitalism 8, 13, 19, 28, 33–4,
   50, 53ff., 71, 73, 76–7,
   96–103, 108, 139, 140, 146,
   148, 150, 160–5, 172–3,
   185, 193, 200, 211–12,
   236–7, 240, 247–8
   factory 96, 100, 219
caring 89–90, 146, 236
censorship 171, 185, 190, 192,
   195, 222, 249
centralization 58–9
changing men 1, 6, 10, 230–1
character 166, 178–9, 210–12
child/children 14, 30, 38, 46, 55,
   61, 111–16, 121–2, 144,
   170–1, 193, 206, 218, 231,
   252
child abuse/violence to children
   121–2, 218, 220, 230, 252
child labour 111, 174
child saving 60, 179
childcare 81, 103, 111–13, 121–2
Christianity 100, 211–12, 214
circuits of desire 205–7
civil disorder 127–8, 133, 138
civil service 20, 72, 135–6, 150,
   153–60, 177
class see economic class
class culture 161–4, 245–6

Classicism 200–2
clubs 20, 140, 200
collectivism 11, 17, 20, 34, 78,
    127, 139, 208, 216, 240
commerce 59, 100, 150, 155, 216
commodification 34, 97, 219,
    235, 252
community 28, 33, 85, 235
conception 78–9, 105, 123–4
consciousness 171, 175, 186–7,
    217, 220, 234
consolidation 22, 228–9
consumption 101–2, 171–2,
    180–4, 193, 216, 230, 250
contagious diseases 103, 241; see
    Contagious Diseases Acts
contradictions 8, 9, 19–22, 76,
    86–7, 117, 144, 175, 191,
    199, 200, 209, 211–12, 218,
    228–31, 245, 253
control 14, 16, 21, 57–8, 97, 126,
    137, 149, 165–6, 168, 195,
    229
crime 111–12, 119–26, 133–4
    see also child abuse, incest,
    rape, sexual violence,
    violence
critique of men 17, 18, 231
critiques 17–19, 43ff., 69, 250
cruelty to animals 121
cultural/culture 12–17, 21, 35,
    45–7, 65, 74, 87, 89–91,
    185, 198–203, 208, 212–14,
    222, 225, 227, 237, 249, 251
cultural reproductive materialism
    89–91, 239
cultural studies 17

death 81, 89, 186, 200, 202–5
deconstruction 7, 8, 18, 23, 42, 45,
    69, 73, 74ff., 228, 231, 250
democracy 128–30
Denmark 63–4
dependence 54, 63–4, 72–3
desire 13, 17, 30, 88–9, 184,
    192–3, 205–7, 216, 223–6
dialectics 70, 89–91
dichotomies/dualities 2, 21, 31,

    43, 46, 74ff., 90–1, 204,
    217, 223, 226
differences/differentiation 1–2,
    7–8, 10, 21, 23, 53–4, 64,
    68, 71, 74ff., 150, 165,
    223–4, 231, 233, 238
disability/disable-bodiedness 3–4,
    78, 233
discipline 210–16
discourse 7, 11–13, 21, 25ff., 45,
    57, 82–3, 88, 90–1, 93–4,
    152, 170–3, 180–1, 199,
    201, 207–8, 214, 217–18,
    220, 235, 239, 251–2
diversity/diversification 22, 27,
    68, 83–4, 104, 106, 199, 209
divorce 118–21
dominance/domination 2–3, 6,
    17–18, 21, 54, 56, 61–2,
    66–7, 76, 80–1, 110ff.,
    142–6, 172–3, 200, 225,
    233, 243
domestic 26, 31, 44, 47, 51–2,
    56, 61–2, 80, 97–8, 174,
    181, 236
domestic servants 181
domesticity 109

economic class 3–4, 13–15, 39,
    49, 58–60, 83, 98–9, 102,
    109–10, 139, 149, 161–5,
    175, 186, 191, 225, 240–2,
    245
economics 26–9, 136
economy 33, 55, 57, 95–108,
    148, 211
    see also capitalism
education 19, 44, 51, 109,
    111–13, 140, 148–9, 152,
    210–15, 240, 251
eighteenth century 13–15, 36,
    55, 109, 111, 128, 187
elections 13, 128–30
emotions 9, 40, 102, 150, 166,
    193, 236, 253
empire see imperialism
employers 58, 66, 97–8, 151,
    161–4

Enlightenment, The 14, 30–3
epistemology *see* knowledge
ethnicity 4, 78, 83, 109, 149
ethnic relations 191, 219
eugenics 116–17, 125
everyday 2, 12, 32
exchange value 19–20, 180
existence 27, 39, 45
experience 1–2, 11, 20, 22, 25–6,
    37, 45, 85–90, 161–2, 164,
    196, 199–200, 204, 217–18,
    231, 232, 234
externalization 16–17, 25, 198,
    207

factory 96, 100, 146, 150–1, 153,
    159–64, 178–9, 181
family 13, 36–7, 44–5, 47, 50–1,
    55ff., 72, 78–9, 84, 96,
    108–15, 119–22, 125–6,
    163, 170–1, 174, 181,
    186–7, 219, 227, 237, 241
  bourgeois 33–4, 37, 39, 108–9
  democratic 62
  patriarchal 36, 108
  see also family patriarchy
family wage 66–7, 99, 114
fantasy 72, 171, 190, 218, 252
fascism 35, 235
father/fatherhood 6, 14, 19,
    36–7, 48, 52, 65, 67, 72,
    76–7, 81–2, 103, 108–15,
    122, 126, 141, 148, 185–6,
    205, 209, 219, 220, 227,
    230–1, 233, 251–2
feeble-minded, the 116, 124
female 2, 218
female sexuality 15–16, 105, 173
  see also women's sexuality
feminine 2, 13–14
femininity/femininities 14, 61,
    87, 219
feminism 5–6, 17–19, 23, 43ff.,
    69, 71, 89, 102–3, 116, 118,
    125, 132, 140, 175, 231–4,
    240–3, 247
  anarcho- 73
  marxist 71

men's responses to 5, 17–18
feminist materialism 91
feminization 151ff., 244
feudalism 46, 59, 72
fifteenth century 13
film 72, 101, 171, 185, 188–95,
    199, 210–11, 221–2, 229,
    235, 249
  stars 192–4, 221
First World War 116, 118, 129,
    132, 135–6, 154, 159,
    201–5, 220
fracturing 16, 22, 75, 88, 209ff.,
    228–9
fragmentation 22, 40, 104,
    171–2, 179–207, 209, 223,
    228–9, 249
France 188–9, 239, 248
fratriarchy 67, 138, 153, 200
frontier 99–101, 193, 249
Futurism 203–3, 221

gay history 107
gay liberation 17–19, 139
gay men 4, 107, 139, 205, 231,
    234, 243
  see also homosexuality
gay studies 17–18
gaze 198, 216
gender 1, 12–17, 45, 49, 57–8,
    76–7, 89, 115, 126, 133,
    141, 213, 233–4, 240, 245,
    253
  class 5–6, 22, 49, 75–6, 225
  construction 44
  critiques 17–19
  division of labour 33, 62,
    66–7, 150–69, 173
  ideology 14–16
  relations 12–13, 43, 109, 152,
    155, 191, 219
gendered/gendering 2, 27, 31,
    35, 41, 43, 45, 65–6, 76–7,
    87, 114, 146, 152, 154, 159,
    163, 167, 222–3, 245
gentlemen 210–16, 242
Germany 100, 211, 235
girls 148, 155, 174, 192–3, 223–4

global *see* world
government *see* state
grand narrative 77, 83

health 44, 51, 103, 110, 116–17
Hegelianism 32, 34, 89
hero 193, 209, 216
heterosexual/heterosexuality 3–4,
    16, 87, 95, 106–8, 115–26,
    171–80, 193, 198–9, 204,
    225, 232, 243, 250
hierarchic heterosexuality 81–2,
    103, 226–7
hierarchy 10, 18, 67, 82–3, 87,
    93–4, 140ff., 173, 199,
    205–7, 212, 216
history/historical 1, 4, 6, 8–10,
    12–17, 19–22, 32, 34,
    38–42, 44–6, 52ff., 69ff.,
    75–80, 84, 86, 91, 93, 95,
    99, 115–16, 140–2, 152–3,
    160, 217, 223, 227–8, 233,
    244
holidays 195–6
homoeroticism 175, 204–7, 216,
    224, 250
homophobia 175, 199, 204–7
homosexual/homosexuality
    15–16, 87, 103, 106–7, 117,
    123, 170–1, 175, 179, 194,
    198, 200, 204, 225, 250, 252
homosociality 174–5, 179, 194,
    199, 205–7
households 13, 59, 65, 73, 84,
    139, 163
husbands 14, 56, 111, 114,
    119–21, 148, 175, 209

ideology 2–4, 7, 9, 14–15, 29,
    44–5, 47, 57, 65, 81–2, 101,
    126, 143, 145, 148–9, 165,
    181, 212, 237, 240, 248
identity 107, 163, 214, 229–31,
    245
images 10, 16–17, 19, 53, 170ff.,
    222, 248
immigration 103, 166, 191
imperialism 76, 78, 97, 99, 100,

139, 146, 149, 200, 211–12,
    236, 239
incest 125
individuals 11, 17, 19, 37–9, 52,
    55, 58, 71, 85, 89, 117, 139,
    171, 185, 208ff., 241
industrialization 13–16, 28, 55,
    62, 66–7, 100–1, 127, 144,
    173
infant death 111–12
infant development 223–4
information 16–17, 101, 137,
    140, 167–9
inheritance 59, 99
institutions 25, 28, 36, 40, 44–5,
    61–2, 70, 80, 88, 93, 95,
    140, 146, 149, 205, 224
intermediate zone 86–7
international competition 100,
    116, 211, 228, 239
internationalization 16–17, 198
intersubjectivity 85, 91
intimacy 36, 88–9
Ireland 127, 134

knowledge 5, 18, 26ff., 45, 55,
    74–5, 124, 180, 232, 247

Labouchère Amendment 15–16,
    123, 126
labour *see* work
labour-power 81, 180
language 18, 32, 41, 61, 88, 178,
    252
law 7, 15–16, 31–2, 41, 44–7,
    59–61, 63, 66, 71, 78, 96,
    103, 108, 110–13, 117–26,
    129, 148, 171, 222, 241
lesbians 4, 15, 139, 243
liberalism 26, 28, 36, 57, 211, 240
Liberals 115, 244
local government *see* state
love 17, 204, 224, 230, 250

male 2–3, 14–15, 32, 95, 160,
    167, 171, 226–7, 241
male sexual narrative 193–5
malestream 5–6, 9, 12, 23, 25ff.,

43, 45, 52, 62–3, 69, 77, 240
man 3, 11, 33, 95, 212, 232
managers/management 28, 72,
    83, 97, 104, 127, 135, 145,
    147, 155, 160–9, 177,
    180–1, 209, 219, 235, 245,
    247
managerialism 163–7
manliness 16, 100, 130, 166,
    186–7, 210, 214
manual labour 150–3, 166
manufacturing 97–8, 101–2
market 26–8, 46, 60, 63, 65, 146,
    245
marriage 13, 29, 39, 46, 48,
    58–9, 103, 108–9, 111, 114,
    119–21, 144, 227, 237, 241
    bar 156, 159, 175
marxism 46, 54, 71, 77, 89, 98,
    165, 172, 240–1, 248, 250
masculine 2, 14, 95
    gender system 45, 51–2
    solidarity 61, 161–2, 252
masculinity/masculinities 1, 5–6,
    9, 11, 13–14, 18, 22–3, 33,
    39, 87, 90, 87–102, 115,
    126, 139, 160, 163–4, 166,
    168, 181, 187, 191, 195,
    199, 202, 219–22, 227, 234,
    239, 245–7, 250
    crisis 16, 101
mass media see media
masturbation 117, 241, 246
material/materialism 1–2, 7,
    12–13, 22, 42, 45, 47, 53,
    58–9, 89–91, 95, 109, 171,
    179, 205, 208, 219–20, 225,
    239
media 19–20, 65, 93–4, 108,
    170–2, 180, 185–9, 200, 222
medieval society 13, 39, 123, 235
medicine 15, 105, 107, 110, 112,
    122, 124, 148, 171, 239, 241
men, able-bodied 82–3
    black 82–3, 138–9
    bourgeois 128, 173
    as bread-winner 113
    as a class/collectivity 50–1, 55,

67, 71, 78, 85, 89, 96, 99,
    205, 208–10, 223, 228–9,
    245–6
    as class traitors 6, 20
    critique of 17–18
    with disabilities 82–3
    dominance/power of 1–2, 5,
    7–9, 18–22, 23ff., 55, 61–3,
    65–8, 71, 80, 90, 96ff.,
    142ff., 175, 185, 205–7,
    225, 231–2, 239, 242–3, 248
    in economic classes 81, 99,
    245–6
    as effeminate 100
    feminized 13, 235
    gay 4, 107, 109, 205, 231, 234
    243; see also homosexuality
    heterosexual 107–8, 193, 205–6
    identities of 231, 245
    images of 187, 191, 193–5
    as individuals 208ff., 228–9,
    245–6
    loss of 35–8, 61
    as managers 127, 155, 161–7,
    180–1
    meetings of 127–8
    middle class 14, 83, 100–2,
    106, 118–19, 134–6, 138,
    147–51, 161–6, 200–1,
    203–5, 210, 215, 245–6
    modern 154, 166, 171, 228
    new 13, 240
    in organizations 140ff., 170ff.
    in private see private men
    psychodynamics of 72, 106,
    171, 217–22, 225, 246
    in public see public men
    as salesmen 182–3
    self-reflection of 185, 220
    selves of 210–16
    sexuality of 117, 123, 170ff.,
    221, 226, 245–6
    in the state 118–19, 122,
    153–60
    types of 22, 81–2, 122–3, 126,
    138–9, 157–8, 161–4,
    207–10
    upper class 83, 210, 215

white 82–3, 100, 200
white heterosexual able-bodied
    3–4, 228
and work 12, 70–1, 98, 131,
    206, 245–6
working class 83, 109, 128,
    130–2, 148–9, 161–4,
    173–80, 191, 242, 245–6
young 109, 138–9, 151, 157
men's movement 18, 101
men's studies 17–18
men's violence 44, 65, 119–37
    see also violence
mental labour 150–3, 166
mentally deficient 116
military/militarism 13–14, 20,
    28, 44, 83, 100, 115–16,
    127–8, 135–6, 200, 214, 220
modern/modernism 6, 9, 11, 16,
    52–3, 71, 117–18, 154, 171,
    185, 195, 199–202, 204,
    216, 227–8, 249
modernization 17, 32–5, 133,
    150–3, 160, 193, 214, 226
monarchy 20, 127, 136–7, 187,
    242
monocultures, organizational
    199–205
monopoly capitalism 53, 55–6,
    77, 80, 96–7, 100, 129, 141,
    170, 219
mothers/mothering 47, 64, 90,
    103, 109–14, 116, 206, 221
movement 18–19, 137–9, 170,
    193, 195–8, 229, 238
multiple perspectives see plural
    perspectives

narcissism 36, 198, 204, 207, 221
narrative 77, 83, 190–5, 197–200,
    207
nation 33, 36, 100, 116–17,
    134–7, 202, 215, 227, 236
naturalism 29–32
nature 14, 32, 35, 47, 198
neutrality 136–45, 166–9
Norway 62–3, 66–7
novel 15, 101, 194, 222, 249

NSPCC 110, 122
nurture 21, 79–81, 84, 89–90,
    103–4, 106, 146, 223–4,
    227, 237

offices 20, 146–7, 150–60, 171,
    175, 183
oppression 17–19, 21, 29, 38–9,
    49–50, 57–63, 70, 73, 80,
    82–3, 171, 220, 226
optimism 33–4, 99
organization(s) 1–2, 8, 10–11, 16,
    18–19, 25, 28, 44–5, 60, 67,
    79, 84, 87–8, 93–4, 104,
    110, 114, 117, 137–9,
    140ff., 170ff., 224, 227, 243,
    247
organization sexuality 170–80
organization theory 8, 28, 235,
    243
organizational processes 170ff.
Other, the/otherness 166, 196,
    199, 206, 223, 227, 233, 246
outer-directed see externalization
overlaps 86–7
owners 97, 99, 145, 155, 165, 209

pain 9, 39, 42
painting 201–3
paradox 9, 18, 36, 87–8, 185
passion 30, 40
paternity see fatherhood
patriarch 3, 20, 58–9, 219
patriarchal discourse 25ff., 233–4
patriarchy/patriarchies 1ff.,
    12–13, 19–21, 43ff., 69ff.,
    74ff., 103, 150, 205, 230–2,
    237, 240–1, 243 252
capitalist 50–2, 56, 70–1, 101
communal 58
private/family/familial 6, 8,
    19, 49, 53ff., 79, 103, 113,
    230
public/social/reorganized 6, 8,
    10, 19–21, 23, 43ff., 69ff.,
    74ff., 93–4, 95ff., 140–2,
    145–6, 153, 166, 170–3,
    183, 185, 195, 197, 199,

203, 208–9, 219–20, 223,
226–8, 236
subversion of 19–20
people work 144, 146–50, 160,
166, 236, 244, 248
perception 210, 222–6
person(s) 62, 88–9, 94, 171,
208ff., 251
personal, the 1, 4–5, 18–20, 26,
35–8, 43–5, 73, 86, 101,
107, 114, 136–7, 197, 204,
238, 251
personality 36, 89, 185, 217–22
pessimism 35–9, 72, 99, 149, 238
phallocracy 48
phallus 88, 126, 190, 206, 218
philosophy 27–8
photography 130, 185–8, 191,
195, 199, 201, 248, 251
pin-up 192, 207
place 25, 78, 83, 187–8, 195–8
pleasure 180
plural perspectives/pluralizing
1ff., 10, 74ff.
pluralism 26
police 20, 110, 115, 118–19, 122,
127, 133–5, 138, 205
political parties 28, 129–32, 143,
241
political science 28–9, 240
politics/polity 1, 4–5, 11–13,
18–20, 22, 28, 43–4, 48, 53,
55, 57, 66, 71, 98, 127–33,
203, 227, 231–2, 238, 253
'population problem', the 100,
116, 118, 242
pornography 15, 53, 171, 221,
229–30, 241, 247
Post Office 155–7, 177, 244–5
postmodernism 9, 16, 20, 38, 45,
49, 75, 90, 153, 195,
216–17, 226–7, 238
post-public patriarchies 228–30
poststructuralism 38, 40, 49
power 1–2, 5, 7, 11, 18–21,
26–7, 34, 40, 45, 52–3, 59,
71, 80–1, 87–8, 101, 110ff.,
142–6, 170, 185–6, 196,

208, 219–20, 225, 243
praxis 13, 17–19, 22, 93, 218,
230–1, 233
pre-capitalist society 13, 58, 66,
101, 109
pre-modernism 200
private domains/private, the 1ff.,
11ff. ,18, 20, 26–7, 30–1,
34–5, 38, 43–5, 54, 57,
69ff., 76, 78–83, 110,
114–15, 124–6, 147, 171,
173, 186, 229, 232, 247
private masculinities 72
private men 6–8, 71–2, 85, 233
processual see organizational
processes
procreation see biological
reproduction
production 16–17, 19, 27, 29, 36,
44, 50, 59–60, 62, 81–2, 88,
97–100, 103–4, 164, 166–7,
175, 235–6, 247
pro-feminism 18, 29, 69, 101,
231, 238
professions 18, 33, 44, 61, 103–6,
108–15, 140–1, 143–4,
146–50, 219, 227, 239, 243,
248
progressivism 32–8, 40, 106, 108,
214, 238
projection 222–6
pro-male backlash 101
property 55, 58–9, 77, 99, 108–9,
111, 120, 128–30
prostitution 103, 117, 122–3,
192, 204, 232, 241
psyche/psychology 10, 85, 93–4,
208–10, 217–19, 223, 235,
246, 251
psychiatry 15, 124, 218
psychoanalysis/psychodynamics
17, 35–7, 72, 91, 94, 137,
185, 209–10, 217–23, 250–1
public domains/public, the 1ff.,
11ff., 23, 25, 31ff., 43ff.,
69ff., 74ff., 94ff., 140ff.,
170ff., 208ff., 227ff., 232,
235, 239, 247

public masculinities 10–11, 23,
  68, 69–73, 74ff., 94ff.,
  140ff., 170ff., 208ff., 232–3,
  238
public men 2ff., 23, 25ff., 47ff.,
  69ff., 74ff., 93ff., 140ff.,
  170ff., 208ff., 227ff., 232–3,
  238
  problem of 11ff.
public-private
  differences/divisions/relations
  6–8, 21–2, 30ff., 43ff., 69ff.,
  74ff., 94ff., 140–1, 186, 217,
  227ff., 236–9, 246
public sector *see* state
public self/selves 210–18
public schools 201, 210, 251
publicization 16, 22, 209, 220,
  223, 228–9
pubs 20, 174, 191, 205–6
purity 15–16, 116–18, 123, 125,
  241–2
pyramids of desire 205–7

qualitative change 170ff.

'race' 83, 100, 116–18, 137, 212,
  250
race suicide 60, 100
racialization *see* 'race'
racism 191
rape 123–5, 220, 241
rationality/reason 14, 30–5, 40, 71,
  77, 144, 153, 166–9, 217, 247
religion 13, 55, 105, 140, 161,
  176, 200, 214, 218
representation 38, 170, 179,
  201–3, 224–5, 229
reproduction 7, 21, 27, 34, 45–7,
  56–60, 80–2, 89–91, 103,
  117, 145–8, 150, 160, 164,
  166–7, 170–1, 209, 216,
  230, 235–7, 239, 252
resonances 87
resource accumulation 84–5
Restoration, The 13
retailing 153, 170–2, 175, 180–3,
  248

rights 60–1, 138
royal commission 118–19
rules 59, 153, 160, 176

Scandinavia 62–4, 236, 238
schools 109, 112–13, 116, 148–9,
  159, 176, 200
science 77, 136, 140, 200, 217,
  221
secretaries 207
  see also typists
self/selves 10, 17, 25, 36, 40, 78,
  85, 89–91, 94, 99, 102,
  117–18, 171, 195, 208–16,
  222–3, 253
senses 10, 210, 222–6
separate spheres 14–16
service sector 97–8, 101–2,
  144–5, 147, 175
seventeenth century 13, 123
sex 13, 171, 208, 210, 222–6
sex-gender *see* gender
sexology 107
sexual abuse 72, 218, 220
sexual difference 13, 74
sexual division of labour *see*
  gender division of labour
sexual harassment 98–9, 171,
  174–9, 181, 183, 205–6,
  247–8
sexual immorality 173–80
sexual politics 15, 17
sexual violence 116–26, 226
  see also child abuse, incest,
  rape, sexual abuse, violence
sexuality 1, 3–4, 10, 13–17, 21,
  29, 39, 53, 65, 68, 78, 80–1,
  84, 89–91, 96, 102–8,
  114–26, 132, 137, 143, 146,
  152, 170ff., 218, 221–4,
  227, 229, 236–8, 240–1,
  247, 249–50
sexualization 171–2, 176–9, 193,
  200
shops *see* retailing
signs/signification 13, 20, 93,
  139, 166–7, 169, 199, 210
silence 18–19, 222–6, 252

sixteenth century 14
size of organizations 10, 140ff., 170
slaves 30
smell 197
social contract theory 28
social interchange 25
social relations 93–4, 95ff., 145
social science 5–6, 25ff.
socialism 17, 63, 76, 98, 128, 134
society 27–30, 37, 55, 143, 165
sociology 27–9
sodomy 14
soldiers 114, 116, 186–7, 250
souls 210–16
space 25, 37, 76–9, 84, 107, 130, 139, 187–8, 195–8, 200, 238
sport 25, 100–1, 138, 187–8, 199–200, 212, 214–16
state, 28, 31, 34, 36, 48, 53, 55, 57–67, 71–3, 77, 80, 82, 95–6, 98, 100, 103, 106, 108–37, 140–1, 144–9, 153–60, 164–5, 172–3, 175–8, 200, 205, 211–12, 219–20, 227, 230, 237, 240–1, 244–5, 248
street(s) 127, 137–9, 205
structural functionalism 28, 31
structure 8, 10, 13–14, 48–9, 65–6, 91, 93, 140ff., 208, 237–9
subjectivity 18, 37, 45, 212–13, 220–1, 228
surplus value 58, 66
Switzerland 31
symbolic 109, 186, 189, 199–203, 206–7, 218
synthesis, 64, 66–8

Taylorism 28
technocratic consciousness 71
technology 11, 20, 67, 97, 145, 147, 161, 171–2, 200, 228, 252–3
themes 20–1
theory 1, 4–6, 17–18, 22, 28–9, 93, 95, 230–2, 235

time 25, 46, 76–9, 84, 130, 139, 195–200
total institutions 149, 224
touch 197, 22
trade unions 18, 63, 66, 97–9, 128, 130–2, 143, 148, 151, 154, 161, 163, 171–2
transcendence 38–40, 231
transport/travel 78–9, 138, 140, 190, 195–8
trauma 220, 251
typists 151, 158, 170

United States 8–9, 16, 56, 99–102, 116, 175–8, 182, 186, 189–91, 239, 245, 251
unities 199–207
universalism 3, 11, 19, 166, 195, 199–205
urbanization 13, 33, 197, 227
use value 19–20, 180

value(s) 19–20, 27, 46–7, 234
venereal disease 105, 122–4
  see also contagious diseases
vice 117, 193–4
violence 3, 14, 16, 19–21, 44, 80–1, 84, 89–90, 96, 103–4, 115–26, 146, 201–6, 218, 220, 223–5, 231, 237, 240
  husbands' to wives 119–21
  men's to children 121–2
  private 115–26
  public 126–37
viriarchy 48
  extended 50–2
visibility 3, 17, 85
visitors 109–10
visual 171–2, 180–99, 201–3, 226
voting 128–9
  see also women's suffrage
voyeurism 195, 226

wage labour 53, 55–6, 58–9, 65–7, 71, 77, 98, 132, 139, 140, 143, 150–2, 173–4
war 14, 116, 186–7, 202–5
welfare 51, 106, 124, 179, 219

state 53, 57, 62–4, 67, 77, 115,
141, 219, 244
western, the 101, 194, 249
white people 3–4, 191
  see also men, white; men, white
  heterosexual able-bodied
white slavery 179, 193–4
wife/wives 14, 56, 119–21, 175,
186–7
women 2, 4, 6–7, 13–18, 38,
43ff., 70, 83, 94, 166,
182–3, 240
  black 4
  as childcarers 113
  citizens 30, 33, 63–4, 72–3,
  113
  clerks 150ff., 175–7
  clients 63–4, 72–3, 182
  as commodities 252
  as customers 181–3
  with disabilities 4
  employees 63–4, 72–3
  exclusion of 110, 147, 154–7,
  173–9, 244, 253
  married 174, 178: *see also* wives
  middle class 118–19, 151–2,
  159–60, 175–6, 182
  new 108
  oppression/control of 29, 38,

57–62, 70, 82, 119–21, 173,
175, 200, 205–6, 243
  in private 31
  in professions 148–9
  in public 26, 30–1, 118–19,
  143–4, 148
  as sex objects 183–4, 201–3
  as signs 225–6, 250
  speech of 124–5
  and work 50, 57, 66–7, 70–1,
  98, 130, 144, 147, 151–8,
  161–4, 166, 173–83, 191,
  206, 235, 243, 247
  working class 4, 98–9, 114–15,
  130–2, 186, 191
women's liberation/movement/
  organizing 44, 61, 102,
  132–3, 139, 143–4, 175, 231
women's power 7, 13, 66
women's suffrage 31, 61, 71, 113,
  118–21, 129, 132–3
world 7–8, 12–13, 78, 249
work/workers 12–13, 22, 27, 35,
  38, 44, 50, 53, 97, 104,
  145–7, 150–60, 173–4, 209,
  219, 227, 236, 245–6
writing 1, 9, 28, 39, 40

youth 109, 200, 214